STANDING TALL

Oregon Historical Society Press, Portland
in association with
University of Washington Press, Seattle and London

STANDING TALL

The
Lifeway of
Kathryn
Jones
Harrison

**CHAIR OF THE CONFEDERATED TRIBES
OF THE GRAND RONDE COMMUNITY**

*For Lucille ~
Enjoy!
Kris Olson*

by **KRISTINE OLSON**

Oregon Historical Society Press
1200 SW Park Avenue, Portland, OR 97205, USA
www.ohs.org

in association with
University of Washington Press
P.O. Box 50096, Seattle, WA 98145, USA
www.washington.edu/uwpress

The paper used in this publication is acid-free. It meets the minimum
requirements of American National Standard for Information Sciences —
Permanence of Paper for Printed Library Materials,
ANSI Z39.48 — 1984. ∞

Cover design: Ashley Saleeba. *Interior design*: Veronica Seyd
Cover photograph: Courtesy of Kathryn Harrison family collection,
photographer unknown

Library of Congress Cataloging-in-Publication Data
Olson, Kristine.
Standing tall : the lifeway of Kathryn Jones Harrison, chair of the
Confederated Tribes of the Grand Ronde Community / by Kristine Olson.
p. cm.
Includes bibliographical references and index.
ISBN 0-295-98582-8
1. Harrison, Kathryn Jones, 1924– 2. Indians of North America —
Oregon — Biography. 3. Confederated Tribes of the Grand Ronde
Community of Oregon. I. Title.
E78.O6O725 2005
979.5004'97'0092 — dc22
2005024160

For Les, auðvitað

To Kathryn Jones Harrison's ancestors and
descendants — may they receive the honor that
is theirs.

*To my ancestors, especially Ole,
and descendants, who launched me on this path.*

Kathryn Jones Harrison Family

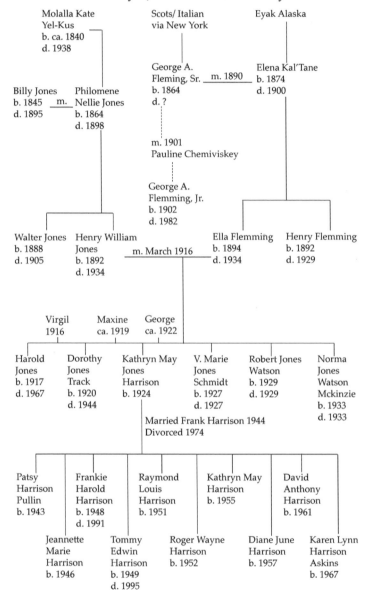

Molalla Kate
Yel-Kus
b. ca. 1840
d. 1938

Scots/ Italian
via New York

Eyak Alaska

George A.
Fleming, Sr. _m. 1890_
b. 1864
d. ?

Elena Kal'Tane
b. 1874
d. 1900

Billy Jones
b. 1845 _m._
d. 1895

Philomene
Nellie Jones
b. 1864
d. 1898

m. 1901
Pauline Chemiviskey

George A.
Flemming, Jr.
b. 1902
d. 1982

Walter Jones
b. 1888
d. 1905

Henry William
Jones _m. March 1916_
b. 1892
d. 1934

Ella Flemming
b. 1894
d. 1934

Henry Flemming
b. 1892
d. 1929

Virgil
1916

Maxine
ca. 1919

George
ca. 1922

Harold
Jones
b. 1917
d. 1967

Dorothy
Jones
Track
b. 1920
d. 1944

Kathryn May
Jones
Harrison
b. 1924

V. Marie
Jones
Schmidt
b. 1927
d. 1927

Robert Jones
Watson
b. 1929
d. 1929

Norma
Jones
Watson
Mckinzie
b. 1933
d. 1933

Married Frank Harrison 1944
Divorced 1974

Patsy
Harrison
Pullin
b. 1943

Frankie
Harold
Harrison
b. 1948
d. 1991

Raymond
Louis
Harrison
b. 1951

Kathryn May
Harrison
b. 1955

David
Anthony
Harrison
b. 1961

Jeannette
Marie
Harrison
b. 1946

Tommy
Edwin
Harrison
b. 1949
d. 1995

Roger Wayne
Harrison
b. 1952

Diane June
Harrison
b. 1957

Karen Lynn
Harrison
Askins
b. 1967

Contents

Foreword

Unlike many Anglo Americans in the United States, I did not grow up with distorted perceptions of Native Americans based on misleading portrayals served up by the entertainment industry. Nor did my perceptions become molded by erroneous prejudices fed to me by my elders. Indeed, my experiences as a young boy, playing in the hills around my uncle's workplace in "Swede Mill" at Valley Junction, established in my young mind the fact that our Native American neighbors were a vital part of the community and commanded respect. As a people long established, they had a unique culture and heritage, and in their way of life they displayed the proud traditions of their ancestors. They seemed to have an intimacy with the environment, a special key to unlocking the secrets of the woods and rivers. I can remember an Indian boy showing my cousin and me, third-graders, where to dig for licorice root, a simple treasure for kids eager to feast on nature's candy.

Sadly, the past 200 years of this country's Native American policy have fostered increasing division over differences in appearance, culture, and religion. Indian nations throughout the Americas were forced on a Trail of Tears in which thousands of Native Americans made their marches toward segregated regions, at times far from home, reserved for them out of greed and fear.

Imagine yourself living in a small town on the outskirts of a large and rapidly expanding city. Your population consists of a handful of families who have lived and worked in this town for many years, as long as any local historian can trace. Your town is largely self-sufficient, but it depends on the surrounding region for some necessities of life. Now imagine that an assemblage of prominent citizens from the city just over the hill pays a visit to your town. With dexterous oratory, they speak to you of their plans to expand their city into your area. To do so, they must harness your rivers for electricity, mine your hills for metal, and cut your trees for lumber. Adding to your astonishment, they tell you that you and your family must move beyond the next ridge-line to a specified area created for the members of your town. Try to imagine your shock and anger at such audacity.

This is not an extreme illustration of what Native Americans in the United States have experienced but a mild and weak attempt to explain the outrages our government imposed on Indians in the nation's early years. How could we expect any people who have endured such assault not to become filled with bitter resentment and fired with a passion for retribution? Only a truly strong and courageous person could rise from these circumstances to become better rather than bitter, to forge a path toward reconciliation rather than retribution.

I am sure there are many historical accounts of people who have taken just this attitude toward injustice. Yet, I would agree with Kris Olson, the author of this biography, in ranking Kathryn Harrison among the most eloquent and determined examples of this philosophy. Within the context of her life as a Native American, she has been a firsthand recipient of raw deals such as termination, the culmination of over a hundred years of broken promises and inept solutions. Within the context of her personal life, she has borne many heartaches, to the extent that one can only weep at their recounting. Through all these tests, Kathryn's calm, steely character has emerged. It is accurate to say of her that she is gentle and pleasant. The wisdom of her years and the fruits of her experience have taught her it is unnecessary to stand always with sword unsheathed. She is kind and warm; this is her natural response to life as she now lives it. Yet, when she wages battle for her people's causes, she exhibits an iron will and a passionate resolve to see justice done.

Whether she sought better medical care for Indian children or the protection of the sacred burial sites of her ancestors, Kathryn Harrison was not to be denied and certainly not to be forgotten. It is no mystery to me how she has risen among her people to become a distinguished leader and tribal elder, commanding respect not only among the Grand Rondes but also among people from all walks of life and throughout this country.

Kristine Olson has researched well and thoroughly and presents the reader with an important model for young, aspiring women in the twenty-first century. They would do well to learn from Kathryn's leadership style. Never overbearing, never scrapping over the trivial issues, she wisely chooses her battles and sees them through to the end of her energies. Kathryn, in her quiet confidence, demonstrates an ability to waste no words but to wield them as a powerful tool when circumstances so demand.

As a matriarch of the Grand Rondes, Kathryn will continue to provide wise counsel for those who will listen. She will no doubt continue her activism on behalf of her people for the rest of her life. In doing so, Kathryn Harrison endows generations of future Native Americans with a legacy that teaches persistence in the face of adversity, consistency against a backdrop of hypocrisy, and, most importantly, love in the presence of animosity.

Since restoration, the Grand Rondes have effectively demonstrated what wise tribal leaders can accomplish with governmental support. The road to gaining such support has never been easy, and at times I am sure it has appeared virtually impossible. But those who take note of the lessons Kris Olson sets forth in this life story will find that it is worth the effort.

This is the challenge for the twenty-first century: full restoration of the rights and privileges due to the first Americans. Now the torch is being passed to a new generation of tribal leaders. It is my hope that the next leaders will be motivated and encouraged to follow in the footsteps of Kathryn Harrison. By continuing to increase awareness of Native American issues among members of Congress and in society at large, I believe we will foster a climate that leads to acceptance of rightful claims for Indian people. May it also lead to long-lasting friendships like the one Kathryn and I have enjoyed through many years.

SENATOR MARK O. HATFIELD
Portland, Oregon

Preface

Shortly after I was nominated by President Bill Clinton to serve as Oregon's United States Attorney, the Grand Ronde tribal attorney called to ask if I would preside at a repatriation ceremony. Seven-thousand-year-old artifacts associated with the aboriginal territory of the Grand Rondes along the Columbia River near what is now the Portland International Airport were to be returned to the tribal leadership by the developers who had unearthed them. The ceremony took place in the state capitol in January 1994.

I walked into a room full of legislators, county officials, Indian drummers, singers, and tribal members with small children. Near the front stood a diminutive woman in her fifties or sixties, with short, curly gray hair and big glasses. She was wearing a shapeless navy suit she could have purchased at any local mall, yet there was something commanding about her. She was introduced as the tribal vice chair. Although the tribal chair was present, she was clearly the spokesperson for the Grand Rondes.

The ceremony began with a traditional Native prayer laced with Christian references, Kathryn's own fusion of tribal legends and Bible stories. Bemused corporate officers of the Columbia South Shore development companies stood on the sidelines. After preliminary remarks by officials, these men stepped forward to hand over plastic baggies filled with what appeared to be dirt and rocks. Then Kathryn Harrison began to speak.

She told what these crude stone tools shaped by the hands of her ancestors meant to her people. Through tears, she said they were symbols of ingenuity and endurance in the face of great odds, telling of courage and connections across generations.

"Someone's grandmother used this bone awl to make a baby's first moccasin," she said. "One of our father's fathers used this stone point to kill a deer to feed his family. These are the treasures of my people, every bit as important as your grandmother's brooch." It was important to pass on these memories and visible reminders to the children of the tribe. There were long silences as Kathryn struggled with her emotions.

I began to cry with her. Others were moved to tears. Even the developers responded to her words. Afterward, people filtered slowly from the room, as if reluctant to leave a hallowed place. Like no other speaker I had ever heard, Kathryn gave strangers in a meeting room direct access to her heart. Thus began a long and intimate association that ranks among the most rewarding of my life.

Kathryn's path and my own crossed often in the next ten years, sometimes in official functions as we improved our government-to-government relationship, sometimes as fellow board members when we decided how to award grants from the Spirit Mountain Community Fund, sometimes in treasured personal encounters. She gave the invocation at my investiture as U.S. Attorney. She routinely includes me and my family in the prayers she says before each meal. After the death of my mother, closely followed by the breakdown of my long marriage, she offered solace as an older woman and surrogate mom who understood broken promises and abandonment.

As our personal and professional lives converged over the years, my admiration for Kathryn Harrison grew. Her life has been intimately interwoven with twentieth-century federal Indian policy. In Senator Hatfield's words, she was "an experiential witness" whose voice projected all that her accumulated pain and passion could produce. The orphaned child of a tribal member deprived of his land, she was raised in abusive foster care and attended an Indian boarding school. Married at an early age to an alcoholic, she raised ten children as a single mother. After the federal government "terminated" tribes, forcing many individuals into destitution in urban areas, she helped hold the Native community together and founded much-needed alcohol and drug treatment programs. Elected to two different tribal councils during their restoration efforts, Kathryn Harrison led both Siletz and Grand Ronde members in their quests for self-determination and sustainable economic development. Today, the eighty-one-year-old former chair of the Confederated Tribes of Grand Ronde still carries her message into classrooms, boardrooms, and other private and public arenas. For her eloquence and perseverance in communicating the story of her people, she is highly regarded across the nation.

Like no other, Kathryn Harrison lent a human face to the story of her tribe's suffering and survival. Someone needed to record her own story for her family and her tribe, and I was an obvious candidate. It was a tall order. Could I do justice to this remarkable life? Was it possible to be objective about someone I hold dear? I was encouraged by the words of Peter Conradi, who wrote in *Iris: The Life of Iris Murdoch*: "Closeness to one's subject is simultaneously a strength and a liability, and I wanted to write the first biography of Iris, but not the last." Conradi's "life" became the standard, a place for others to begin.

I asked Kathryn if she would help me gather and write her life story. She bowed her head, took my hand, and gave thanks. "I had hoped to preserve some part of my history for my family and for my community," she said.

Thus we began this work of love and exploration.

KRISTINE OLSON
Portland, Oregon

Acknowledgments

Many have helped to further this venture—assisting in archival research, gathering materials, providing photographs and family records, offering hours of taping recollections, reliving painful memories, and commenting on very rough early drafts. The staffs of the Benton and Lincoln County and Oregon Historical Societies were unfailingly courteous and energetic in their searches for information. The newsroom staff of the *Newport News* lugged dozens of large ledgers down from their storeroom and copied many originals from the bound volumes. The Lincoln County Clerk's Office combed through boxes of voter registration cards and death certificates and taught me how to find old, handwritten land records.

Everyone named in this book deserves individual thanks. Several spent hours with me (often feeding me to boot) to ensure that I got things right. I am particularly grateful to these patient people: Les AuCoin, Len Bergstein, Kathryn ("Kat") Brigham, Diane Harrison-Samson, Tony Johnson, Judy Juntunen, Robert Kentta, Verna Miller Kentta, June Olson, Dee Pigsley, Patsy and Gene Pullin, Marie Schmidt, Sue Shaffer, Jeff Van Pelt, and Bob Watson. Several people served as critical readers, providing insight and the incentive to persevere: Sam Deloria, Walter Echo-Hawk, Elizabeth Furse, Dave Hatch, Mark Hatfield, Jennifer Jasaitis, Adair Law, Susan Marmaduke, Harold "Ole" Olson, Louis Pitt Jr., Lynell Schalk, Don Wharton, and Elizabeth Woody.

Lauri Smith, Kathryn Harrison's assistant, contributed invaluably to our Monday taping sessions, providing quiet space and water and preserving us from interruptions. Cynthia Conner, my assistant, was indispensable to the book's creation, shepherding the text through its first round of revisions and tracking down elusive people and documents.

Once the research was completed, the task remained to enliven my lawyerly text. I have learned so much about the art of writing from Karen Kirtley. The director of the Oregon Historical Society Press, Marianne Keddington-Lang, and her associate, Eliza Jones, provided the final polish.

Most of all, I must thank Kathryn Harrison, who lived this story and gave me the incomparable gift of allowing me to review every detail of her life. She carved out the time to meet with me weekly, and she rummaged through many a box of memorabilia to provide essential details. I have cherished the process of working with Kathryn as she remembers and reassesses the moments of her extraordinary lifetime. More than anything else I have ever done, recording her life has been an honor and a pleasure.

Part One

Ancestors to Adulthood
1843–1945

Map by Dean Shapiro

WASHINGTON

PACIFIC OCEAN

Columbia River

Buxton

Portland

Oregon
City

Grand
Ronde

Willamette River

Chemawa
School

Salem

Logsden

Newport

Corvallis

N

W   E

S

Eugene

Coos Bay

OREGON

1

Survival

There's more to us than the casino. We've come back to take our place in the community. —Kathryn Harrison

The cavernous Spirit Mountain Casino opened in 1995 on Grand Ronde Indian lands sixty-five miles southwest of Portland, Oregon, and half an hour from the Pacific Coast. Within five years it was the state's foremost tourist attraction, drawing more visitors than Crater Lake and the Columbia River Gorge. In addition to 90,000 square feet of casino gaming, the Spirit Mountain complex includes a hundred-room lodge, five restaurants, and a children's play center. The bingo hall doubles as a showplace for visiting entertainers, who have included Ray Charles, Joan Baez, and Willie Nelson. Tribal representatives join federal and state government officials in crediting Spirit Mountain with a burst of economic prosperity for the Confederated Tribes of the Grand Ronde Community, which owns and operates the complex.

From the beginning, the Grand Ronde Tribal Council, under the leadership of Kathryn Harrison, agreed that profits from the casino would fund health, economic, educational, social, and cultural programs for members of the community. In 1997, the council established the Spirit Mountain Community Fund to support nonprofit programs and projects for the eleven counties in their Bureau of Indian Affairs service area of northwest Oregon. Six percent of the casino's annual profits now go to the charitable fund, which has given out over $30 million to charities around the state. Spirit Mountain has succeeded beyond the wildest dreams of its founders, who sought to help tribal members escape the poverty that had gripped them for generations.

In September 2001, the casino concert hall was the site of a retirement celebration for Kathryn Harrison. Hundreds of guests and the wealthiest tribal government in the Pacific Northwest assembled to pay tribute to the woman who, for two decades, had led the Tribe's comeback. Had it been built, Kathryn would have preferred the Grand Ronde Interpretive Center as the setting for her retirement party. She has always been a reluctant champion of the gaming facility; and a tribal cultural center, drawing some of the visitors that now gather daily around the casino's one-armed bandits, would have been her milieu of choice. Still, she realizes that the casino's proceeds have made it possible to restore the community infrastructure for her people. Tribal ranks and jobs swelled as the Grand Rondes built a health clinic, education center, elders' housing, administration building, and hotel.

Organizers of the gala evening in Kathryn's honor attended to traditional culture, something she had always emphasized. To soften the garishness of the bingo hall, giant trees sculpted of metal were spaced around the room. On each dinner plate lay an invitation covered with a miniature pheasant-feather fan that the children and the elders in an after-school program had painstakingly assembled. Within elaborate origami folds, the program announced corporate sponsors and the evening's speakers and paid tribute to Kathryn Harrison, retired chair of the Confederated Tribes of Grand Ronde, who "over the course of many years . . . has demonstrated passion, determination, courage, spirit and strength to build the Grand Ronde Community and preserve her Native American culture." Ceremonies included Indian drumming, children performing in the traditional Chinook tongue, speeches by Oregon senators, and a touching video of reminiscences.

When Kathryn was called to the stage, the guests grew quiet. She began, as always, by acknowledging her parents. Although they died within days of each other more than seventy years ago, she gratefully bore witness. "They gave me what I needed to sustain me for the rest of my life," she told us. "I knew I was an Indian." Kathryn recalled her ancestors and their traditional foods, the Christian practices that had meant so much to her, the sweat lodges of her people. She had never lost faith and pride in her Native heritage, and she had spent decades of her life embodying it for others.

Later, some neighboring tribal representatives grumbled that the program was "too glitzy" and displayed how an "assimilated" tribe had lost touch with its roots. True, it was not a traditional giveaway in a longhouse, presided over by elders, but an extravaganza orchestrated by professional event planners and emceed by a local television personality. All the same, Kathryn set an appropriate tone with her combination of humility and dignity. She reveled in the personal recognition, but she leavened it by poking fun at herself. When she first met noted Native American author Sherman Alexie, she told us, he was surprised at her small stature. "Why, you're just a half-pint!" he declared. "We need to add water!"

Fondness and respect for Kathryn were palpable in the room. No one who drove the long distances to Grand Ronde on the night of the tribute did so out of obligation. Despite a life plagued by poverty, illness, domestic violence, alcoholism, and the wrenching deaths of her two oldest sons, she was widely loved and acknowledged and she had succeeded at what few women could hope to accomplish.

In Kathryn's experience, it is the women who hold families together and the family, above all, that gives meaning to life. As Kathryn said firmly at the conclusion of her retirement tribute, "As a mother of ten, grandmother of eleven, and great-grandmother of twelve, I would like to say that my proudest achievement is my family."

Kathryn Harrison's maternal grandfather, George A. Flemming Sr., was a New Yorker born to Scottish and Italian immigrants

FLEMMING ISLAND, SOUTHEAST OF ALASKA'S KENAI PENINSULA

in 1864. Seizing an opportunity to settle in the newly acquired Alaskan Territory, he traveled by rail from the East Coast to Seattle, then walked to Prince William Sound, where he tried his hand at fox ranching on an island later named for him.

George's fur trade prospered at the turn of the nineteenth century.[1] He also worked for the Alaska Pacific Steam Whaling Company and later started one of the barge lines out of Valdez on Prince William Sound. According to his descendants, George built the first paddle-wheeler to go upriver from Cordova at the head of Orca Inlet. Flemming Spit in Cordova is named after him. He married a woman known as Lena, an Eyak who was baptized in the Russian Orthodox church and given the name Elena Kal'Tane. They had two children, first a son they named Henry, then Ella, Kathryn's mother, born a couple of years later in 1894.

Lena and her people fared far worse than the newcomers to their homeland. Not many years before George Flemming made his trek to Alaska, the aboriginal population numbered about 67,000. When the Russians occupied Alaska in the 1860s, whole island populations of Aleuts were annihilated by fur traders.

> The Eyaks . . . provided, in our own time, a prime example of the death of a culture. Previously, they had been among the few Athabascan people to make their way to the coast, and isolated by glaciers and hemmed in by alien tribes, the Eyaks developed a unique language and lifestyle. The land they claimed could have supported almost 1,000 people, and there was half that number of Eyaks at the coming of the whites. The beginning of the end for them came in 1891, with the establishment of four canneries in the area.
>
> Dr. Michael Krauss, linguist who recorded the Eyak language when but half a dozen members survived, found it was a "classic pattern of exploitation." The canneries hired only males and almost no Indians, and the outsiders who worked there brought with them opium and liquor. Epidemics were also introduced. By 1905, not more than 50 Eyaks were left.[2]

The Eyaks' culture was systematically erased. In the last quarter of the nineteenth century, the Alaska Commercial Company began removing ceremonial objects, items of cultural patrimony, and human remains (which they referred to as "mummies") from the Aleuts—now the Chugach—of which the Eyaks were a part. A company ledger lists "an expense of $12 for securing masks and mummies on September 28, 1875."[3]

While George was away, Lena and Ella stayed on the isolated island. Through the long winters, Ella fell asleep many a night to her Eyak mother's version of "Two Old Women," a tale mothers repeated to their daughters over generations.

> As winter approached, the People were trekking across the tundra, realizing that they had not been able to store enough food to see them through until Spring. After much deliberation, they reluctantly left their two oldest members—two women—behind.

Frightened almost to paralysis, the two elders slowly mustered the courage to try hunting and building shelter for themselves.

Rising above abandonment, betrayal, fear, loneliness, and anger, the women supported each other to survive the harsh winter. As the People staggered back after the snow-melt to find what they anticipated would be the elders' remains, they found instead two strong, forgiving women who took the People in and provided for them with loving care. The women became revered leaders, renowned far and wide.[4]

The old women were Ella's role models. Raising and harvesting foxes in the bitter cold was tedious and demanding, and the child had little to fire her imagination aside from her mother's storytelling. Her playthings were dolls of fur and leather and the wood pelt-stretchers used to dry furs for sale. George, determined to widen his children's horizons, planned to send both Ella and her brother to an Indian boarding school for a more formal education.

Lena died when Ella was six, perhaps in childbirth or in one of the flu epidemics that ravaged the Native populations. Shortly afterward, George married a Russian woman, Pauline Chemiviskey. When her first child, "Young George," was born, Pauline may have decided that George's Indian offspring were too much for her to handle. For whatever reason, the decision was made to pack the children's things and send them away from family and home. Henry was the first to go, leaving Ella bereft of her only playmate.

Then, in 1902, George rowed Ella, his eight-year-old daughter, from Flemming Island to nearby Cordova, where she was to catch the steamer south. Tears streamed from her eyes as George pinned a note to her dress: "Please see that my little girl gets to the Salem Indian Boarding School. Please notify George Flemming at Flemming Island, Alaska with questions."[5]

Ella's destination was Salem, Oregon, where a school for Indian children had been founded twenty years earlier. Chemawa, as the school is named, is the Chemeketa word for "happy home," an irony for its homesick young boarders. The school primarily trained them to adapt to the white culture's ser-

OHS Neg. OrHi 101581

GEORGE A. FLEMMING SR. IN ABOUT 1902

vice industry to become farmers' helpers, truck drivers, laundry workers, waitresses, maids, barbers, and mechanics. The first generation of students, most of them from Washington, constructed the buildings and planted the gardens, and the inaugural Chemawa class graduated in 1886, having completed the sixth grade. As the school grew, it accepted younger and younger children like Ella and expanded into the tenth grade. Henry was at

Chemawa when Ella arrived, and she was relieved and happy to see him, the only familiar face.

In 1902, Alaskan students were a rarity and a curiosity at Chemawa, and the surrounding white community considered "half-breeds" such as Ella social outcasts. An official history of Oregon written in the early 1900s reveals the inhospitable setting into which Ella was deposited:

> The heaviest penalty the servants of the Hudson's Bay Company were obliged to pay for the wealth and authority advancement gave them was the wives they were expected to marry and the progeny they should rear. . . . I never could understand how such men . . . could endure the thought of having their name and honors descend to a degenerate posterity. Surely they were of sufficient intelligence to know that by giving their children Indian mothers, their own Scotch, Irish or English blood would be greatly debased. . . . Perish the Hudson's Bay Company thrice over, sooner than bring upon my offspring such foul corruption, sooner than bring into being offspring of such a curse.[6]

Ella ached for her island home and her Eyak mother. At Chemawa she encountered teachers whose mission was to erase her Native culture from her memory, but the survival-by-sharing values of the "Two Old Women" legend sustained her. The child had already learned the most important lesson of her people—that "during the time of hardship . . . we could best survive by working together. . . . The important thing about being Indians was the willingness to share whatever we had and the determination to survive with renewed intent."[7] On reservations and in Native villages across the continent, Indians saw communal survival as their paramount edict.

Today, Kathryn Harrison aches for Ella, her own mother. Her bitterest disappointment in life has been losing her mother, not just to early death but to the mists of the past. It has been impossible to trace that part of her family's history. Kathryn mourns the loss deeply, for herself and for her descendants. She does have dim memories of her Uncle Henry, Ella's older brother, from her childhood. He had remained in Corvallis after his years at Chemawa and had died at an early age. Ella's half-brother, George Jr., chose to remain on Flemming Island all his life, a reclusive fisherman and cannery watchman. He died in the Cordova Community Hospital in 1982, an eighty-year-old widower.

Kathryn continues to search endlessly for information about her Eyak relatives and hopes she might someday learn about the Scottish and Italian immigrants who bore "Old George." Of all the genealogical lines, however, that of the Eyaks is among the most difficult to pursue. Their language has virtually disappeared from the consciousness of the earth, surviving only in musty anthropological files. According to the August 2000 *Harper's* magazine, only one Eyak speaker remained at the time:

> [She was] eighty-one years old, and there is no other native speaker of Eyak on earth. What must she think of us? Neither T.S. Eliot nor Claude Levi-Strauss knew how the world would end, but the last speaker of Eyak knows: it will end in silence. . . . The Eyak fell into silence in the old way, caught between two larger nations on the south coast of Alaska, crushed to a whisper.[8]

If Kathryn has one hope for this biography, it is that it will help bring her mother—and her mother's mother—back to her before she dies. She wants them to survive at least in memory, against all odds.

2

Harry Jones, Valedictorian

The Northwest Ordinance of 1787 promised that Indian lands "shall never be taken from them without their consent; and in their property, rights and liberty, they shall never be invaded or disturbed." Another U.S. promise bites the dust! —Kathryn Harrison, December 10, 2000

Kathryn knows much more about her father's history than about her mother's. Henry "Harry" William Jones was descended from Molalla Chief Yel-kus, who was forcibly removed from his tribal lands and marched on Oregon's "Trail of Tears."[1] Harry was born on the Grand Ronde Reservation in 1892. His father, Billy Jones, died at age fifty when Harry was three years old, and his mother, Philomene Nellie Jones, died three years later. Harry and his older brother Walter were raised by extended family. Walter died when Harry was thirteen, and Harry inherited their parents' land at Grand Ronde—a house, a barn with its twenty acres, and other family lots in the area.

In his early school days at Grand Ronde, Harry was known as a child with promising intelligence, but he bristled at the attitudes of those responsible for educating the "savages." In 1902, when he was a fifth-grader, the Bureau of Indian Affairs issued new instructions to the mostly Catholic staff at the reservation schools:

OHS Neg., OrHi 101593

HARRY JONES AT CHEMAWA, JUNE 1910

The wearing of long hair by the male population . . . is not in keeping with the advancement they are making . . . in civilization. . . . You are to induce your male Indians to cut their hair, and both sexes to stop painting. With some of the Indians, this will be an easy matter; with others, it will require considerable tact and perseverance. . . . A non-compliance with this order may be made a reason for discharge or for withholding rations and supplies . . . and if they become obstreperous about the matter, a short confinement in the guard-house at hard labor with shorn locks should furnish a cure. . . .

Indian dances and so-called Indian feasts should be prohibited. In many cases these dances and feasts are simply subterfuges to cover degrading acts and to disguise immoral purposes. You are directed to use your best efforts in the suppression of these evils.[2]

Both Harry's parents had converted to Catholicism — Philomene was from Siletz, where the missionaries had seen to that — but Harry left the church as a youth, later explaining to his children that he had witnessed too much "meanness" from the priests and nuns. He balked at eating the greasy canteen food and thought the monks who prepared it paid too little attention to sanitation. The young man's independent ways set him at odds with those trying to execute directives from the Bureau of Indian Affairs.

So Harry, too, was sent off to boarding school at Chemawa. The school's ledger shows that when Harry entered the school at age thirteen, he was five feet three inches tall and weighed 128 pounds. When he arrived in 1905, Ella Flemming was already established at the school. Tall and thin and wearing her fur-trimmed Alaskan clothes on special occasions, she must have seemed elegant and exotic.

The only extended family member who kept in touch with Harry at Chemawa was his mother's aunt, Molalla Kate, a free-thinking matriarch who was by then married to her fourth husband and living on the Siletz Reservation. Kate took an interest in Harry, writing him letters and occasionally sending him spending money. In the winter term of his freshman year, when he came down with the flu, Kate wrote the superintendent of Chemawa: "Let me know if his case is doubtful or hopeful and also the length of time of his illness. . . . I am very anxious about him and I thought it would be best to investigate the matter by writing direct to you." She was right to be worried about her great-nephew. Students from the Siletz Reservation had been dying at Chemawa in significant numbers, mostly from cholera and tuberculosis.[3]

Nevertheless, young Harry thrived at Chemawa and became a "big man on campus" despite his small stature. He graduated in June 1910, at the age of eighteen, with the highest grades in the class. There were eight students in Harry's graduating class, four men and four women. They posed for a formal portrait in the attire worn by most students at private prep schools of the era. In his valedictory address, entitled "The Outlook," Harry spoke boldly to the audience of faculty, staff, tribal leaders, and community guests:

> As the Indian was driven back, back, towards the setting sun, his hatred towards the white men increased. The hunt-

ing grounds which had been his were his no longer. The Great Spirit had forgotten the redman. The sadness of disaster predominated in the Indians' music—the weird, minor strains which were sung by the mothers to their little ones—colored the life of the Indian, and only gave place to the terrible war chant . . . which their young men defiantly sang, in a despairing, futile hope of regaining the power of their ancestors. This hope died hard, but it—DIED.

No more will the Indian live his life as did his forefathers. This is generally understood by all Indians—even those who have been most corrupted by the evil habits learned from the white man.

As the Indian was brought to bay, he looked around and saw the white man everywhere. He has submitted to the inevitable, and is now beginning to know that . . . the White man's God . . . intends that all men should be brothers. Instead of looking on the White man as an enemy, we turn to you for help. Will you be our brother?

As Harry noted, "Even an educated Indian has been looked upon with suspicion and a lack of confidence by the western people." All the same, he proclaimed, "I am not sorry that I am an Indian. This is the era in which the Indian can prove his worth."[4]

Harry's teachers encouraged him to go on to college, unusual advice to give an Indian student at the time. So, he stayed at Chemawa for two years after graduation while he attended Capital Business College in Salem. He studied at Washington State University in Pullman off and on for two years—until he ran out of funds. He hoped to sell some parcels of his inherited property at Grand Ronde to finance his education, but in 1915 BIA authorities labeled him a "spendthrift" and judged him incapable of managing the land that was his. Harry Jones, valedictorian of his graduating class at Chemawa, was declared "incompetent."

Many Indian landowners were declared incompetent in the years around 1915 in order for government agents to reclaim the land and sell it to white settlers.[5] The same thing was happening at the nearby Siletz Reservation. It was a deliberate policy dating from the previous century, when so-called assimilationists

OHS Neg., OrHi 101592

HARRY AND ELLA JONES AFTER THEIR WEDDING IN ALASKA, 1915

first teamed with timber companies to break up the tribal land base. It was a long story.

The Northwest Ordinance of 1787 promised that Indian lands "shall never be taken from them without their consent; and in their property, rights and liberty, they shall never be invaded or disturbed." One hundred years later, in 1887, the Dawes Act led to the loss of more than 90 million acres of Indian land, almost two-thirds of their most recently legitimized holdings.[6]

Under the Dawes Act, reservations were divided into private land "allotments."[7] At Grand Ronde, 270 allotments totaling slightly over 33,000 acres of the reservation were created. Each head of household was awarded 160 acres; other adults received 80 acres, and children under eighteen were assigned 40-acre lots. Family parcels were not necessarily contiguous. The remaining land on the reservation was considered "surplus" and offered for sale to non-Indian bidders at $1.50 per acre. In a 1900 amendment, Congress dispensed with the minimum amount for bidders. Accordingly, in 1901, U.S. Inspector James McLaughlin declared over 25,000 acres of the Grand Ronde Reservation as surplus and sold it for just over one dollar an acre. Timber, mining, railroad, and other commercial speculators bought most of the land. Proceeds from the sales were supposed to be used to support Indian programs, but Congress failed to follow through on this purpose.

Under the Dawes Act, individual allotments were held in trust for twenty-five years, during which they could not be sold, leased, or exchanged without permission from the superintendent of the Bureau of Indian Affairs. This provision was intended to protect Indians from being defrauded of their land, but it usually presented an opportunity for the superintendent to evaluate the Indian owners' ability to properly manage the property. Not surprisingly, the politically appointed superintendents favored the companies, with their proven talents for land management.

Thus, under the strict terms of the Dawes Act, Harry Jones should have inherited 160 acres from his parents, 40 acres from his deceased brother Walter, and his own 40 acres, for a total of 240 acres. Instead, he ended up landless. The twenty-five years that Harry's land was held in trust would have expired in September 1916, when he would have owned the land outright and could have sold parcels at will. It was not coincidental that the BIA administrator declared him incompetent in November 1915.

While Harry was at business college and at WSU, he corresponded faithfully with his fellow Chemawa student, Ella Flemming. Although Ella was also a good student, she could not stay to complete her education at the Indian school. Her father's hands were badly frostbitten the winter after Harry graduated, and she had to go home to Alaska to help at the fox ranch. In farewell, her classmates signed an autograph book that Ella treasured — one of the few mementos of her mother that has passed down to Kathryn.

When Harry found himself stymied in his efforts to pursue his college degree, he went to Alaska to claim Ella. They were married aboard an Alaskan steamer on March 23, 1916, at Cordova. Harry returned with Ella to the Grand Ronde Reservation to seek employment painting the homes of the new white settlers, who, as they usurped his land, at least provided him with some temporary income. In December 1917, the couple had their first child, a boy named Harold after his father.

The following year Harry and Ella left the reservation to try their luck in Alaska, hoping to work on a steamer line or in one of the canneries. Their second child, Dorothy, was born in Alaska in April 1920.

Within a few months the family moved again — this time to the Siletz Reservation to be near Harry's great-aunt, Molalla Kate. A son George, named after Ella's father, died as an infant.

Among the Siletz, Harry rediscovered his roots, as Aunt Kate taught him and Ella to fix traditional foods, brain-tan deer hides, and follow cultural lifeways. Kate was a godsend to the struggling young parents, who did their best to subsist on the resources of the land. In honor of the intrepid Molalla Kate, they pledged to name their next daughter Kathryn. "With such a resourceful ancestor," they told themselves, "we'll never have to worry about her."

3

Kakwa Anqati
(As It Was in the Past)

Grizzly's demise, and hence the birth of the Molalla Nation, came about when he met Coyote who was on his way to "make the world" according to an old Molalla tale. The great bear demanded a fight, but Coyote cunningly challenged him to a red hot rock swallowing contest instead. But Coyote cleverly swallowed strawberries while Grizzly gulped down hot stones that burst his heart. After much thought, Coyote skinned and cut up Grizzly, and while scattering his body to the winds, he foretold that the Molalla people "will think all the time they are on the hunt."—Smoke Signals, September 1, 1998

An elderly woman in full Native regalia stares frankly at the camera in one of the last surviving photographs of Kathryn Harrison's great-great-aunt Molalla Kate. By then a resident of the Siletz Indian Reservation, Molalla Kate was a well-known character in Oregon pioneer lore. The niece and adopted daughter of legendary Chief Yel-kus of the Northern Molalla Band, or Molels, Kate was born around 1840 in the hills east of the Molalla River.

The first official Euroamerican contact with the Northern Molalla band was recorded by the man who was to become the Oregon Territory's first governor, Joseph Lane. In a letter to the secretary of war, the supervisor of the commissioner of Indian

OHS Neg. OrHi 101586

MOLALLA KATE IN ABOUT 1934

Affairs in those days of Indian wars, Lane colored his report with his hopes for land settlement and his stereotypes of "hostiles": "The Mole Alley Indians range in the Cascade Mountains and claim no land in the Valley. Their whole number is about 120 warriors. They are a brave and warlike people and not fond of Americans. They are well-armed and live principally by the chase."[1]

Loosely translated, their ancestral name, Mol-el, means "land of elk and berries." Prior to white settlement, the Molallas had followed their traditional seasonal pathways throughout the

Willamette Valley and on the west slopes of the Cascade Mountains, trading and fishing at the falls in Oregon City, hunting and
gathering roots and berries in the nearby prairies and forests. In
their early dealings with the Indians, the settlers acknowledged
the Molallas' rights:

> When [John Dickey's] wagon train arrived in Oregon in
> 1845, the area west of the Molalla River was the only settled
> land. John . . . set out to meet with the Molallas and bargain
> for the right to settle on the prairie east of the river. For goods
> amounting to something less than two hundred dollars, plus an
> agreement that the Molallas could pass through and camp on
> the land as they had always done, John had his land.[2]

Shortly thereafter, settlers invaded the traditional hunting
grounds of the Molallas, and Molalla Kate witnessed the first
enclosing of her people by fence-building veterans of the Oregon Trail.

Initially, the tribe welcomed the newcomers, who presented
trading opportunities. They respectfully nicknamed one pioneer, William Hatchette Vaughan, "Uncle Billy" and "Sage,"
for example. When Vaughan died of smallpox, even though the
Molallas themselves were greatly decimated by this infectious
disease, they "mourned [his] death and wrapped him in a ceremonial blanket before he was buried."[3]

For a while, settlers and tribal people coexisted amicably, but
pressure soon mounted to remove the Indians from the fertile
Willamette Valley. Treaty negotiations, begun in 1850, identified
all the land east of the Molalla River as exclusively tribal. The
1851 treaty, in which the Molallas tried to reserve some of their
traditional territory for themselves, was negotiated by the U.S.
Willamette Valley Treaty Commission but was never ratified by
the U.S. Senate. At that time, the "Moolal-le" tribe ceded land
described as

> commencing at the entrance of the creek known as Abernathy's
> Creek, Into the Willamette River, about a mile below the falls
> of said river, at Oregon City; thence up said creek, running in a

southeasterly direction, to the summit of the ridge dividing the
waters of the Clackamas River from those of the Moolal-le River; thence along the summit of said ridge to the summit of the
Cascade range of mountains; thence along the summit of said
range, in a southwardly direction, to a point due east from the
headwaters of Silver Creek; Thence in a westerly direction to
its headwaters; thence down said Creek to the point where the
eastern boundary line of the Santiam Band of the Callapooyas
crosses said creek, . . . thence along said line to the point where
the same reaches the Willamette River; thence down said river
to the place of the beginning.[4]

In 1851, the federal representative, Superintendent Anson Dart,
listed the Molalla population as consisting of 40 men, 60 women,
and 23 children. Chief Yel-kus and eleven-year-old Molalla Kate
were among them.

Responding to settlers' growing demands, a harsher treaty
was imposed on the Molallas in 1855, totally dispossessing them
of their lands. Chief Yel-kus, on behalf of his people, signed a
treaty agreeing to be relocated to the Grand Ronde Indian Reservation. Then the U.S. Army began its roundup in earnest. A
year later, the army "removed" Chief Yel-kus's band to a reservation farther west, along with thirty-three other bands and tribes
from western Oregon and northern California.

Molalla Kate was fifteen years old. With her twelve-year-old
stepbrother Henry, she traveled by foot on a branch of Oregon's
"Trail of Tears," a sixty-mile trek from her home. The Molallas
left their ceremonial sweat lodges and their ancestors' resting
places. Grandmothers abandoned their beadwork, young mothers relinquished their favorite gathering baskets, men left their
hunting gear behind, and young children chose a single toy to
take with them. The Indians could take only what they could
carry, and for some that meant their babies and a few clothes.

Joel Palmer, the superintendent of Indian Affairs for the
Oregon Territory who negotiated this final treaty, rued the dev-
astation of the forced march and tried to provide for the Indians
once they reached his home in Dayton. He arranged for the "old,
infirm and helpless" to be loaded onto oxcarts and driven the last

Dean Shapiro

TRIBES AND BANDS OF TRADITIONAL OREGON

thirty miles up the Yamhill River from Dayton to Grand Ronde. Palmer lamented that in July 1856 "there were well over fifteen hundred Indians there from among the Willamette, the upper Umpqua and the Rogue Rivers peoples . . . Clackamas and Oregon City people. . . . Some had been there since April amid much disorganization, confusion and suffering."[5] The need for food and shelter was now paramount, as cold and rainy weather would soon be upon them.

A local historian recounted the story of Zella Shaver Muller, who was raised on the east bank of Oregon's Molalla River. Zella remembered the day in 1888 when she and her childhood friends discovered an abandoned Indian village on the river's edge.

> One day when we were spending an afternoon with our grandparents, we went down to the river with Mother and Aunt Ipha. While the grownups picked berries on the hillside,

we went down below and found the two sweathouses, the long-house, and an old canoe. Everything looked as if the Indians had just left it. We were especially fascinated with the sweat-houses. We had to try each stone seat to see which fit us the best. . . . On the day we found the Indian camp and explored it, Mother and Aunt Ipha scolded us. They said that if we played in the sweathouses we would surely catch smallpox.[6]

Little Zella was right: the Molallas had abandoned the camp suddenly, but it was not from Indians that the pioneer children caught smallpox. To the contrary, Euroamerican immigrants had transmitted the disease to Indian people, and it killed tens of thousands of them in Oregon well into the 1870s.[7]

A hundred years later, Hoxie Simmons, Molalla Kate's son-in-law (married to Lizzie Smith, the daughter of Kate's third marriage) told about the Indians' departure from their ancestral grounds:

Chief Yelkes [*sic*] was offered certain sums of money to lead their tribe to the reservation at Grand Ronde, with prom-ises . . . that after five years, they could return to their ancestral lands. . . . Molalla Kate told how there were many tents at the reservation and the Indians were very crowded and unhappy there, and that after the five-year period was up, when they were not released from the reservation . . . her family . . . left the reservation in the dark of the night and made their way back to the . . . former hunting grounds of the Molallas where they remained for some years and then finally moved to the vicinity of Oregon City.[8]

Historian Patricia Baars picks up the story with a photo-graph of Molalla Indians camped near Dickey Creek east of the Molalla River around 1860. Molalla Kate would have been about twenty years old. Yel-kus had warned the white settlers about hostile Indians and fought on the settlers' side against Crooked Finger and the Klamaths in 1848. In appreciation and in a rare departure from their countrymen's prevailing attitudes, the set-tlers allowed the Yel-kus family to return. William Vaughan, the

Dickeys, and their neighbors welcomed the two returning children of Chief Yel-kus into their homes. Henry Yelkus, known to the local citizenry as "Indian Henry" and mistakenly said to be the "last Molalla," lived in the area until his death in 1913. An account of the smallpox patients in the *Corvallis Gazette* on February 6, 1869, names eight whites, one unnamed "colored," and "three squaws." This kind of prejudice was common in Oregon at the time. In 1866, the Oregon legislature prohibited whites from marrying anyone with one-quarter black, Asian, or Hawaiian blood or any person who was more than one-half Indian. Such a marriage was a misdemeanor that carried a penalty of imprisonment for up to one year. Joel Palmer, then a state senator and trustee for the Indians, voted in favor of the law. Molalla Kate dismissed the statute with abandon, and it had no impact on her later marriages.

To the dismay of the returning Yel-kus family, fenced pastures and plowed fields had mushroomed since the Molallas had been "removed" from the area. Kate went to Oregon City to find work and soon married. Her first husband was a Molalla, but the marriage was short-lived and Kate promptly married again. Her second husband, Matehes Williams, was Mexican. That marriage ended quickly as well; rumor had it that domestic violence provoked Kate to leave. In 1868, Kate went home to her mother's people, the Wascos, in The Dalles to give birth to her first son, Mattias.

Ever resourceful, "thinking while she was on the hunt," by 1880 Molalla Kate was living in the Salem area with her third husband, an Irishman named James Smith. Kate's son and their daughter, Lizzie Smith (born in 1878), went to the Chemawa Indian School. When Kate's third husband died in 1881, she made her way to the Siletz Reservation, though her name was never officially entered on tribal rolls there.

In 1894, when Kate was about fifty-four years old, she married her fourth and last husband, Louis Chantal (Chintelle), in Grand Ronde's Saint Michael's Catholic Church at the foot of Spirit Mountain, with Father Croquet presiding. The couple remained together for over forty years. Louis ran the mail route between Grand Ronde and Siletz, and, according to Patricia

Baars they "homesteaded land beside a stream in the Coast Range, a place that must have reminded Kate of her earliest home."[9]

There, at Logsden, Oregon, near the Siletz River, eight-year-old Kathryn Jones first met her great-great-aunt Molalla Kate. Kate was ninety-two and nearly blind, yet Kathryn remembers her as commanding and vibrant. Despite her failing eyesight, Kate navigated around her homestead with ease. She made wonderful biscuits with ingredients by "handful" measures, and she always had milk souring on the back of her wood stove, which she used to make pungent cottage cheese. For extra income, she and Louis tanned hides.

The Jones family lived within walking distance of Kate's homestead, and Harry took his children to see his great-aunt once a week. Like their father, they called her Aunt Kate. Whenever they arrived, Kate was waiting in a long, traditional dress. She told them to line up. Then she felt their faces, one by one, exploring the contours with her capable fingers and paying a moment of special attention to each child. Afterward, the children usually went out to play, while their father and Kate chatted in Chinook Jargon, properly called Chinuk-Wawa. Originally the trade language that had allowed Indians to communicate with French and English merchants and with people who spoke different languages, Chinuk-Wawa had become the universal language among northwestern tribes.[10]

Kate kept a basket of trade beads for making jewelry by her side, and on special occasions she presented gifts of beadwork. On Kathryn's tenth birthday, ninety-four-year-old Kate surprised her with a necklace she had strung herself. Kathryn was touched and marveled anew at Kate's big, familiar hands. Kate loved Royal Anne cherries, and Kathryn imagined that they had caused the many brown spots on her great-great-aunt's face. She was fascinated by Kate's traditional clothing and by her flattened forehead, carefully and deliberately reshaped in her infancy by a Chinook cradleboard, according to custom.

In June 1934, Kate gave a week-long interview to Smithsonian anthropologist Philip Drucker. Detail by detail, in her people's language, she explained Molalla ways. About mourning customs, for instance, she said: "[Female survivor] visits grave

a_{ts} — *sister*	b_{astən} — *white person*	ch_{inuk} — *chinook*	ćh_{ux} — *chip*	d_{akta} — *doctor*	dr_{et} — *true*
mƏkmək — *eat/food*	g_{idəp} — *get up*	h_{ihi} — *laugh/play*	ıxt ıkta — *one what*	K_{əmtəks} — *know*	kʰ_{iyutən} — *horse*
kʷ_{anisəm} — *always*	kʷʰ_{ata} — *quarter*	Ḱ_{aw} — *tie*	Ḱʷ_{as} — *afraid*	l_{ulu} — *carry*	ɬ_{ush} — *good*
m_{iɬayt} — *stay/live/sit*	n_{anich} — *see/look*	lagOm — *pitch*	p_{aya} — *fire*	pʰ_{ikʷ} — *back*	ṕ_{əq} — *hit*
q_{usax} — *sky*	qʰ_{ata} — *how*	q́_{əl} — *hard*	qʷ_{inəm} — *five*	qʷʰ_{etɬ} — *hang*	q́ʷ_{əɬ} — *knock*
lip_ret — *priest*	S_{kukəm} — *strong*	sh_{ush} — *shoes*	t_{əmtəm} — *heart*	tʰ_{at} — *uncle*	t́_{aləpas} — *coyote*
pʰot_{ɬan} — *portland*	t́ɬ_{ap} — *find*	ts_{əqʷ} — *water*	t́s_{əm} — *mark/spot*	U_{lali} ɬU_k — *berry broke*	W_{awa} — *talk*
X_{ulxul} — *mouse*	xʷ _{ɬxʷap} — *hole*	X_{alaqɬ} — *open*	x́ʷ _{itsxʷət} — *black bear*	y_{aʔim} — *tell*	ili?_i — *earth*

CHINUK-WAWA LANGUAGE CHART

five mornings after death. Puts beads on top. Goes around all night—doesn't sleep. Woman's hair cut short. Washes hair with piece of deerskin (doesn't touch with hands), doesn't paint or comb. Uses scratching stick for one year."[11] Her patient testimony preserved many facets of Kathryn's cultural heritage.

As a young teenager, Kate had worked as a nanny for Dr. John McLoughlin, the man sometimes called the Father of Oregon, and his Native wife, Marguerite. A handmade doll attributed to Molalla Kate is now in a display case at the John McLoughlin House National Historical Site in Oregon City.[12] The doll has a beautiful painted face and wears a beaded and fringed buckskin dress much like the one Kate wore when she

KATE IN PROFILE IN 1934

posed for photographs in full regalia. Also on display is a pair of
finely crafted women's moccasins that Kate made, probably for
the McLoughlins' widowed daughter Eloisa. The moccasins are
decorated with handcut glass beads in subtle pink, white, and
blue, forming a large star pattern across the instep. Kate's artistic handiwork bears this misleading inscription:

These things were made by Mrs. Kittie Chintele [Kate Chintelle], the last of the Molalla Tribe. She grew up in Oregon City and knew Madam McLaughlin [*sic*], who taught her many things.

Dorothea Nash Francis, 1939
Donor Information Card

Kate Yel-kus Davenport Williams Smith Chintelle died on September 17, 1938, at the age of ninety-eight. She is buried in Siletz, Oregon, at the Paul Washington Cemetery. Resourceful and defiant to the end, Kate had "squatted" on her property for seven years after the bank foreclosed on it. Louis, her husband of forty-four years, died two months after Kate and was buried by her side.

When Patricia Baars, Molalla Kate's storyteller, first met Kathryn Harrison in 1992, she was struck by several qualities that Kathryn and her great-great-aunt shared. Both Kate and Kathryn had "a sense of self, earned with difficulty over the years"; both bore the marks of someone who had "survived and prevailed through the vicissitudes life handed out," including finding themselves in marriages where they got so desperate they felt they had to leave their husbands. Displaying uncommon resiliency and the ability to straddle two worlds, both were women who "look at life realistically and do what they need to do . . . purposeful, determined . . . *anyone's* role model."[13]

4

Orphaned

Who will tell our stories? Who will sing the songs? — Kathryn Harrison, 1934

Jobs at the Siletz Indian Reservation were scarce, and even with Molalla Kate's help, Kathryn's parents struggled to support their growing family. In the early 1920s, Harry and Ella, with three-year-old Harold and baby Dorothy, moved inland to Corvallis, where Ella's brother Henry worked on a sheep ranch. In Corvallis, they lived in a two-story house on Thirteenth Street, near Oregon State University. Harry painted houses, signs, murals, cars — anything to make ends meet. Ella did housework for white families and also worked as a seamstress.

On March 28, 1924, Harry and Ella had a second baby girl. They named her Kathryn May Jones in honor of Molalla Kate. The same year, Congress passed the Indian Citizenship Act, providing that "all noncitizen Indians born within the territorial limits of the United States be, and they are hereby, declared to be citizens of the United States." The Jones family finally became American citizens, and Kathryn was the first member of the family to have a citizen's rights from infancy.

Harry and Ella were active in the Methodist church in Corvallis, and Kathryn was baptized there in November 1926. Her earliest memories from childhood center on the church. Both

KATHRYN MAY JONES, CRADLE ROLL CERTIFICATE, 1926

her parents sang in the choir, and their lilting hymns were part of family life, along with saying grace at meals and kneeling for bedtime prayers.

Kathryn's most vivid early image of her "Poppa" is of Harry wearing paint-covered overalls and a painter's cap. He kept his paints in the garage, and he and Ella told the children again and again to stay out of them. But Kathryn was drawn irresistibly to the gold leaf he used for painting signs. Once, when she was old enough to know better, she got into the forbidden paint and earned herself a spanking.

In the early days of the Depression, Ella put all her resourcefulness at the service of her family. "Mama could always make something out of nothing," Kathryn recalls. She would get old coats from the church people and cut them down to size. She made whole outfits for Kathryn, with cotton bloomers to match. Kathryn was constantly climbing on things and ripping her bloomers, so Ella teased her by threatening to make "ticking bloomers" out of the tough striped fabric used to make pillow and mattress covers. Many an evening Kathryn fell asleep to the steady lull of the sewing machine treadle as her mother sewed through the night.

On special occasions, Ella would tell the children stories of Alaskan life and tales from her family's fox ranch. Then she would open her steamer trunk, a treasure chest filled with furs and, tucked away, a special box with a carefully arranged Russian tea set and a metal pot cradling brass holders for crystal glasses. Kathryn especially loved the sleek sealskin hat her mother had preserved and the black bear rug with felt lining and a waxy tongue. Ella herself had shot and killed the bear.

The railroad tracks ran near the house, and hobos often came knocking at the door for a meal that Kathryn's mother scraped together for them. Money was tight, and Ella earned extra income by serving for special events at nearby Oregon State University. Kathryn soon discovered she could go to the university and get extra snacks from the party trays. She would knock on the door where she knew her mother was working and ask, "Is Mrs. Jones there?" and the women inside would give her samples of the evening's delicacies. In those years, Kathryn remembers, she ate enough stuffed green olives to last a lifetime.

In 1927, Kathryn's younger sister Marie was born at home in her parents' ground-floor room in a house they rented near the university. Bob followed in 1929, soon after Kathryn started kindergarten at Roosevelt Elementary. Kathryn remembers happy family gatherings, when her parents sang and made music—her father playing a guitar and her mother a ukulele. Dorothy was in third grade, and she, Kathryn, and Marie slept together in an upstairs bedroom. Their oldest brother, Harold, had his own room upstairs. He would pretend to get up in the morning by throwing his shoes on the floor and then roll over and drift back to sleep. Kathryn wondered how he continued to get away with it.

In Kathryn's childhood, Corvallis was a classic country college town. Weekends brought parades, dancing around the Maypole, campus concerts, and football games. As the Great Depression approached, people lined up at the courthouse for flour and at the Sunnybrook Dairy for milk. Outlying farmers brought in surplus crops.

Kathryn's favorite entertainment was going to the movie serials on Saturdays at the Whiteside Theater. Admission was a nickel, and Kathryn often scrounged for that last penny on Saturday mornings. Each episode would end at an exciting moment so the audience would want to return the next week. Saturday nights, the family would wash, iron, and mend their best clothes in preparation for Sunday services.

A solemn family ritual took place at least once a year when Harry took the entire family to the cemetery at Siletz, a day-long trip. There he erected a freshly painted wooden cross on two small graves, where Maxine and George, the two children who had died in infancy, were buried. The children helped clean the grave sites and decorated them with fresh flowers. The ritual linked Kathryn to the ancient Indian tradition of the "grave-tender." The person who held this honored position rode circuit on horseback among the widely scattered graves of his people, tending them with care. In the absence of a designated grave-tender, Harry took on the role and shared it with his children.

Ella and Harry now attended a Pentecostal church, and the family devoted Sunday nights to Bible study. Kathryn's father developed a talent for "chalk talks." Working quickly with chunks of colored chalk, he illustrated Bible stories, bringing "Jonah and the Whale" or "Daniel in the Lion's Den" to life with vivid words and a few deft strokes of color.

In 1930, when Kathryn was six, the Spanish Colonial–style Full Gospel Assembly Church was constructed at Fourth and Adams Streets. Harry painted the murals on the arched back wall of the assembly hall. After joining the congregation, Harry and Ella were re-baptized at the traditional Native gathering place near the confluence of the Willamette and Mary's Rivers.

Despite all the efforts of Kathryn and her parents to fit in, they were often abruptly reminded that they were viewed as different in the eyes of others, especially with the cruel taunts of her classmates. Kathryn's first recollection of being treated as Other came in elementary school, when someone on the playground called her a "dirty Indian." The Jones children were the only Indians in their grades, and Kathryn's father often came to school to defend them. At the same time he tried to prepare them

Courtesy of Kathryn Harrison

HARRY AND ELLA'S RIVER BAPTISM NEAR CORVALLIS, 1932

for the inevitable discrimination they would face. "You have to excel," he told them at home. It was the only way to counteract the fact that when any of them went downtown to the five-and-dime store after school, they were the last to be waited on.

Still undaunted, Kathryn auditioned for the 1932 third-grade production of "Goldilocks," staged as an operetta. Her parents rehearsed her well: she sang loudly, and she was not shy. Despite her own dark locks, Kathryn was selected for the lead. Her mother bought her new buckled shoes and made her costume, a white wool pleated skirt and a fancy jacket with a hood. She even curled Kathryn's hair in corkscrews, laboriously winding the locks around her fingers. The play was so successful that the children performed it again in the downtown auditorium.

Kathryn's triumph as Goldilocks was her swan song in Corvallis. In 1933 came rumors that the federal government was giving out "Indian money" (probably as part of the New Deal and the Indian Reorganization Act). Harry and Ella had baby Norma in February of that year, and life in Depression-era Corvallis was getting harder. So Harry packed up the family in the old Essex "crank car" and headed back to his roots and his great-aunt Molalla Kate at the Logsden homestead near Siletz.

ELLA WITH THE CHILDREN IN CORVALLIS, MARIE ON
RIGHT, BOB IN FRONT AND BABY NORMA

Harry and Ella told their children that it would be good to
be with their own people again, and they promised to build a
"fabulous log house" in the woods. They piled their household
goods into a homemade trailer, hitched it up, and set out over the
Coast Range. Kathryn remembers having to unhook the trailer
and pull it, because the old Essex didn't have enough power to
lug it uphill. In a square basket that Grand Ronde basketmaker
Bill Simmons had made for the family, Ella had packed Indian
bread, canned fruit, and homemade jams for the family to enjoy
along the way. Harry and Ella didn't know that the federal bank
had foreclosed on Kate's property due to failure to pay taxes.
Fortunately, the Lincoln County sheriff allowed the family to
"squat" on the land in the absence of a buyer.

The family liked Logsden, though they lived in an old chicken
house at first, with furniture—including a rocking chair and

an old-fashioned fainting couch—piled up like chicken crates. Molalla Kate and her daughter, Lizzie Smith Simmons, welcomed them back, and they knew all the families along the road. A refreshing creek ran through the land, and berries abounded in the fields. Lincoln County records show that Ella and Harry registered to vote Republican right away, despite their support for some of the New Deal programs.

Kathryn spent a lot of time at Lizzie's big house and sometimes borrowed food from the root cellar Lizzie and her husband Hoxie supplied. Their daughter Pearl was a little older than Kathryn and became a favorite Auntie. Lizzie would make huge breakfasts of biscuits, venison, farina, fried potatoes, and eggs. A beautiful woman with smooth skin, she carefully washed her face in cold water every morning. Kathryn took up the practice, which became a lifetime habit.

In 1933, Harry began building a log cabin on land listed in the Lincoln County records as "Section 34, T9S, R9W," by Rock Creek. He did not peel his logs, and he chinked them with moss in the Alaskan fashion. Downstairs he built a kitchen, a bedroom, and a greatroom with floor-to-ceiling French windows, where the family held prayer meetings. The greatroom was furnished sparsely, with a round wooden table, claw-footed matching chairs, and Harry's favorite wooden rocking chair. Upstairs were the children's bedrooms.

Next Harry built a sweat lodge between the cabin and the creek. Only the men of the family used it, and for once Kathryn didn't mind being excluded. If you poured too much water on the hot rocks, she remembers, everyone choked on the steam. Harry insisted that the boys use the sweat lodge, and they began to dread the after-sweat dip in the cold water of the creek.

By the summer of 1934 the family had moved into the cabin. Kathryn helped her mother carry firewood and wash clothes in the creek. Ella gave each of the children a part of the garden and let them decide what they wanted to plant. Kathryn chose dahlias and carrots, but she kept digging up the carrots to see how big they were, so none of them grew to maturity. Ella surrounded the house with colorful cosmos flowers, which she could see from the windows of the greatroom. Dahlias and cos-

OHS Neg. OrHi 101574

KATHRYN AND BOB, 1931

mos were Ella's favorites and became Kathryn's too. In memory, she always associates them with her mother.

Harry continued his artistic pursuits. He would dry "punks" (ledges of lichens) he had cut off trees and logs and paint on them. He took on numerous WPA projects around Newport and between projects painted dolls and other toys for the children. He and Ella caught and dried eels and fish, and Kathryn stayed with four-year-old Bob when they rented fishing boats at the coast. The rest of the family would pile into a rowboat and paddle a few hundred yards out, while Kathryn and her little brother stayed wistfully on shore.

Kathryn began fourth grade in a two-room schoolhouse with four grades and one teacher in each room. Miss Wilson lived right across the road from the school, while Mr. Hobart commuted from Newport.[1] The children's typical lunch was venison with gravy, which each child carried to school in a five-pound tin lard bucket to heat it on the pot-bellied stove. During the

Depression, Kathryn wore shoes with cardboard in the soles. The students combined to stage plays and memorized poems such as "Old Ironsides." Kathryn played the part of a child in "The Old Woman Who Lived in a Shoe," and Dorothy was the baker-woman in "Sing a Song of Sixpence." Kathryn loved spelling and reading and looked forward to monthly issues of a farmer's magazine that included word puzzles. Reading about Portland's annual Rose Festival, she imagined herself a festival princess but then immediately knew this could never be. Over the years, if she mentioned feeling like an outsider to her mother, Ella would say, "You always have to earn your place."

Each summer the family went to a hops harvest gathering in the fields between Salem and Independence. Camps were divided between Grand Ronde and Siletz pickers, and occasionally other Oregon tribes would join them. In the hot August days, whole families joined in contests to see who could pick the most.

Kathryn hated the job of stripping hops. One woman from the Coeur d'Alene tribe minced no words in her description of that hard labor: "Stripping hops is backbreaking work: dirty and hot and the vines are so sharp you wear out a pair of leather gloves each and every day, first one side and then the other, and the vines whip across your face if you aren't careful and leave a long, red welt that stays for a long time and looks like an angry scar."[2] Kathryn did not have gloves, so she wrapped black friction tape around her fingers for protection. Because the workers were paid by the pound and had to get their "tickets" punched at the end of the workday, they worked all day long. She could hardly wait for the evening's entertainment when the camps came alive with dancing, boxing matches, traveling salesmen hawking their elixirs, and stick games with pickers from the Warm Springs Indian Reservation.[3] The children would be treated to cream pies and orange popsicles miraculously delivered from ice chests that had withstood the heat of the day.

It took some effort for the Jones family to get to the hop fields. Harry cursed at the old Essex as he cranked it up, while Kathryn pushed on the spark valve. They could count on having at least one flat, so the family would have to save up to be sure they had an extra inner tube and tire-patching supplies. While her father was fixing a tire on the road, Kathryn would ask him questions about the surrounding vegetation, and Harry would identify licorice ferns and Indian celery for her. The Siletz Indian Boarding School had extinguished most of the traditional lessons, because the staff frowned on "barbarian folklore"; but Molalla Kate had passed her cultural training along to Harry, and he passed it on to his children.

All of the Jones children lived at home and went to public school in Logsden and Siletz. Harold was particularly adept at art projects, once carving an intricate Viking ship and making a bow and some arrows. His social life was better than it had been in Corvallis — so good that one night he stayed out too late and got in trouble. Ella sent him to the barn to see Harry, who delivered a resounding spanking. Later, Kathryn found out that both had faked it. Harry had thumped on the floor, while Harold had hollered.

As much fun as school could be, the Jones children dreaded their lessons in American history. "Oregon Indians Were True Savages," read a heading in the standard history text Kathryn used in grade school at Logsden. They lacked "more than the rude beginnings of civilization. [They were] always poor, always hungry and miserable." Kathryn was bewildered to read that the Indians had "vanished": "The remnants of that savage people which made an attack on Captain Robert Gray in 1788 are now extinct. Nought of them remains but the names they gave to the geography of Oregon." As a final eulogy, she read this update: "Now, his [the savage's] thousands of warriors and hunters, his dark-eyed maidens and careless children are no more."[4]

Harry kept up his ties to Grand Ronde. He was considered a leader and was selected in 1934 to testify on the tribe's behalf at a congressional field hearing at Chemawa Indian School on the Indian Reorganization Act, another BIA scheme to "civilize" the Indians. The IRA would substitute Anglo-style governments for the longstanding methods of rule that had served tribes remarkably well over the centuries. Tribal leaders were understandably leery but knew that this proposal came with promised benefits. The dilemma was reflected in the closely divided plebiscites on the issue. Harry's words are recorded in the *Congressional Record* for March 8 and 9, 1934:

> What assurance have we, as the people, that these gentlemen here assembled will declare to us a . . . firmer and surer bill, or contract, or agreement or treaty, whatever it may be, than [Joel] Palmer? . . . That is the question. I think every one of the older men who may speak having to have an interpreter, want to be governed by the treaty rights. . . . I believe there are those here that will benefit by this measure or bill. There are those of us who are still doubtful, still wondering if we are going to benefit by this bill or whether we will stand in the future as perhaps we have with the past treaties. How much better off will we be then if we accept it now? . . . We have formulated an answer to this question because we believe that when we accept or reject that we can still be considered a people that have attempted all along to cooperate with the government in its proposed plan. At one time there were twenty-three tribes on the Grand Ronde Reservation. Now the reservation is comprised of an area of eight by twelve miles.

In the final tally, the Siletz voted against the act. At Grand Ronde, the act passed by a narrow margin, because unmarked absentee ballots were counted as "yes" votes. At several reservations around the country, the federal government used this method of tallying to secure compliance.

One day in the fall of 1934, when Harold was seventeen and Kathryn was ten, Kathryn came home from school with a fever. She became dehydrated and developed sores in her mouth. Soon her hair began to fall out in patches, and she began to hallucinate. She thought she heard the door opening constantly and Aunt Kate walking in, asking her questions. Kathryn was sick for several weeks. A visitor told her that an article in the local paper warned of a virulent flu outbreak and reported that "one of the Jones girls has it."

MARIE (LEFT) AND KATHRYN HOLDING BLUE COAT HER
MOTHER MADE, 1934

All her life Kathryn has carried the emotional burden of believing she was the one who brought the deadly virus home. But infections were rampant in the Indian community, and several people that same fall came home from the hops harvest with an intestinal virus. The pickers reported a rumor that the water supply in the fields was contaminated.

Dorothy and Harold soon came down with the illness, and Ella was up all night feeding the wood stove and tending her sick children. Harry was the next to get it, early in November. Kathryn could hear him struggling at night to get to the cold outhouse. Finally, Ella began to show symptoms.

In early December, family friends came from the BIA clinic at Siletz to transport the sickest members of the family into town for medical care.[5] The clinic was staffed by two midwives, a visiting nurse, and old Dr. Burgess, who came up from Toledo once a week. Kathryn stood in the greatroom of the log cabin and watched as her mother was carried out in a long basket, weakly waving goodbye. Harry and the sickest of the children, Dorothy and Harold, trudged after her to the waiting truck. Ten-year-old Kathryn, seven-year-old Marie, five-year-old Bob, and two-year-old Norma stayed behind. A few days later Bob, too, was taken to the infirmary. He was allowed to see his mother briefly. She lay her hot hands on his face, told him to take care of himself, and said that she loved him.

About a week later, Agnes Isaakson, a family friend, took Kathryn to the clinic to see her parents. She wasn't allowed in, but she peeked through a window and saw her mother in the far corner of a large room. Ella's face was pale, but her cheeks were bright red. She lay very still, and Kathryn couldn't tell whether she was asleep or too sick to move. Agnes took Kathryn, Marie, and little Norma home with her so they wouldn't starve trying to cook for themselves.

Only a few days had passed when Agnes came into Kathryn's bedroom and told her that her mother had died. Holding back a flood of tears, Kathryn went to find her favorite blue wool coat — the "coat with the lapels" that her mother had made for her. She hugged it, a precious remnant of her mother's love, and vowed, "I'll never let it go." The women tending Ella at the clinic reported that when they went to tell Harry his wife was dead, he said he already knew.

The following week, Maude Lane, who lived next to the clinic, was asked to tend Harry. Hoxie Simmons had been sitting with him but had to leave for an errand. Maude provided a detailed account of the morning:

> I went in and talked to Harry and asked him "How are ya this morning?" He said "Not so good," and he told me "My mouth is just burning up." He said, "Do ya know where that cream is that they rub on my mouth?" and I said, "I'll find it."

So I found that bottle that had that stuff in it—kind of like a cream that you put on your lips—and I put that on his lips. I was standing there, and he kept talking to me.

Pretty soon he turned over, and he said "I hope Ella's getting better." And I said hm-hmmm. I didn't know what to say, so I turned around, and I put the lid on the medicine and put it back. Pretty quick, he turned over, and he said, "My goodness, my lips are just burning again," so I put some more of that on his lips. Then he said, "I just don't feel good," and I thought, "My God, what if something happens and I'm here?" I was already eight months pregnant, and—I didn't know—I just hoped that Hoxie [Simmons] would come back, because he said he would come right back from going down to the store.

So anyway, Hoxie never came back . . . and Harry turned over and he grabbed my hand. He just held my hand. . . . Pretty soon he was gone. . . . And there I was: I didn't know what to do. There was no phone, or *nothing*.[6]

Ella Flemming Jones died on December 13, 1934, at the age of forty. Her husband Henry "Harry" William Jones died six days later at the age of forty-three. Kathryn cried to Agnes, "I hate God!" But Agnes shushed her, saying, "That's the devil talking to you!"

Funeral services for Ella and Harry were held at the Pentecostal church in Siletz. Kathryn and Marie were the only children there. Dorothy and Harold were still sick, and Bob and Norma were too young to attend. Kathryn, approaching her mother's body in an open casket, was shocked to see that she was wearing a stranger's dress. She cried out, "My mother never had a blue satin dress with a lace collar. Who did that to her?" Again, she was quickly shushed.

The *Lincoln County Leader*, on December 20, 1934, reported that "funeral services were held for Mrs. Harry Jones Saturday morning at the Full Gospel Tabernacle. Mrs. Jones was dearly loved by all those who knew her and is survived by her husband and several children. The entire family is ill." Harry's obituary appeared in the January 3, 1935, issue: "about a week after Mrs. Jones passed away her husband also passed away. He was laid

ELLA IN LOGSDEN

to rest by the side of his wife. In the passing of Mr. and Mrs. Jones it leaves a family of six children who are recovering from their illness and have been up and around the last few days." The children had become the Jones family orphans.

Kathryn longed for her mother from the depths of her soul. "I just felt so lost," she recalls. "I didn't know where to go, what to do. All I wanted was to feel Mama's arms, hear her voice. I wanted to sleep all the time because maybe Mama would come to me in my dreams."

5

Homeless

The Congress hereby declares that it is the policy of this Nation to protect the best interests of Indian children and to promote the stability and security of Indian tribes and families by the establishment of minimum Federal standards for the removal of Indian children from their families and the placement of such children in foster or adoptive homes which will reflect the unique values of Indian culture, and by providing for assistance to Indian tribes in the operation of child and family service programs. —Indian Child Welfare Act of 1978, Sec. 1902, Congressional Declaration of Policy

Five-year-old Bob was collected one day shortly before his parents' funeral by a Mrs. Watson, known to the children only as "that Catholic woman who went to the Siletz butcher shop." She arrived on Agnes Isaakson's doorstep flashing papers that she said granted permission from the Bureau of Indian Affairs to take Bob to Newport, where her husband was working on the construction crew for a town bridge. Kathryn and Marie cried hysterically as Bob was driven away. They had no idea when or where they might see him again.

The first summer after their parents died, Kathryn and Marie were sent to Chemawa to have their tonsils removed. There they were allowed to visit their older sister Dorothy and also baby Norma, who had grown so chubby that she couldn't cross her legs on the little nursery chair. The girls at Chemawa gave Kath-

OHS Neg. OrHi 101596

KATHRYN IN FRONT OF LESLIE MILLER'S
HOUSE IN LOGSDEN, 1936

ryn and Marie dresses they had made in home economics classes. When it was time to leave, both Kathryn and Marie dissolved in tears.

Shortly after that visit in summer 1935, Norma was delivered to the Albertina Kerr orphanage in Portland. Harold ran away from Chemawa and went south to Klamath Falls, then to Arizona. Sixteen-year-old Dorothy wanted desperately to reunite Kathryn, Marie, Bob, and Norma, but she was a boarding-school student and didn't know how to begin to accomplish such a task. Her sense of family, so crucial in Native American culture, was beginning to fracture.

No one knew much about Lillian Watson, the woman who took Bob away in the winter of 1934–1935. She sometimes came

to Siletz to play cards. The people who had met her described
her as excitable and easily angered when the cards were not falling her way. She dyed her hair bright red and was rumored to be
a former "woman of questionable virtue."[1] Her only son, a child
of unknown origin she had brought into her current marriage,
was mentally ill.

Later the family learned that Lillian and Carl Watson were
friends of a butcher who had briefly employed Harry Jones as
a sign painter, which may explain how Mrs. Watson learned of
Harry's death and the children's dispersal. The Watsons were
living temporarily in Newport, where they supplemented their
construction income with BIA payments for tending Indian children. It was in their interest to increase their per capita payments by having extra children in the household, and "old Lil,"
as the townspeople knew her, had come for Bob even before his
parents were in the ground. When she learned that Norma was
at Albertina Kerr, she got BIA permission to "rescue" the child.
Albertina Kerr records show the release of "baby Norma, at the
request of the Superintendent of Department of Field Services,
Bureau of Indian Affairs," on September 24, 1936.

A year later, in the summer of 1937, Lillian Watson again
appeared on Agnes Isaakson's doorstep with an official letter to
the effect that Kathryn and Marie Jones were to return home
with her to Buxton. "Home" at that time was a shack in the forest, followed shortly afterward by a log cabin the Jones children
labored to build. When Kathryn visited sixty-three years later,
she still remembered every plank and stone.

Kathryn and Old Lil were at loggerheads from the beginning. Mrs. Watson (as Kathryn still calls her) made deroga-
tory comments about Indians. Kathryn took offense and talked
back. Mrs. Watson assigned Kathryn to washboard duty. She
beat Kathryn, and the young girl tried to run away. Kathryn
later learned that Dorothy often wrote her at the Watsons'
address, but Old Lil never showed her the letters. The first
Christmas at Buxton, Dorothy sent presents for each of her
siblings. Mrs. Watson rewrapped them and presented them as
her own gifts for the children. If the children made the mistake
of speaking fondly of their birth parents, she would scream

KATHRYN IN 2000 REVISITING THE WATSONS' CABIN, WHICH SHE
HELPED BUILD AS A CHILD IN 1937

that if they didn't "move on into the white world" they would
end up on Skid Row.

Carl Watson was a nightmare in the flesh. Serving as a
Marine in World War I, he had been shot in the mouth (twenty
years later he drew a 25 percent military disability). His interest
in his three foster daughters was primarily sexual, and at every
opportunity he attempted to molest them. Marie remembers him
chasing her around in the garage and catching her by her hair.[2]
The girls went to great lengths to avoid being alone in the house
with Mr. Watson. It infuriated and depressed Kathryn that she
was helpless to protect her younger sisters. All she could do was
run and try to protect herself.

During the Depression, when BIA or Catholic Charities officials would pay formal visits to the Watson foster home, Old Lil
would get the girls "all dolled up," Kathryn remembers. They
showed no outward signs of the frequent abuse, so the officials
would report that all was well and the abuse would start all over
again. Kathryn asks now, "Who would have believed a little

Indian girl if she had complained?" After all, her foster father was a war veteran.

Kathryn fled to Chemawa as soon as she graduated from ninth grade. When she arrived, on June 30, 1939, her guardian was listed as "Superintendent, Siletz—Grand Ronde Agency." Once again, "no home" appeared in the address blank. Kathryn had spent two degrading years as a ward of the Watsons with no home worth mentioning.

In 1978, the Indian Child Welfare Act became law.

> The Congress hereby declares that it is the policy of this Nation to protect the best interests of Indian children and to promote the stability and security of Indian tribes and families by the establishment of minimum Federal standards for the removal of Indian children from their families and the placement of such children in foster or adoptive homes which will reflect the unique values of Indian culture, and by providing for assistance to Indian tribes in the operation of child and family service programs.[3]

The provisions came too late to save the Jones girls from the humiliations of life in their foster home.

Bob's experience with the Watsons was radically different. A handsome boy who embraced the idea of assimilation, Bob occupied a privileged place in the Watson household. In view of Lillian's son's disability, he was treated as a favorite. Though he realized that his sisters did their best to stay out of Carl Watson's reach, he did not learn why until many years later.[4]

Bob had only the haziest memories of his own parents, and the Watsons were the only parents he ever really knew. He lived with the Watsons while he worked his way through college at Willamette University in Salem. Norma, too, struggled, staying in the home until her junior year in high school, and she and Bob became especially close. Although the Watsons never formally adopted Bob, he assumed their surname. When Carl Watson took a new job as a prison guard, Bob followed him. Later Bob would become director of the Oregon Department of Corrections, which oversaw the operations of the state prison.

6

Chemawa Revisited

A quitter never wins and a winner never quits. —Kathryn Jones's motto
in the 1942 Chemawa yearbook

Kathryn remained at Chemawa throughout her high school
years. Even though she did not land at the school until she was
a sophomore, she was a bright, popular student who quickly
became immersed in activities. She was in House Council, YWCA,
Girls Quintette, and Glee Club in 1940–1941. In keeping with
her Goldilocks debut, she starred in both the junior and senior
plays. She wrote for the school newspaper and yearbook and
was home-room president her senior year. She enjoyed singing,
dancing, and cheerleading and especially loved singing traditional songs with classmates from all over the western United
States and performing the Corn Dance with friends from New
Mexico. "The whole school was involved in that pageant, even
the little kids," Kathryn recalled. "We made our own dresses of
unbleached muslin, fringed edges everywhere. Superintendent
[Paul T.] Jackson took video footage of the dance."

Kathryn's friends dubbed her "Jonesy" and knew they could
count on her for a cheerful boost. Despite constant messages
from the dominant society that Indians were lazy, dull drunk-
ards, Kathryn reminded everyone within earshot that Indians
could do anything they set out to do. Do it they did during Kath-

ryn's school years. Chemawa had a first-place basketball team, a semi-finalist in Western Division wrestling, a state finalist in boxing, and a Big Nine boxing champion. For a small rural school in 1940s Oregon, Chemawa made its mark. Instead of fulfilling its mission of assimilation, the school unintentionally reinforced a sense of Indian identity. Many of Oregon's tribal leaders are alumnae.

At her first school Christmas in 1939, Kathryn found herself at loose ends. Her sister Dorothy, officially her surrogate parent, was a live-in employee in a home in Astoria and could not receive overnight guests, so the Jones family had no place to gather for the holidays. Sybil Woods, a Chemawa classmate, invited Kathryn to spend the vacation at her home. So Kathryn and Sybil took the mail boat up the Rogue River from Port Orford and walked through the woods to the family's log cabin. Kathryn remembers a delicious Christmas dinner at the Woods' home and a dance with Sybil's large family in an old schoolhouse.

Several Chemawa students, including Kathryn, stayed at the school in the summers, because they enjoyed each other's company in the more relaxed months or because they had no other homes. At least at Chemawa, they were paid for their work. Most of the girls worked in the laundry or the dining room, and students who proved themselves were invited to work for the teachers. "You had to be trustworthy and work your way up," Kathryn said. "This was a privilege. Otherwise you were forced to depend on money from home."

One year Kathryn worked for a teacher one night a week and on weekends. Among other duties, she remembers washing the teacher's long cotton socks and hanging them on the line to dry. Later she worked at the home of Superintendent Paul T. Jackson, a well-liked man who took an interest in the students and proudly videotaped special school events.

"Superintendent Jackson's home was a nice cement house," Kathryn remembered. "To me it was like a palace. I was in awe of the furnishings. I had to learn how to do the laundry, set the table, make beds with mitered corners—do all the things they were too busy to do." One of Kathryn's duties was to carry scraps from the school dining room for the Jacksons' tiny dog.

She had a special bucket for the task and grew fond of the dog, "a little mutt that knew its place."

During "off hours" every other weekend, the students could take a chartered Greyhound bus to nearby Salem to shop or go to the movies. One of their challenges was learning to manage the little money they had. During the school year, the girls' field trips to Salem often entailed learning some kind of social skill. Wearing hats and gloves, they went to a formal tea—a "silver tea"—and learned how to "pour." In accordance with BIA imperatives, they were also farmed out to upper-class white homes to learn proper etiquette.

> Whether Indians wish it or not, they must become a part of the life around them. . . . It is our task then to help the Indian girl equip herself to meet the demands of modern living—vocationally, spiritually and socially. We must help her to fit herself, and the gifts she brings out of her own rich heritage, into the communities of which she is to be a part.[1]

In 1941, the summer after her junior year, Kathryn worked for a doctor in Oregon City doing housework and answering the telephone, much as her Aunt Kate had worked for John McLoughlin in Oregon City almost a century before. The doctor and his wife had no children and took Kathryn under their wing. "They were always telling me, 'Don't be afraid to get out in the world,'" Kathryn recalled with a smile. At summer's end, they invited her to stay with them and offered to send her to college.

Kathryn was tempted by the generous offer—this was her opportunity to go to college and receive a four-year liberal arts education—but she was afraid that if she left her community of Indian friends, she would never return to them. She recalled years later: "I had a gut feeling that if I took them up on it, I would end up in the East and never get back to my people." At summer's end she said goodbye to the doctor and his wife and returned to Chemawa, where she rejoined Lillian "Dada" Case, her longtime roommate. Later, Kathryn saw this decision as a crossroad in her life, and she has never regretted the path she chose.

KATHRYN AND FRANK AT CHEMAWA, 1941

Near the end of her junior year, Kathryn began dating Frank Harrison from Montana's Rocky Boy Chippewa Reservation. Frank was another popular student—a strong personality and a talented clarinetist who loved to perform in public. Their courtship was mostly clandestine, since Chemawa had strict rules for male-female interaction. The school administrators posted a list of couples for the school dances, and the only permitted time they had together was when the boys picked up the girls at their dorm and walked them over to the gym. The girls were chaperoned when they took trips to town, although on their senior class trip to Silver Falls they were allowed to walk with their boyfriends on the trails.

The Class Prophecy section of the Chemawa yearbook for 1942, the year Kathryn graduated, foretold that her future would be intertwined with Frank's. Jonesey would be "a popular singing star . . . singing that number one of the Hit Parade—'Down with the Rising Sun' . . . the featured songstress in 'Frankie' Harrison's popular orchestra." Kathryn's teachers had loftier aspirations for her. Her official student rating form bore the note: "Could be strong leader."

Frank was slated to perform a Verdi clarinet solo at commencement, but late in his senior year he was expelled for drinking. He and some of his friends had broken into a nearby winery and had gone drinking down in Pigville on the Chemawa campus, where they raised hogs. Kathryn clung to the belief that Frank would mend his ways as he matured.

Kathryn has many fond memories of Chemawa: "For me, coming from a foster home, my best memory was knowing that is where I was going to go. When [the bus] pulled up to that driveway leading to Winona Hall, I knew I was going to be among my own people and things would be okay." Her worst memories of Chemawa were the good-byes at the end of each school year.

> We would sing "God Be With You Till We Meet Again."
> We held hands. We knew it was going to be hard, but it was our tradition. We never got through it. It was always too hard. Then school ended. Some of the students were leaving on the bus that brought them. You always knew when to be ready. They would post it—Flathead bus is leaving on such and such a day. Some would go by train. The rest were left behind, and there were quite a few. The train whistle became the loneliest sound of all when you knew they were taking your friends away.
>
> I remember standing at the window many times listening to that [whistle] and crying. . . . Chemawa is where I gained my self-esteem. I had none when I got there.

Kathryn is not alone in this feeling. In twenty-three interviews that Sonciray Bonnell conducted with Chemawa alums for

FRANK IN UNIFORM WITH KATHRYN HARRISON AND PATSY, 1944

her master's thesis at Dartmouth College in 1997, she found they "were able to view Chemawa in a positive light, because students molded their boarding school experiences to fit their needs. Students created their own families (friends), community (school), and resisted the institutional suppression. . . . The net result was that the school tended to increase, not decrease, their feelings of Indian identity." This is not the prevailing view in Indian Country. Most of the literature about Indian boarding schools dwells

on the homesickness of the students and the relentless control of
BIA administrators, even to the point of denying parents' requests
to visit their children.[2] Wilma Mankiller, who was principal chief
of the Cherokee Nation, wrote of her father's experience in the
1920s:

> Back in the bad old days, the BIA representatives who main-
> tained boarding schools . . . would go hundreds of miles and re-
> turn with native children. The philosophy, reflecting an errant
> missionary zeal, was to get native children away from their fami-
> lies, their elders, their tribes, their language, their heritage.[3]

Kathryn's situation was entirely different. She was fleeing a far
more abusive home when she went to Chemawa, and she had no
other home to long for.

Kathryn's first positive experience with the power and comfort
of women came when she was a high school student at Chemawa. After her abusive foster home placement, Chemawa was
a refuge. Soon Kathryn found herself relying on her roommate
Dada Case and friends such as Cecilia Bearchum and June Simmons, trusting they would provide a lifelong safety net.

In later years, Dada and June would provide housing for
Kathryn's growing family and support in times of crisis. Cecilia was often there to share laughter and tears and professional
interests. The four women kept in touch through constant correspondence, no matter where life took them. June kept a scrap-
book of Kathryn's achievements and hung a newspaper photograph of Kathryn on her living-room wall, as a proud sister
might do.

During the time that Kathryn and Dada were roommates,
World War II began. In 1940, Congress passed the Nationality
Act, reconfirming Indian citizenship (cynics would say in order
to subject Indian males to the draft), although several states
still refused to allow Indians the right to vote. Chemawa grew
its own food, and at first it was largely unaffected by wartime
shortages and rationing. Kathryn's graduating class yearbook,
The Chief, bore the following dedication:

> WE, the senior class of 1942, do hereby dedicate our yearbook to the AMERICAN INDIANS in the armed forces who are giving so unselfishly of their services to our country, and who are gallantly showing the loyalty of our race to our country.

By 1942, more than 25,000 Native Americans were in combat, and 40,000 were employed in wartime industries.[4]

Upon graduation, Kathryn again found herself with no place to go to. She decided to marry Frank, although she knew he was about to go overseas with the army. At least then, she thought, she could live with his family in Montana.

Mrs. Black, a staff member at Chemawa, had arranged a post-graduation job for Kathryn at the home of a Portland family; but the day before she was scheduled to leave Chemawa for Portland, Kathryn ran away. She was determined not to end up in another abusive foster home. The staff tracked her down and found her working at the National Laundry in Portland. Mrs. Black wrote up an official Chemawa runaway and character complaint report, but Superintendent Jackson simply wrote "Graduated" on the bottom and filed it away without taking any action.[5]

Immediately after graduating, Frank and Kathryn tried to get a marriage license, but they were turned away because they were underage (Kathryn was eighteen and Frank was seventeen). Already pregnant with their first child, Kathryn visited Frank's home in Montana, where his obviously drunk grandmother greeted her. She decided to return to Oregon to make her own way.

While Frank went off to basic training in the East, Kathryn moved to Portland and got a small apartment on Southwest Tenth Street. She worked as a waitress at a Chinese restaurant, the Golden Wheel on Broadway. Her classmate and relative from Siletz, June Simmons—Lizzie and Hoxie Simmons' granddaughter and Molalla Kate's great-granddaughter—was working at a Jell-O factory in northwest Portland. When June decided to return to the reservation, she got Kathryn a job on the

OHS Neg., OrHi 101638

KATHRYN'S SISTER DOROTHY WITH BABY ROY IN
MONTANA, 1943

assembly line, weighing the Jell-O packages. Throughout her pregnancy Kathryn worked there, standing all day.

Patsy was born on June 8, 1943. When Kathryn went into labor, her old roommate Dada was with her, and they rode the trolley up to Wilson Memorial Hospital. Kathryn was stunned that no one offered her a seat. The army shipped Frank back from his training post on the East Coast to see his newborn baby before he left for the war in Europe. Kathryn moved with her infant into a rooming house in northeast Portland, but the baby's crying disturbed the other tenants and she was asked to leave.

By this time Kathryn's older sister Dorothy was also a "war widow," with a husband overseas and a young child. In late summer of 1943, Dorothy insisted that Kathryn come to live with her in Wolf Point, Montana. Kathryn and Frank were finally married there in the county courthouse on February 16, 1944, when he was home on a hardship leave. Thus, Kathryn became eligible for military benefits.

Marie, their younger sister, joined Kathryn and Dorothy in Montana. Mrs. Watson had stopped receiving BIA payments

when Marie turned sixteen and she had no more interest in foster parenting, so Dorothy sent Marie money to take the train to
Montana. She arrived just after her junior year in high school,
with a trunkful of children's clothing she had worn in Old Lil's
charge, a useless collection of pinafores and rompers. Kathryn and Dorothy shared their clothing with her, and Dorothy
arranged for Marie to get a temporary job at J.C. Penney's so
she could re-outfit herself for her senior year in high school.

With typical care and foresight, Dorothy borrowed money,
using her husband's horses as collateral, to arrange for Marie to
attend college at Haskell Indian College in Lawrence, Kansas.
There Marie registered in business classes that equipped her to
become an executive secretary. After she earned her two-year
degree, she was offered several jobs and chose to go to Chicago.
Dorothy did not live to see Marie matriculate. In the winter
of 1944, she came down with the flu, and complications led to
pneumonia. She died at the age of twenty-three.

After her sister died of the same disease that had claimed their
parents ten years earlier, Kathryn and eight-month-old Patsy
were alone again in Montana. Dorothy's own child, Roy Track
Jr., was raised by his paternal grandparents and had a long
career as a broadcaster in Arizona. He resumed contact with his
Oregon family after Kathryn located him in the late 1980s, when
she attended a conference in Phoenix. For many years, Roy
served as emcee for the annual Grand Ronde powwow. When
he died in May 2005, Kathryn mourned him like a lost child.

Dorothy's husband's family took all the clothing and furniture from Dorothy's home, including Kathryn's beadwork and
other personal belongings. Kathryn, without so much as a surrogate parent, moved into a temporary shelter and depended for
a time on hand-me-downs from a nearby Presbyterian church.
She had attended this church with Marie after Dorothy's death,
so the parishioners knew her and sympathized with her predica-
ment. Soon she was working as a housemaid for the minister of
the church and his family.

The Synod sent supplies of food, toys, books, and clothing
for distribution to the Indians in the area, but Kathryn soon dis-

covered that the minister was selling the goods and using the money to support his church. Despite his purported rationale that this would help the Indians become more self-sufficient, Kathryn had had enough.

The following summer, destitute and again homeless, Kathryn headed back to Oregon with two-year-old Patsy to live at Siletz with June Simmons, her old classmate. Frank joined her at Siletz when he was shipped home from Germany. He had been scheduled to go overseas in the Pacific, but the war abruptly ended after the United States dropped atomic bombs on the Japanese cities of Hiroshima and Nagasaki.

Frank received an honorable discharge in September 1945, after serving almost two years in the European war theater. His homecoming was a mixed blessing for Kathryn. Like so many of his fellow combat veterans, Frank returned from the war a confirmed alcoholic.

Part Two

Searching for Home
1946–1981

7

Cast Adrift
and "Terminated"

*There is simply no evidence that termination in any way or measure had
a positive effect on . . . Western Oregon Indians.* — Report to the U.S.
Congress, American Indian Policy Review Commission, Task
Force No. 10, 1976

Although Kathryn Harrison has unusually vivid recall of her
early years, she draws a blank when she tries to recover her
third and fourth decades. Her life from 1946 through 1966 was
marked by biannual pregnancies and childbirth and backbreaking migrant labor at minimum wage, with no permanent home
for an anchor. This period in her life paralleled the horrific federal policy that terminated many tribes and again forced Indians
off their traditional lands, splitting families and destroying cultural ties. Throughout this period, Kathryn was learning firsthand about life steeped in alcoholism.

When Frank returned from the war, he was not welcomed
to any community as patriot or hero. Instead, he found signs on
stores and movie houses in the West warning: "No Indians or
Dogs." An indication of the national attitude toward its Indian
war veterans came with an incident reported in newspapers
around the country. The body of Sgt John Rice, an American
GI killed in action, "had been brought home for burial in Sioux

City, Iowa, but . . . at the last moment, as the casket was to be lowered into the grave, officials of the Sioux City Memorial Park . . . stopped the ceremony because Sergeant Rice, a Winnebago Indian, was not a 'member of the Caucasian race.'"[1]

Closer to Kathryn's home, a woman in western Oregon published a collection of "folk sayings" her family knew and used in the 1940s. After each quotation of conventional wisdom, she offered an explanation in parentheses:

~ There's no good Indian but a dead Indian. (This attitude is ungenerous, but it is derived from the experience of some of the early settlers.)

~ He's an Indian giver. (He is a person who gives something and takes it back again; an ungracious giver.)

~ He's off the reservation. (. . . derived from the sometimes wild behavior of Indians when permitted to leave their reservations and enter the white men's towns.)

~ He was drunker than an Indian. (. . . a person obstreperously drunk.)

~ He works harder than an Indian. (. . . ironically said in western Oregon where most of the Indians worked very little.)

~ Wild as an Indian; sly . . . as an Indian. (. . . examples of numerous uncomplimentary comparisons).[2]

When Frank Harrison returned from the war to apply for jobs in the logging industry, after-work watering holes—typical rural taverns—barred Indian patrons. He told his young wife they would have to pose as Mexicans or Hawaiians to go out for a beer on a Friday night. Sometimes Kathryn tried to keep up with him, only to make herself sick. His barroom friends knew her only as the "party pooper." Usually she refused to go, so he went alone. Soon Frank was downing many beers each evening, while Kathryn waited at home with the children.

In May 1946, a second daughter, Jeannie, was born. Kathryn was working at the lumber mill in Toledo, Oregon, painting preservatives on logs for the navy. With no protective clothing and no EPA at hand, she was exposed to the toxic wastes typical of the era. Frank was working odd logging jobs driving trucks, and the family was still living with June Simmons at Siletz. Eventually they found a place of their own in mill workers' housing the company had constructed in Siletz during the war.

"With the savings I had in the bank, we bought a car," Kathryn remembers. "I learned to drive—just got in the car and learned. I probably drove illegally for a while. It was a green Plymouth coupe, and the girls could sleep up on the shelf in the back. The car was a necessity. It was not a luxury, and not the best one in town, but we were proud of it, our first car."

After eighteen months of eking out a living at Siletz, the struggling family moved to the Umatilla Indian Reservation in Pendleton, Oregon. Kathryn's oldest brother, Harold, was living there, working in the timber industry at the Harris Pine Mills. Harold found a job for Frank and babysat with the two girls. Kathryn worked in a pea cannery and sometimes drove the company truck through the pea fields at night. Frankie Jr. was born at the hospital in Mission, just outside Pendleton and a few miles from the reservation, on January 15, 1948.

Exactly a year later another child, Tommy, was born. Because he and Frankie had the same birthday, the Harrisons always called them the "twins." Frank moved the family back to Portland, where his cousin lived. He talked about taking classes funded by the GI Bill, but his drinking drowned his dreams. Friends described Frank as having "gypsy feet," because he seemed unable to stay in any place or job for very long.

By April 1951, Frank and Kathryn were back in Pendleton with her brother Harold. She dates that move by the birth of her son Raymond. Ten months later, in February 1952, Roger was born in Silverton, where the family had gone with the promise of a logging job for Frank. Kathryn helped make ends meet by making her six children's clothing. That ended when Frank pawned her sewing machine. After a short stay in Silverton, the family moved back to Siletz. Kathryn was ashamed to keep showing up destitute. She thought with despair: *My own family are no better than the hobos Mama used to feed out the back door in Corvallis. At least the, people had the excuse of the Depression. But these are the booming post-war years.*

In Siletz, the Harrisons turned to Kathryn's old neighbor and first surrogate mother, Agnes Isaakson. Agnes's niece, Joanne Miller, agreed to house Kathryn and her growing family in a small rental house behind Monroe's Mill at Logsden. All Kathryn can remember of those days is being home with all her babies. Frank would promise to return from the lumber camp on Friday with his paycheck and take them all to a movie. Kathryn would bathe and dress the children and line them up on the sofa, where they waited for their father to appear. More often than not he did not come home, and she would put them to bed before he showed up drunk.

Frank took the car, so Kathryn and the children were often stranded at home. She was proud when nine-year-old Frankie bicycled to the baseball games at Siletz, a seven-mile round trip. Baseball was his passion, and Kathryn was glad he could pursue his dreams.

Frank was abusive when he was drunk. Often, when he came home after a long night of drinking, Kathryn would hide in the chicken coop with her children until he had slept it off. When the boys tried to protect their mother, Frank would spank them. Frank didn't "look Indian," but Kathryn did. When she tried to stand up to him, he would scoff: "You'll never make it without me. You're just another Indian."

Kathryn packed and unpacked, wishing for a way out, but she knew that no shelter beds were available for such a large family. She relived her helplessness at the hands of her foster father Carl Watson and felt humiliated that she still lacked the resources to protect her family.

Kathryn first spoke publicly of her history as a victim of domestic violence at an inter-tribal conference titled "Intimate Abuse," which the Grand Rondes sponsored on March 2, 2000. Her daughter Patsy (also an elder at Grand Ronde by that time) was in the audience, admiring her mother's willingness to speak out. Kathryn recalled memories of her own parents holding hands and holding the Bible together as they read, and she spoke of her profound shock at discovering in her own marriage that a husband's hands could also be used for beating his family.

As World War II ended, fifty delegates attended the first meeting of the National Congress of American Indians.[3] Kathryn remembers a rush of pleasure as she read about the event. Across the nation, Indians were attempting to stand up to the dominant culture. Congress established the Indian Claims Commission, and Native people started pressing for compensation for lands taken from them. As the BIA spent half a million dollars moving Indians to urban areas to facilitate the Eisenhower assimilation policy, the National Congress of American Indians publicly blasted relocation as "cultural destruction."[4]

In many respects, between 1850 and 1950 the United States treated Native Americans much as Europe treated its Jewish and Gypsy (Roma) populations. Even before the Holocaust, official policy targeted Jews, Gypsies, and homosexuals. German Jews were forced to change their names and cut their hair, and they were forbidden to speak Yiddish or to wear traditional headgear. Ondrej Gina, director of the Roma Cultural Union, speaks indignantly of European repression of Gypsy language, songs, and culture (as well as sterilization incentives). The inscription found in the Jewish Museum in Vienna is apt: "Tolerance is intolerant; it demands assimilation."

When the Eisenhower administration began to implement its insidious assimilation (termination) policy toward Indians in 1954, the only home Kathryn had ever known—the Siletz Indian Reservation—ceased to exist. She was reduced to doing seasonal work, picking fruits and vegetables around Hillsboro, Oregon, and despairing about her children's future. She had just turned thirty when a "government man" came to the door to inform her about the "benefits" of termination. Although the new policy was presented as an enlightened route to assimilation, Kathryn sensed that this was just another budget-cutting measure.

With a few choice words, the congressional language adopting termination was benign:

> Whereas it is the policy of Congress, as rapidly as possible, to make the Indians within the territorial limits of the United States subject to the same laws and entitled to the same privileges and responsibilities as are applicable to other citizens of

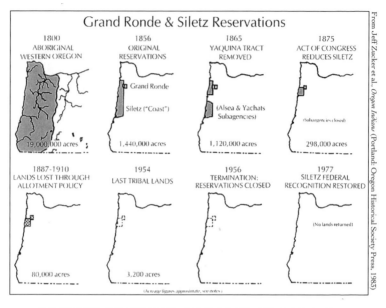

THE REDUCTION OF SILETZ AND GRAND RONDE LANDS IN OREGON,
1800 TO 1977

the United States, to end their status as wards of the United States, and to grant them all of the rights and prerogatives pertaining to American citizenship; and whereas the Indians within the territorial limits of the United States should assume their full responsibilities as American citizens: Now, therefore, be it Resolved by the House of Representatives (the Senate concurring), That it is declared to be the sense of Congress that, at the earliest possible time, all of the Indian tribes and the individual members thereof . . . should be freed from Federal supervision.[5]

The official language was lulling, but its import was dire for tribal people. This was a policy designed to allow the federal government to wash its hands of its "Indian problem." Instead of empowering Indian individuals, it shredded their safety net. Government health, education, and social services programs were suspended at the tribal level, tribes lost their official voices, and cultural networks were decimated. Perhaps most devastatingly, the Indian land base was further undercut. Congress passed the Siletz and Grand Ronde termination bills in 1954, abdicating federal programs in Indian Country and selling off almost a million acres of Indian trust land in Oregon. The Grand Rondes were reduced to two and a half acres of land (their cemetery alone).

> At the time of Termination . . . at least 2,081 Indians at Grand Ronde and Siletz were affected by the closure of their reservations and withdrawal of services. . . . Confusion resulting from hazy explanations of termination legislation, suspicion of the circumstances in which tribal "approval" of the Act was obtained, and misunderstanding about remuneration for tribal lands persist among Oregon Indians.[6]

Vine Deloria Jr., an insightful and unsparing analyst of federal Indian policy, provides a concise requiem for tribal sovereignty and identity: "The impact of termination . . . was unmistakable and significant. If the policy did not completely destroy Indian culture, it encroached substantially upon Indian attempts to remain Indian."[7] Alvin M. Josephy Jr., a national award-winning journalist and historian, is searing in his observations of western Native people reeling under the new policy:

> In the 1950s, numerous Indian peoples were scandalously defenseless and put-upon. The only Americans without freedom, self-government, and the right to manage and control their own affairs, they were still beset by bullying government bosses, imperious missionaries, and thieving whites, and on their reservations were still victimized by grinding poverty and by political, social, and economic problems that appeared beyond the abilities of the government to solve. . . .
>
> During the decade of the 1950s, the federal government made things worse, adopting a cruel and fraudulent "termination" policy that pretended to "free the Indians" by ending the reservations and terminating all government relations with the tribes. . . . One by one, in the course of the decade, tribes were

"terminated" against their will, losing their lands and natural
resources to scavenging non-Indian ranchers, bankers, real estate speculators, timber companies, and other white interests
and being forced to make their living competitively in the white
man's world, whether they were prepared to do so or not. . . .

The implementation of the termination policy brought so
much suffering and hardship to the affected tribal peoples
and so many new social-justice and welfare problems to cities,
counties, and states overwhelmed by the needs of the "freed"
Indians that before the end of the decade, the policy was quietly
abandoned by the Eisenhower administration. In time, some
of the terminated tribes . . . were able to regain the recognition
and rights that they had lost, but the termination period was a
traumatic experience for an entire generation of Indians.[8]

Kathryn and her children were among the traumatized.
Young Frankie heard at his Hillsboro middle school that checks
were being sent to all tribal members to compensate for the termination of the federal government's trust responsibility. Kathryn wanted nothing to do with the new policy, but he begged her
to let him walk to the local post office to check the mail. Kathryn
relented, so Frankie and Patsy made the trip and brought home
checks for $35 for each of the four oldest children in the house-
hold.

Later in life, Kathryn asked her older children what they remembered of their early years. She hoped they would say something
about the fresh popcorn she made or cookies she baked so the
house would be filled with a good smell when they returned from
school in the afternoon. Remembering instead the non-stop piles
of laundry, Jeannie replied: "*Tide!*"

Patsy ruefully admits that alcohol abuse and her father's job-
lessness obliterated her childhood. Only one year was she able to
stay in the same school for the entire grade. She didn't make any
real friends until fourth grade, and she doesn't remember any
toys. Christmas was not a time when "little girl fantasies" were
fulfilled—one year she got a hairbrush, another year a bracelet
made of pennies—but her mother made an effort to see that the

family had a Christmas tree and that everyone had at least one gift under it. If necessary, she rewrapped previous gifts so each child would have a present.

Patsy recalls when she encountered racism for the first time in school. Like her mother, she was called a "dirty Indian" on the playground and came home crying. Kathryn visited the school the next day. After recess, she addressed Patsy's class: "This is my daughter. She has a name. You can call her 'Patsy,' but you cannot call her other names. She may not have many clothes, but what she does wear is washed every night. She is *not* a dirty Indian!" This was not the only time Kathryn rose to her daughter's defense, and Patsy has always been thankful for this model.

What Patsy remembers most vividly from her childhood is living in shacks with no heat, sometimes no running water, no real floors, and furniture made of boxes. She remembers living next door to people who smelled horrible and fought constantly. One time, she went without food for three days in a row. When Kathryn opened a box of macaroni and cheese and discovered it had worms in it, she cooked it anyway, because it was better than nothing. The family relied on Department of Agriculture handouts and sometimes scavenged through the dumpster at the local supermarket.

Patsy's most lasting image of Kathryn as a young mother is that of a woman too shy even to talk with neighbors. Yet, when Kathryn had an external motivation, such as standing up for her children, she was transformed. Patsy recalls one time when she was driving with her parents. One of Frank's drinking mates was in the front seat, and he reached around to touch Patsy. Kathryn rose up, pointed straight at him, and shouted: "Don't you *dare* touch her!"

In August 1955, a seventh child, Kathy (named for Kathryn), was born in Hillsboro. An eighth, Diane, was delivered in November 1957 in Silverton, where Frank was driving a dump truck. Both Kathryn and Diane almost died in childbirth and were revived with blood transfusions. Today, Kathryn has hepatitis, which she traces to the contaminated blood supply.

Having no permanent address, the family's mail went to a post office box in Salem. At least that way, Kathryn could attempt to keep in touch with her tribal community and the developments at Grand Ronde. Grand Ronde elders contacted Kathryn there and urged her to have her children officially enrolled at Grand Ronde in case the federal government offered compensation beyond the $35 checks they had received.

Throughout this period, Kathryn treated others respectfully but had little regard for herself. She has cloudy memories of wandering through Idaho, stopping at thrift shops to find clothes for the children, eating handouts from churches. She bore three more children, and the days and months blurred as the family moved from state to state in search of jobs.

The Harrisons landed temporarily in Arizona, where Frank drove tractors in the fields while Kathryn and the children picked vegetables. They lived in a sparsely furnished farm shack and hauled their own water. Deadly flash floods, compounded by soil erosion, kept them constantly on edge. They were living in Buckeye, Arizona, outside Phoenix, when sixteen-year-old Patsy announced that she was leaving the family to marry Gene Pullin, a singer and guitar player with his own country-western band. Patsy was working as waitresses and singing with Gene's band on weekends.

"Gene played a little bit of everything — guitar, violin, drums," Kathryn says. "He was self-taught. He could sing too. It was a chance for Patsy to make a little money. I thought Gene was all right. I didn't blame Patsy. I wished I could get away too."

Gene remembers his shock when Patsy took him to meet her family. "Picture the *Grapes of Wrath*," he said. "They lived in a shack with walls you could see through."

Patsy hoped to become a professional singer, and she and Gene often performed together. Her debut song in the early years — with words she sang from the depths of her heart — was "Won't You Come Home, Bill Bailey?" Patsy and Gene were married on May 8, 1960, and for over four decades, they have sung country western ballads together.

Jeannie, too, fled to an early marriage. She was a junior in high school, but the family moved around so much that she couldn't keep up with her credits. So she quit school and married a man from Brownsville. "He was all right," Kathryn remembers.

"A mechanic, a good worker, and for a while they were happy. They had three children close together, two boys and a girl. The kids went to school in Brownsville. Her husband's dad owned his own machine shop, and he worked with him and finally took it over."

By 1960, Arizona had lost its allure for the family. Picking cotton and berries could not sustain Frank, Kathryn, and the six Harrison children still at home, and Frank's other job prospects failed to materialize. At their lowest point, Kathryn remembers that her only shoes were plastic flipflops, and they were held together by a safety pin.

Penniless and with great difficulty, Frank, Kathryn, and their remaining children made their way back to Oregon. In November 1961, David was born in Oregon City. Logging jobs led the family south to the Lebanon area, where the older boys, Frankie and Tommy, were able to attend one school for longer than a term. Both were athletes. Frankie lettered in track and basketball, Tommy in wrestling and boxing. During the termination era, the BIA had been quick to eliminate terminated tribal members from eligibility for its federal programs. As a result, children of Grand Ronde tribal members were not admitted to the Chemawa Indian School, so the Harrison children could not attend their parents' alma mater.

Kathryn spent her fortieth birthday in the Mill City area by Detroit Reservoir but remembers nothing of significance until 1966, when Frankie graduated from high school. Then the family moved back to the Umatilla Indian Reservation to be near Kathryn's older brother. The Umatillas had escaped the misfortune of termination and remained somewhat intact as a native community.

The Umatilla Reservation land around Mission, in the northeast corner of Oregon, was the closest place of the heart Kathryn had left in the world. Her brother, Harold, had married a Umatilla tribal member and lived on the reservation. When Harold's wife, Naomi Kash Kash, looked out the window and saw Kathryn, Frank, and their brood coming up the driveway, she moaned, "Oh no! Here they come again!" But she and Harold took the Harrisons in, and Harold dutifully tried to find Frank a job.

Kathryn's faithful Chemawa roommate, Dada, had also married into the tribe and was raising a family there. Roger Harrison, who was then fourteen, was close to Dada's son Jeff. Another Chemawa classmate, Cecilia Bearchum, had returned to Pendleton with her daughter after splitting up with her husband. The three families attended powwows together and went camping and berry-picking, giving Kathryn a welcome sense of community. She gained a namesake in Harold's daughter, Kathryn "Kat" Jones, who has gone on to become a leader of her tribe.

This homecoming was not to last. Frank was still drinking and could not hold a job. The Pendleton Police Department would pick him up on a charge of "Driving Under the Influence of Intoxicants" and send him home, still drunk. Kathryn longed to make a break with the help of a battered women's program, but with all her children she felt trapped. When asked why she continued to have babies when times were so rough, Kathryn says, "Ironically, one of the reasons I kept on having all those kids was economic. There was barely enough money for food, rent, or clothing. Who could afford contraceptives?" Finally, bitterly, she concedes: "A lot of those babies were fights that I lost."

Kathryn echoes the words of the oppressed wife in Barbara Kingsolver's *The Poisonwood Bible:*

> I didn't set out to leave my husband. Anyone can see I should have, long before, but I never did know how. For women like me, it seems, it's not ours to take charge of beginnings and endings. . . . I only know the middle ground where we live our lives. We whistle while Rome burns or we scrub the floor, depending. Don't dare presume there's shame in the lot of a woman who carries on. . . . To resist occupation, whether you're a nation or merely a woman, you must understand the language of your enemy. Conquest and liberation and democracy and divorce are words that mean squat, basically, when you have hungry children and clothes to get on the line, and it looks like rain.[9]

In 1967, the Harrisons' tenth child, Karen, was born. The only glimmer of a chance to make a living came through an invitation from Patsy and Gene to join them in Ketchikan. So the family moved to Alaska, where Kathryn's mother had been born. While they were living near Patsy, Kathryn learned that her fifty-year-old brother, Harold, had been killed in a car accident in Pendleton. He died violently and suddenly, and the news shook Kathryn to the core.

At forty-three, with her older brother and sister now deceased, Kathryn Jones Harrison became the elder in her family. The time had come for her to build a future for her five children who still lived at home and begin to shape her own life—a life bereft of parents, older siblings, meaningful work, economic resources, and a sober, supportive spouse.

Frank taunted: "You'll never make it without me." Kathryn was determined to try.

8

Self-Determination

*The story of the Indian in America is something more than the record
of the white man's frequent aggression, broken agreements, intermittent
remorse and prolonged failure. It is a record also of endurance, of survival,
of adaptation and creativity in the face of overwhelming obstacles. It is a
record of enormous contributions in this country—to its art and culture,
to its strength and spirit, to its sense of history and its sense of purpose.*—
Richard M. Nixon, July 8, 1970

The late 1960s and early 1970s were defining years in the development of national Indian policy, with the ascendancy of the American Indian Movement (AIM) and the federal government's declared shift to tribal self-determination. In a special message to Congress on July 8, 1970, President Richard M. Nixon spelled out the need for radical change:

> The first Americans—the Indians—are the most deprived and most isolated minority group in our nation. On virtually every scale of measurement—employment, income, education, health—the condition of the Indian people ranks at the bottom. This condition is the heritage of centuries of injustice. From the time of their first contact with European settlers, the American Indians have been oppressed and brutalized, deprived of their ancestral lands and denied the opportunity to control their own destiny. Even the Federal programs which are intended to meet

their needs have frequently proved to be ineffective and de-
meaning. . . .

It is long past time that the Indian policies of the Federal
government began to recognize and build upon the capacities
and insights of the Indian people. Both as a matter of justice
and as a matter of enlightened social policy, we must begin to
act on the basis of what the Indians themselves have long been
telling us. The time has come to break decisively with the past
and to create the conditions for a new era in which the Indian
future is determined by Indian acts and Indian decisions.[1]

In those years, Kathryn Harrison, too, made a decisive break
with her past. It was a time of liberation for her, as she regained
some positive sense of Indian identity and self-esteem and took
her first concrete steps toward economic self-sufficiency. As a
mother of ten and approaching fifty years of age, Kathryn went
back to school, divorced her abusive husband, and returned to
work at the Siletz Reservation of her childhood, coincidentally
when the Siletz were seeking restoration of their tribal status.

Kathryn and Frank remained in Alaska until Tommy graduated from high school in 1968 and Raymond in 1969. The Vietnam War was raging, and both Frankie and Tommy signed up.
Because two brothers could not be in combat at the same time,
Tommy volunteered to go to Vietnam instead of Frankie. Frankie
was sent to Germany. Kathryn worked at a cannery and spent
most of her waking hours praying for Tommy's safe return.

Living with Frank in Alaska, Kathryn felt as if she were
drowning, "going down for the third time." He would disappear
for weeks at a time, and then she would track him down through
the unemployment bureau, where she knew he would go to col-
lect checks. At home he was frequently drunk and threatening.
One day, sixteen-year-old Roger rose to Kathryn's defense and
finally decked his father. In the past Frank had kept the upper
hand. Now Roger knocked him flat.

Kathryn realized that she could no longer subject her children to this brutal life. She felt doubly humiliated because Frank
kept disappearing when the rent was due, and she could not

pay it with her own small salary from the cannery. All the while, others would say to her, "How could you think about leaving? Frank is such a nice guy." Kathryn would respond, "You don't always know what goes on behind the scenes of a marriage."

Kathryn's third son, eighteen-year-old Raymond, was working at a lumber mill and earning a moderate income. It was Raymond who gave his mother the money to leave. By the time she finally separated from Frank, Kathryn says, "he had knocked me down so far that I came to believe it."

In 1970, Kathryn mustered the will to return to Oregon alone with the five children who remained in her care. She recalled: "I called Jeannie in Oregon and said, 'I'm leaving your dad.' Then I told the kids, 'Those who want to come with me, come now.' They all came." At first she went to Albany, where Jeannie lived with her family. Then she found a temporary home with her old roommate, Dada, in Salem. Kathryn always knew her Chemawa friends would see her through times of trouble.

Frank tracked her down and appeared at the door, demanding to see Kathryn. Dada, lying to protect her friend, told him Kathryn was no longer living there. After a few months, Kathryn found cheap housing in a cabin at Agate Beach, near Newport and the old Siletz Indian Reservation.

Patsy and Gene remained in Alaska but kept in touch with Kathryn and worried about her. They knew she wouldn't fare worse without Frank, because she could qualify for food stamps and job-placement programs. Gene says proudly that everything Kathryn did from that point forward she did herself. Her children watched anxiously as she struggled to find ways to provide shelter, food, and clothing for the family, and they learned a lot about gumption in the process.

In the spring of 1970, Kathryn began a concerted correspondence in search of family records. She particularly wanted to document her father's academic path and tribal enrollment for her children. In May, she wrote Dr. Earle Connette at Washington State University: "Would you be able to tell me where to find the subjects taken and any accomplishments of one of your alumni of early 1900? . . . I can only tell you his name was

John Herald "Harry" William Jones—he was my father, now deceased; was very artistic."

The university replied a month later, enclosing handwritten notes indicating that Harry was a freshman from 1913 to 1914 but that he left his studies there incomplete. Also included was a copy of his transcript, which showed that Harry received an "A" in Bookkeeping, a "B" in Commercial Services, and a "D" in Drawing. Convinced that Harry must have gone elsewhere after this failure to recognize his artistic talent, Kathryn got in touch with Oregon State University in Corvallis, but they could find no record of him.

After Kathryn settled in the Newport area, she was determined to find work and to support her family. First she applied for welfare and went to the vocational counseling center. She was practically toothless at the time, and she knew it would be futile to apply for so much as a waitress position. With every pregnancy she had lost a tooth, and her nutrition was so poor that much of the calcium in her body had gone into the development of the fetus. She couldn't afford dental care, so as her teeth loosened she had sometimes pulled them out herself. The vocational counselor's first step was to set up appointments for Kathryn to go to the dental college in Eugene and be fitted for dentures.

With new dentures in place and her confidence on the rise, Kathryn took the state aptitude tests. Her scores were so strong that the counselor assured her she would be competent at just about anything she decided to study. The counselor suggested computer training at Lane Community College, and Kathryn enrolled, with trepidation, in September 1970. She was intimidated by the math requirements but decided to give it a try.

Frankie and Tommy were stunned when Kathryn told them she planned to return to school. From their posts in the military overseas, they wrote with alarm: "You can't go back! You'll be the oldest one there!" Frankie offered to get a hardship leave to come home and help her, but Kathryn refused. "I've got to do it on my own," she replied.

As Kathryn adjusted to student life, she became aware through friends of the daring actions of the American Indian

KATHRYN (AT LEFT) AT HER LANE COMMUNITY COLLEGE GRADUATION, 1972

Movement. On July 4, 1971, members of AIM staged a counter-celebration at Mt. Rushmore, and on Thanksgiving that year they painted Plymouth Rock red. Kathryn was amused by their media strategy and was encouraged by Native people's newfound assertiveness. It would not have occurred to her to join their occupation of Alcatraz or the BIA headquarters in Washington, D.C., but she welcomed the political push of their collective efforts. Each of these actions allowed her children to walk a little taller.

During her college years, Kathryn re-established contact with the Chemawa Indian School. She went to her first alumni reunion in June 1972 and was promptly appointed alumni historian. There she and Cecilia Bearchum, her friend from Pendleton, compared life stories and drew strength from each other. Both women had married alcoholics, raised many children chiefly alone, and became working mothers interested in Indian health care.

Kathryn soon switched to the nursing program at Lane Community College, where she excelled. In 1972, she became the first Native American to graduate with a degree in nursing.[2] Her family gathered for her graduation, including her brother Bob

Watson, who met her children for the first time. Patsy, who came from Alaska for the ceremony, saw him wave and wondered who he was. Once she got to know him, she hoped he might become a father-figure in her brothers' lives.

Kathryn passed her state boards and was offered a job at Sacred Heart Hospital in Eugene. By then her children were settled in school at the coast, and she had reunited with her old friends at Siletz. She took a job as a licensed practical nurse at Lincoln County Hospital and moved her family to a rental house within walking distance of the hospital.

Ten childbirths had taken a toll on her body. She had no car and had to walk everywhere, including two miles down the main street of Lincoln City to pay her utility bills. After one bill-paying expedition, she collapsed on the way home. When she finally got a ride to the hospital, she told the doctors it felt as though her "insides were coming out." She was diagnosed with a prolapsed uterus and gallstones, requiring immediate surgery and a long recovery period. The doctors warned her that no future employment could entail standing for long.

After this setback, Kathryn returned to Siletz and applied for a counseling position in the new alcohol rehabilitation program at the tribal center. She got the job and bought a secondhand car to commute. The center was forty miles up the curvy Siletz River Highway from her home in Lincoln City. Kathryn says she learned firsthand, day after day, why the Native name for the Siletz River was *ceeleste*, which means "crooked river." The road was dangerous, and she feared she would encounter a drunk driver careening down the shoulderless pavement at night.

Kathryn was now contending with three alcoholics in her life. Like their father, both Frankie and Tommy drank their way home from military service. Looking back, their sister Diane recalls that Tommy was never the same after he came back from Vietnam: "He would wake up in the middle of the night screaming. He would hit the floor if a balloon popped at the supermarket."

Frank had followed his wife back to Siletz. While Kathryn was developing a community education campaign and delivering "scared straight" lectures to high school students about the scourge of alcohol, he kept landing on her doorstep or falling asleep in her driveway, drunk. The children would see him asleep in a car on the street and beg Kathryn to reconcile with him. When she banned him from the house, her daughters wouldn't speak to her. It was only after the Harrison girls experienced for themselves the repeated broken promises and the embarrassment of having to make excuses to Frank's employers that they understood and forgave their mother.

Kathryn persuaded Frank to accompany her to the Alcoholics Anonymous program she conducted at Siletz, but he sat seething in the tribal community kitchen the entire evening. All the way home he ranted at her. Finally, Kathryn exploded: "Enough!" She told him she would never again receive him at her house. If he wanted to see the children, he would have to meet them at a nearby motel. "This is *my* house!" she shouted—although to this day she has never actually owned her own home.

Kathryn had stayed with her husband slightly more than three decades. "There were some good times with Frank, early on," she admits. "There was music in our home, and we sang with the children like my folks did. Frank taught Patsy to sing harmony and probably spurred Patsy's interest in a professional music career. The kids may have some good memories of him teaching them to drive or taking them fishing. But . . . I let him define me as nothing." Living with Frank was like raising an eleventh child. Nonetheless, he provided Kathryn with a semblance of a stable family and the comfort of shared history.

How did she summon the strength to sever that long-term tie? Learning more about the pathology of alcoholism through her work at Siletz was a partial nudge. Early memories of her childhood home with loving, church-oriented parents who taught admirable values and reliance on natural resources reinforced her resolve to recover that healthier way of living for however many vital years she had left.

At her insistence, Frank finally came to Kathryn's office at Siletz and delivered divorce documents. It was 1974, Kathryn was fifty years old, and despite his dire warnings, she was on the verge of making it without him after all. Frank filed the divorce in Goldendale, Washington, where he was living in the mid-1970s.

The Harrison children believe their mother shocked Frank by actually signing the divorce papers. He ignored the terms of the decree and never paid child support for any of his offspring. As far as Kathryn is aware, Frank never apologized to the children for anything he put the family through. "Is it so hard for an adult to say I'm sorry?" she wonders.

Some of the daughters remember changes in their father's behavior after the divorce. Up until that time, he had smoked three packs of cigarettes a day. In the early 1970s, he quit smoking and drinking cold turkey and began to take his responsibilities as a father more seriously. He married a second wife, a devout Mormon. At first the relationship was strained, as his wife said his Indian children were cursed by God. The Book of Mormon described them as "filthy," "loathsome," and "full of idleness and all manner of abomination," and she tried to keep them out of her home.[3] Eventually, Frank learned to stand up to her. Whenever his second wife said disparaging things about Kathryn in his children's hearing, Frank would stop her. In his own way, too little and too late, he tried to make amends.

The boys were hard hit by their parents' divorce. Kathryn learned years later that after the decree was final, Frankie, Tommy, and Raymond made a pact never to marry. They were determined not to perpetuate a pattern of abuse.

In autumn 1974, Kathryn and Cecilia Bearchum made plans to attend a workshop for professional Indian women at the intertribal Daybreak Star Center in Seattle. The two old friends met in Portland to travel together. En route they talked nonstop about the end of their long marriages and their renewed sense of self. They vowed never to remarry, never again to burden themselves with enabling relationships, and to keep their eyes on the road ahead instead of the road behind. Both Kathryn and Cecilia had become confident, hard-working Indian women, and they had high hopes for the future.

Thus, Kathryn began her work of personal and tribal restoration at Siletz, where she had begun her life as an orphan forty years earlier. She was not always accepted there, but she lived by her mother's admonition that whenever she felt like an outsider, she had to earn her place.

9

Siletz (and Self) Restoration

The Congress hereby recognizes the obligation of the United States to respond to the strong expression of the Indian people for self-determination by assuring maximum Indian participation in the direction of education as well as other Federal services to Indian communities so as to render such services more responsive to the needs and desires of those communities.
— The Indian Self-Determination Act of 1975

Word reached Siletz in 1973 that Congress had restored federal recognition to the Menominee Indian tribe of Wisconsin, as the Nixon administration began to push Congress for repudiation of the disastrous termination policy. Leaders at Siletz decided to vie to be the second nationally re-recognized tribal government. Kathryn Harrison was prepared to play a role in the struggle.

Although it took Congress five years to fully accept and implement President Nixon's policy reversal, they did so with clearly worded and moderately well-funded legislation. It was a good start. Once the Siletz managed to achieve restoration of their tribal status, they would be in a position to take advantage of the Indian Self-Determination and Education Assistance Act of 1975. The act provided for, among other things, "an orderly transition from Federal domination of programs for and services to Indians to effective and meaningful participation by the

Indian people in the planning, conduct, and administration of those programs and services."

With the encouragement of the person she took as her mentor, Art Bensell, chair of the Siletz Tribal Council, Kathryn worked on fundraising for restoration efforts and then ran for Tribal Council herself. A number of candidates sought three positions in 1975, so the winners would be the top three vote-getters. Although Kathryn was considered an "upstart" by many at Siletz who did not remember her parents, she did well enough to secure a seat on the council. Another member of this political "freshman class" was Delores ("Dee") Pigsley, a lifelong tribal member and daughter of a former tribal chairman. Dee would figure prominently in Kathryn's later career at Grand Ronde, as they both chaired their tribal governments into the millennium. She and Kathryn were friendly rivals.

The Siletz leaders had their work cut out for them. The BIA had proposed a Byzantine code of regulations to establish criteria and procedures for tribes seeking restoration of federal recognition. Essentially, tribes were required to prove to the Department of the Interior (and subsequently to Congress) that even though the federal government had declared they no longer existed as a political body with a relationship to the federal government as of 1954, they had maintained their culture, lands, and form of government in defiance of that policy.[1] Many of the Siletz, in refusing to be "relocated and assimilated," had pursued a wise course for twenty years.

Art Bensell, Kathryn, and her colleagues at Siletz went into high gear, mounting a full-fledged political campaign. They knew they would have to sustain the effort over at least a three-year period and as many sessions of Congress as it took, because the Department of the Interior was then bogged down in "acknowledgment" proceedings for tribes that had never had a formal relationship with the federal government. For lack of a legislative or regulatory road map, tribes seeking re-recognition used this acknowledgment process as a guideline for the case they would make to Congress for restoration of federal status. Once again the BIA was the biggest obstacle to getting anything accomplished in Indian Country.

According to the BIA acknowledgment process, tribes were required to

1. establish that they had been identified from historical times until present as "American Indian" or "aboriginal."

2. show that a substantial portion of Siletz members lived in a specific area of the community which is viewed as Indian, and that the tribe's members are descended from a tribe with historical occupation in the same place.

3. prove that there existed then, and had existed throughout history a tribal political authority or some consistent method of dealing with group problems and making group decisions. [These criteria were imposed despite the U.S. government's best efforts over the last century to undermine tribes' ability to fulfill them.]

4. provide copies of the tribe's governing documents, such as constitutions, bylaws, charters, etc.

5. provide a current list of the group's members, according to its own membership requirements.

6. prove that the tribe's membership is not composed of individuals who are members of another federally recognized tribe.[2]

Oregon Senator Mark O. Hatfield (R) spearheaded the Siletz Restoration Act with the help of Oregon Representative Les AuCoin (D). Leaning heavily on the assistance of tribal legal advisors (especially Charles Wilkinson, professor of law at the University of Oregon), the tribe prepared an impressive thirteen-point volume of testimony for the Senate Committee on Interior and Insular Affairs, aimed at convincing Congress to overturn its 1954 termination decision. Kathryn and other members of the Tribal Council went to Washington, D.C., to testify on March 30, 1976.

Kathryn's role, as secretary of the Siletz Tribal Council, was to talk about tribal identity (BIA criterion number one). Although she had her testimony written out, she was terrified of public speaking in general and this audience in particular. She worried that she would be interrupted and grilled with questions or

KATHRYN (CENTER) AND PAULINE RICKS (SECOND FROM RIGHT) TESTIFYING
IN SUPPORT OF SILETZ RESTORATION

that she would simply freeze and have to be prompted. Her final address was a combination of her own organization and ideas and those suggested by the attorneys and political advisers.

Kathryn began the only way she knew how, by recounting her personal history. She told of her parents' death and her foster home placement (omitting her abuse at the hands of the Watsons). "I felt rebellious at being asked to give up my Indian heritage," she said. She spoke of the importance of being able to attend Chemawa as a member of a recognized tribe: "Here, for once, I belonged." Paying homage to the intact Indian culture at Siletz, she said, "I never had to wonder if my relatives and the rest of the Indian community in Siletz would be there." She remembered reveling in the traditional activities of basketmaking, Indian dancing, rodeo, and pageants. Then she chronicled the losses of the termination period, the school dropouts, the alcoholism, early deaths, and poor nutrition and medical care.

On impulse, she then abandoned her notes and spoke from her heart:

My Indianness is as strong as ever these days as I work around the Siletz community as a member of the Lincoln County Mental Health Advisory Board, as a member of the Board of Directors for the Home Health Agency. . . . I see so much that could be accomplished. With restoration, our work will be just beginning. . . .

There is a growth of pride in the eyes of our young people as they share . . . the culture of the tribe. Since the restoration bill started . . . there is a new spring in our step, a feeling of expectation in the air, a hoping that maybe this time the Indians will acquire something—something desperately needed. And it will be our own.[3]

Presenting this testimony reminded Kathryn of her father's appearance before the congressional committee that considered the Indian Reorganization Act in 1934, just months before his death. Some of the issues at hand were depressingly reminiscent of that earlier struggle to persuade the federal government to live up to its responsibilities and promises. The message echoed through the years: Native Americans sought to be recognized and then to be left alone to manage their affairs.

In the months that followed, Kathryn felt cast off by the Siletz. Labeling her a Grand Ronde, a member of a neighboring but still unrecognized tribe, a few vocal participants at General Council meetings objected to her growing role in tribal affairs. Kathryn was cruelly reminded, again, that she was an outsider, as her mother had been before her. Although she believed she had honored her mother's advice by "earning her place" at Siletz, she realized that the Grand Rondes were her closest people, since her father had been enrolled there. Her chief concern was to provide a more accepting environment for her youngest daughter, Karen, who was then almost ten years old and the only child still at home.

In June 1976, Kathryn participated in the American Folk Life Festival in Washington, D.C., on the National Mall. She roomed with fellow Siletz Tribal Council member Dee Pigsley at Georgetown University and spent the week with national and

OHS Neg., OrHi 101580

KATHRYN AT COOS BAY, CHRISTMAS 1978

international tribal leaders, demonstrating the various Indian cultures through dancing, storytelling, cooking fry bread, and conversing with tourists from around the world. Kathryn did not mind being on display, as long as she was educating others. During that week she made up her mind to leave Siletz and return to her father's birthplace in search of her tribal home.

The Siletz achieved restoration in 1977. Instead of savoring her political success and running for another term on Tribal Council, Kathryn moved on. She felt prematurely uprooted, she said, like one of those carrots she had planted and plucked out of the ground when she was a child playing farmer at Logsden. Just as she began to take shape, her growth was thwarted. She left Siletz disappointed but without rancor. In retrospect, she saw her experience with the tribe as a spur toward following her own destiny.

Thrown back on her own resources in her mid-fifties, Kathryn looked to three external lifelines. First were her connections with tribal elders and the spirit of continuity they represented. Second was the network of independent women who had figured so prominently in her survival. And third was the sustaining force of tribal traditions.

Pauline Ricks had served on the Siletz Tribal Council with Kathryn, though she lived in Springfield, about a hundred miles away. During the long hours they spent working on restoration for the tribe, the two women had formed a bond of mutual respect. When Pauline learned that Kathryn intended to leave the coastal reservation, she invited her and Karen to live in a small trailer on her land. Kathryn accepted gratefully.

Pauline headed the Lane County Title IV Program (of the Indian Education Act), and she was an inspiration to Kathryn. When the Siletz were terminated, Pauline wisely invested her savings in real estate. Her mother, Angeline Bell, lived with her and kept up the traditions of basketmaking and storytelling. Pauline taught young Indians protocol: how to behave at powwows and ceremonies and how to show proper respect for elders. Kathryn admired Pauline's knowledge of the old ways and her adherence to core beliefs.

Soon Kathryn found an apartment nearby and a halftime job working for Lane County Nutrition Services. Karen was in fourth grade, and other Siletz and Grand Ronde tribal members were living in the Eugene-Springfield area. One of Kathryn's responsibilities in the nutrition program was arranging Meals on Wheels service for senior citizens. She enjoyed connecting with tribal elders through the program, but Springfield never felt like a permanent home.

Kathryn developed an especially rich relationship with an elder named Esther LaBonte. Esther had known Kathryn's father, Harry Jones, and enjoyed telling tales about him as a young boy. She chuckled as she described strong-willed young Harry driving the Catholic missionaries at Grand Ronde to distraction. In the dining hall, for instance, when the clergymen pressured him to "make a clean plate," Harry would refuse and point to the cook's dirty hands. Listening to Esther's stories, Kathryn regained a sense of her father's forceful character. She loved to prolong these moments.

In 1978, Congress passed the American Indian Religious Freedom Act (AIRFA). Kathryn's father had always striven to blend the best of Christianity with traditional Native ways, and Kathryn wished such legislation could have taken effect in his lifetime. The same congressional session produced the Indian Child Welfare Act (ICWA), giving preference to tribal families for Indian foster-child placement. Kathryn applauded the legislation and reflected on the difference it might have made in her own life. National Native American events increasingly caught her eye, and she longed to take part in them.

The summer before Karen entered fifth grade, Kathryn heard that some acquaintances, Annabelle Dement and Jerry Running Foxe, were soon to stage an Indian Olympics in southern Oregon at Coquille. Her oldest son, Frankie, was in charge of some of the games. When he told her that they needed a good cook with an understanding of nutrition for the athletes, Kathryn applied for the job and got it.

Annabelle Dement quickly recognized Kathryn's talents and persuaded her to apply for a job conducting a survey for the Coos County Council on Alcoholism. Its purpose was to do a needs assessment for alcohol and drug-treatment programs directed at Native American users. Kathryn embraced the project with zeal and moved with twelve-year-old Karen to the small southern coastal community of Charleston. They lived happily there for two years, as Karen began middle school.

Kathryn's survey results conclusively demonstrated the need for more alcohol and drug programs tailored to the local Indian population. So, after the nine-month needs-assessment process, she moved into a permanent job as an alcohol counselor. That job quickly expanded into working at the Coos Bay Detox Center, first at a halfway house for addicts in recovery, and then most memorably at a newly constructed sweat lodge, christened Lampa Mountain by the alcoholics who sought release in its steam.

Reminiscent of the sweat lodge her father built in the 1930s by Logsden Creek, Lampa Mountain was homemade. Kathryn and her clients threw blankets over the top of bent saplings tied down with colored cotton and cast tobacco in each of the four directions, honoring the tribal traditions of Lakota medicine men. They sought a blend of healing practices. When room allowed, they invited non-Indians to join them.

Turning again to the company and support of women, Kathryn found a mentor in her boss, Joanne Wright. When Kathryn questioned her own ability to handle the multitude of assignments in the Coos Bay alcoholism program, Joanne had a ready answer. Kathryn asked, "Why would I want to take on a bunch of drunks in Detox when I just got rid of one?" Joanne laughed in response: "That's why you're an expert!"

At both the halfway house and the sweat lodge, Kathryn developed messages about the pride of "Indianness." Speaking of the benefits of feeling alert enough to appreciate the natural world, to heed the lessons imparted by elders, to remember and be able to sing the ancient songs, Kathryn once again called on her Chemawa cheerleading persona. She did not mince words about her own experience. She told them about how she used to drink, trying to keep up with Frank only to get sick, and reminded them that the people who used to call her a "party pooper" were now either dead or dying of alcoholism and its related diseases.

As she relived this part of her past, Kathryn realized she was still carrying much of it with her. "All that hate—every day! I finally said to myself, I might as well still be with him; he's still controlling my life!" Her co-workers understood her rage. They gave her materials advertising a "Spiritual Gathering for Native Americans" with traditional drumming and dancing, scheduled for the following month near Tulsa, Oklahoma. Intrigued, Kathryn checked it out with friends who had attended in the past. Joanne told her that she couldn't spare her just then, but Kathryn, feeling an inexplicable urgency to go, replied, "So fire me!" The next day, Joanne provided travel money and vacation time. All her emotional momentum propelled her to Tulsa. Karen wanted to go, too, so Kathryn began packing her dance shawls and Indian jewelry, anticipating without any particular reason a "giveaway." She and Karen carpooled with co-workers.

At the gathering grounds outside Tulsa, people camped around their vehicles. Traditional dancing was underway—men only, with the women on the sidelines. Not just one, but three medicine men joined the dancers. Kathryn surprised herself by thinking, *If they can't exorcize Frank, no one can.*

Summoning drums called the participants to council. People from all over the United States and Canada gathered in a circle, and the organizers assigned campground chores alphabetically. Karen, a budding teen, wanted to receive an Indian name in order to be more accepted by her peers. In a traditional naming ceremony, she was dubbed Pipestem.

The first night of the gathering, the medicine men grouped people according to the issues they wanted to tackle. Kathryn described hers as being "divorced but still eaten up by hate." She didn't want her children to be poisoned by her hatred of Frank, she said, because he was their father. She felt embarrassed as others described more intractable problems, such as the death of a child.

Kathryn's co-workers were returning to Oregon early the next day, but Karen wanted to stay, so Kathryn stuffed what little money she had left into her bra and remained at the camp. The following night, the three medicine men called all the women into a sweat lodge. Kathryn heard a drumming noise outside that sounded like kids banging on the canvas covering with sticks. People described it as "hearing the elk running." Later, she became convinced that the energy within the enclosure had generated the noise.

When the medicine men directed Kathryn to look into the sweat-lodge fire, she distinctly saw a turtle. As she left the gathering, one of them told her, "We didn't promise that release would come right away, but it will come."

Soon after Kathryn returned home, Patsy called from Alaska with a question for her mother. "What will last from the experience?" she asked. "The image of a turtle," Kathryn said. Patsy commented that the turtle was an appropriate totem for her mother, because it symbolized both doggedness and flexibility, two essential survival skills. From that moment on, the tortoise was Kathryn's personal totem. In her book, *All Our Relations*, Native leader Winona LaDuke cites the turtle as a universal symbol of resourcefulness, perseverance, and adaptability.[4]

Many Indian women treasure this symbolism and sew turtle designs into their personal regalia.

A week or two later, on a Saturday morning, Kathryn felt as though an invisible hand guided her to her desk. On "auto-pilot," she began writing a letter to Frank. "I have hated you all these recent years," she wrote. "But I've just realized that in order to forgive you, I have to first forgive myself." Kathryn had to acknowledge her own responsibility for the alcoholic home in which she raised her children. In those few paragraphs written to Frank, she came to terms with aiding and abetting his disease and abuse. She felt compelled to mail the letter immediately. She told Karen she had to post an urgent note and left to walk to the mailbox. As she dropped the letter through the slot, a weight rose from her shoulders.

In retrospect, Kathryn views her personal exorcism as a natural progression through distinct stages. When she first left Frank, she felt relief to be rid of the burden of his presence. Slowly that relief turned into anger at herself and him for wasting thirty years of her life. Then came the realization that as long as she hated Frank, he would remain an oppressive influence in her life. Finally, when she was able to forgive herself for her complicity and begin to forgive him, she could let go and advance freely. Kathryn's Christian upbringing also came to the fore in this stage of her life. She simply let go of vengeance, excusing herself from embracing Frank at any time in the future. She would always know that Frank's behavior was why her girls married young, why her boys volunteered for war, why her older boys never married.

Kathryn credits the American Indian Movement and the Indian students' occupation of Alcatraz for helping her sons see possibilities beyond the limitations of their childhood. Two unlikely compatriots join her in this assessment. Mark Hatfield, Oregon's senator for thirty years, asserts that "we needed AIM to animate the public. . . . AIM awakened citizens."[5] Wilma Mankiller, principal chief of the Cherokee Nation and one of the students at Alcatraz, experienced the Native action as a "watershed event in her life."[6] Suddenly, Indians justified in their demands had the nation's attention. The Sioux were awarded $100 million for the Black Hills, a landmark decision.[7] Surely the Harrison kids could get the small amount they were due.

In 1980, Kathryn was almost sixty. She had one child at home, and she was still deciding what to do with her life. She kept running into elders who had known her father. By the end of what she calls her "forgiveness summer," she knew she had one more move to make. She asked Joanne for a raise and got it, but to Joanne's surprise Kathryn then resigned and left her things in storage in Coos Bay. She needed to go home to the Grand Rondes, even though no tangible home existed and she could find only a low-paying job to finance one. With Frank's influence finally neutralized, she was ready to take her proper place in Indian Country.

Ever since the Siletz success, the Grand Rondes had struggled to make a case for their own recognition. Upon learning of Kathryn's return to her father's tribe, Cecilia Bearchum commented: "Isn't that just like Jonesy—always wanting to help make something happen."

Part Three

Leader as Elder
1982–2005

10

Grand Ronde Re-Recognized

I am watching your eye. I am watching your tongue. I am thinking all the time. —Chief Jo Hutchins, 1869

By 1982, Kathryn was settled at Grand Ronde. First she worked as a tribal enrollment clerk, then as community organizer charged with mustering support for federal recognition of the Grand Ronde tribal government and as Tribal Council member. Frank Jr. served on the council alongside his mother. Frankie had worked hard, attending Southwestern Oregon Community College in Coos Bay and then Oregon State University in Corvallis, where he majored in forestry. He helped Kathryn and fifteen-year-old Karen make the move to Grand Ronde. He got a job logging, but his real passion was photography, and he spent his weekends on nature shoots. He also looked after his mother, now an elder in the tribe, and helped her financially. With Patsy still in Alaska, Kathryn found herself relying on Frankie more and more.

Kathryn was immensely proud that her oldest son and youngest daughter were recovering their Indian past and taking leadership roles in the tribe. Those of her children who could afford it chipped in to begin payments on a trailer for Kathryn to park on a piece of land on Ash Avenue in Grand Ronde. It was a two-bedroom single-wide, cold and drafty, and Kathryn cherished it.

It was the closest thing to a home she has ever owned. Karen lived there with her and attended the local high school.

To mark the new year in January 1982, Kathryn wrote her congressman, Les AuCoin, seeking his support for tribal restoration. Surprisingly, given his support for the Siletz and his later enthusiasm for the Grand Rondes, his first reply was brusque:

> As you may be aware, I am keeping in touch with your Tribal Chairman, Marvin Kimsey. I have told him that *until* the tribe formulates a substantive draft proposal for restoration, I am not in a position to help out. At that time, I'd be glad to take a look at your plans. . . .
>
> Please understand also that my primary concern for this year is the economy. As our country and more particularly Oregon have so many economic problems, I believe we must first solve them before we can accomplish anything else.[1]

Kathryn had first approached Mark Hatfield, Oregon's ranking senator, who told her that Congress was mostly concerned that it would be inundated with "many more tribes, waiting in the wings wanting to be federally recognized." He advised her to circumvent the BIA and to "play it politically."[2]

Shortly after he retired from the Senate in 1999, Senator Hatfield said that in his thirty years of service performing congressional oversight, he had never been impressed with the BIA's competence as a federal trustee for the tribes.[3] Most leaders in Indian Country subscribe to Hatfield's view. Winona LaDuke, a tribal leader from Minnesota and Ralph Nader's running mate in the 1996 presidential election, characterized the BIA as a "colonial holdover" suffering from "a little conflict of interest problem, in that it cozied up" to other bureaus within Interior that had agendas often antagonistic to the tribes. Voicing the conventional wisdom of her Indian colleagues, she described the BIA as stumbling through its existence "with the mandate of taking care of something the government doesn't want."[4]

In *Blood Struggle: The Rise of Modern Indian Nations*, Charles Wilkinson writes:

When I first began to work with Indian people, I was surprised about their emphasis on the BIA. . . . In time, I began to appreciate the reality and symbolism that the federal agency represented. For more than a century, day after day, month after month, for the entire lives of thousands upon thousands of Native people, the BIA had been their keeper, their master. It mattered little that some good souls in the agency worked to protect tribal rights and traditional practices. The oppression, the confiscation of land, the plots to eviscerate a worldview — all had been carried out under the auspices of the BIA. Things could not be made right until the brute within was removed.[5]

Hatfield had referred Kathryn to Congressman AuCoin, warning that "if your local congressman can't go along, it's sunk." As he himself admits, AuCoin was a hard sell. In an interview in 2000, he was a little sheepish as he recalled his first meeting with Kathryn, who had traveled to Washington, D.C., in 1982 with tribal colleagues to try to enlist his support.

This followed the previous Congress' passage of the Siletz Bill. The Siletz Bill was one of the most rigorous legislative policy challenges I faced as a very young member of Congress. The combination of ignorance, bigotry, opportunism and avarice was really mind-numbing, and I was pretty exhausted after getting the Siletz Bill passed. The only thing I knew about Grand Ronde was the general location of their tribal facility. All they had was five [*sic*] acres, just a cemetery.

So you had this young member of Congress who felt that he had . . . done a fabulous, wonderful thing. . . . Then the Siletz issues crowded out lots of other things on my slate. . . . Then comes a group of tribal members who are descendants of several bands, and they . . . want tribal restoration.[6]

In later years, AuCoin readily confessed his ignorance about his Grand Ronde constituents. He described a "Winnebago office tour" of his congressional district, during which he "set up shop for two hours at a wide spot in the road in Grand Ronde." He saw no evidence of a tribal community there. Thus he assumed that when the Grand Ronde representatives came to see him in his Washington office they were an assorted group of tribal remnants who had seen what happened with Siletz and wanted a piece of the congressional appropriation pie.

Skeptical at first of their ability to produce the evidence demanded by the BIA's restoration criteria, AuCoin tried to dampen the Grand Rondes' optimism. He wanted to impress them with the difficulty of merely getting to the stage where he would draft legislation. By his own account, it was a "tough meeting":

> I didn't give them in the beginning any reason . . . to believe that I was automatically going to draft this bill. Instead, I told them that they had to do a lot of footwork and local work to demonstrate the historical case and also go to church groups, to community groups and build the constellation of allies, like the Siletz had done, to help make it politically feasible to run this bill through.
>
> I also had this nagging doubt that this collection of bands of tribes was bona fide, and I just had to be honest about that. That was my ignorance. . . . I really thought this was a reach. . . . I pretty much approached that meeting with piercing eyes and straight talk . . . and I think it was sobering. I did tell them at the end that if they were to do these things, then come back, I would be open to commencing a serious conversation with them.[7]

AuCoin's disheartening message left Kathryn undaunted. Tribal leaders got to work in a little shack on the cemetery grounds, the only ancestral land remaining to the Grand Rondes. With little heat and virtually no logistical support (they had to write a grant for typewriters), they undertook the slow, methodical task of assembling the historical record of their people, beginning with the Treaty of 1855. In a twist of fate, they found themselves relying on Catholic church records of births, deaths, marriages, and schooling on the early reservation. Someone found Chief Jo Hutchins's 1869 speech to Grand Ronde BIA Superintendent Meacham and tacked it up for inspiration:

I am watching your eye. I am watching your tongue. I am
thinking all the time. Perhaps you are making fools of us. . . .
We are not dogs. We have hearts. We may be blind. We do not
see the things the treaty promised. Maybe they got lost on the
way. The President is a long way off. He can't hear us. Our
words get lost in the wind before they get there. Maybe his ear
is small. Maybe your ears are small. . . . Our ears are large. We
hear everything.[8]

For the most part, the BIA records were useless. They were
internally inconsistent and shoddily kept. Often they appeared
to have been altered or fabricated to accomplish specific ends,
such as the findings of incompetency at the turn of the century to
justify land grabs. In 1977, the American Indian Policy Review
Commission (AIPRC) had reported to Congress on the economic,
social, and political conditions of Native Americans as "managed" by the federal trustee (the BIA).[9] They found that few, if
any, of the federal government's promises to improve Indian
welfare and sovereignty had been fulfilled. This was no news to
Kathryn and her colleagues working on Grand Ronde restoration.

Their challenges were threefold. First, the Grand Rondes had
to overcome opposition by the neighboring communities, who
were threatened by rumors of impending tribal land acquisition.
Second, they had to garner the support of other tribes, who were
fearful that the federal government might reduce their own mea-
ger benefits if another tribal entity lobbied for its share. Third,
they had to convince Congress that this bill was not a Pandora's
box, opening the way for a myriad of illegitimate claims. The
Grand Rondes knew they had to mount the argument that theirs
was a distinct and justified case for federal recognition of a full-
fledged, pre-existing tribal government wrongfully terminated
thirty years before.

At the urging of Charles Wilkinson (who lent help on both
Menominee and Siletz restoration issues), Grand Ronde leaders
turned to the Native American Program of Oregon Legal Services (NAPOLS) for assistance in planning a strategy and marshal-

ing the necessary evidence of legitimacy. NAPOLS, in turn, prepared a grant proposal. Congress had funded NAPOLS in 1978 to serve Indians living on or near the reservations of the then-recognized tribal governments of Umatilla, Warm Springs, Burns-Paiute, and Siletz. Then, two years later, NAPOLS received additional funding from the National Legal Services Corporation to serve terminated tribes in Oregon. Unfortunately, they did not have enough long-term funding to sustain a tribal termination reversal campaign.

NAPOLS hired a first-year law student, Elizabeth Furse, to serve as "Restoration Coordinator." She was an experienced Indian rights advocate, having worked with tribes in both Oregon and Washington on fishing rights and other resource disputes.[10] In NAPOLS' grant proposal, they asked the Campaign for Human Development for $80,000 to begin their "Self-Determination for Terminated Tribes Project." An implementation plan was developed for Grand Ronde, including an ambitious timetable spanning the years 1981–1982.

Tasks outlined included community contacts; collection of materials on tribal history; "doorbell ringing" to build support within the tribe; federal and state legislative contacts; bill drafting; tribal travel to Washington, D.C.; statistical collection and analysis; testimony preparation; editorial conferences with newspapers; development and presentation of a slide show; local fundraising; visits with coordinators and consultants; and tribal meetings to keep members informed of progress. A large portion of the responsibility to carry out these directives fell on Kathryn's shoulders.

Church groups were the primary means of support for this initiative, so NAPOLS staff concentrated on making educational presentations to Church Women United, Ecumenical Ministries of Oregon, and other religious organizations. Elizabeth Furse first made the ninety-minute trip from Portland to Grand Ronde to begin the work on tribal ground in early 1982. There she met Kathryn Harrison and was immediately impressed by her calm resolve to accomplish the formidable tasks.

Kathryn had prepared a job description for herself and a list of contacts. First came lining up the support of the four Oregon tribes that the federal government currently recognized—Warm Springs, Umatilla, Burns-Paiute, and Siletz. Kathryn made presentations to each of their governing bodies, making the rounds in her Plymouth Scamp (Frankie dubbed it her "restoration car"). Frankie often accompanied her on long trips so she wouldn't have to travel the back roads alone.

The Umatillas furnished the only firsthand review of Kathryn's performance. In 1982, Kathryn ("Kat") Jones Brigham—Kathryn's brother Harold's daughter and Kathryn's namesake—was herself appearing before the Umatilla Board of Trustees on a fishing issue, and she noticed that Kathryn Harrison was on the agenda and wondered why her Auntie would be addressing the Umatilla tribal government. Kat could see that Kathryn was not yet comfortable with public speaking—her voice was shaking and her hands trembling—but when Kathryn began to speak about the effects of termination on her personally, as well as on other tribal members, she held the council spellbound. The Board of Trustees unanimously voted to issue a letter of support for the Grand Ronde restoration effort. Several members of the board said that they "didn't realize how good the Umatillas had it" in not being terminated. Kat says that she was "so proud of Auntie."[11]

When Elizabeth Furse heard the saga of Kathryn's destitute life during the termination years, she said to Kathryn: "What's remarkable is that a life can *contain* all that. Today, people think of you as a strong, serene leader." Kathryn was astounded at her ability to stand up and present the Grand Ronde case. "Ten years ago," she said, "I had no teeth and couldn't even be a waitress talking to just one table of people!"

Next on Kathryn's list were all the organizations, public and private, in the area around Grand Ronde. In that first year of restoration work, she addressed the Polk and Yamhill county commissioners; the city councils and chambers of commerce of Sheridan, Willamina, McMinnville, Lincoln City, and Dallas; the altar societies and elders of churches, synagogues, and Mormon wards; hospital staffs in Lincoln City, McMinnville, and Dallas as well as statewide health organizations, school principals, counselors, and senior classes; college gatherings in Portland, Eugene, and

OHS Neg. OrHi 101614

GOVERNOR VICTOR ATIYEH APPOINTING KATHRYN TO THE STATE
HISTORIC PRESERVATION BOARD, 1982, WITH HER DAUGHTER KAREN

Corvallis; and the League of Women Voters, Business and Professional Women, attorneys' bar associations, commercial fishing
groups, and many more groups that went unrecorded. Much to
her surprise and pride, when she concluded these talks by asking
for letters of support, she was never refused.

Before she won them over, many of Kathryn's audiences were
not receptive. Vocal opposition came from those who feared that
the restored tribe would immediately start amassing land and
remove it from the tax base. Oregon historian Stephen Dow
Beckham, then a professor at Linfield College in McMinnville,
was asked to address the concerns expressed at public meetings about national AIM activities and rumors of "costs" to tax-
payers if the tribal governments were officially recognized. He
especially remembers one specific query: "What more do these
people want? They got citizenship."[12]

Kathryn helped organize fundraisers in Grand Ronde in
support of restoration. There were bazaars, raffles, quilt projects, bake sales, old photograph displays, and movie showings
of *Windwalker* and *Three Warriors*. Kathryn fondly recalls "how
many of each other's cakes and cookies we bought" when they
could have knocked on any door and been invited in to share a
treat for free.

Next Kathryn needed to cultivate the local, regional, and state newspapers. She worked with the editorial boards of each one. She also sought and obtained the approval of Oregon's Republican governor, Victor Atiyeh. He was warm and receptive to their efforts, given his positive experience with the Confederated Tribes of Warm Springs. When Kathryn finally approached Congress with a draft of the restoration bill in hand, she wanted to have her ducks lined up—and she did, flocks of them.

Congressman AuCoin remembers that by the time the Grand Rondes came back to him, they had prepared "a very sophisticated case statement based on a lot of footwork in the local area. . . . That was the strength that catapulted the cause forward." At this juncture, he was impressed enough to agree to serve as their legislative champion. It was 1983, Kathryn was fifty-nine, and she reckoned that restoration would be a great way to celebrate the beginning of her seventh decade.

The year began with an apparent boost to restoration efforts nationwide when President Ronald Reagan released his Indian Policy Statement in January 1983. He expressed concern that not much had happened in the last thirteen years to implement President Nixon's self-determination message. He attributed that failure to the BIA's "excessive regulation and self-perpetuating bureaucracy," the perspective of a Republican states' rights administration that was seeking to lift the heavy hand of the federal government.

President Reagan emphasized tribal economic development, along with reinforced tribal governance. Although this was sweet music to their ears, tribal leaders were mindful of past federal performance and feared that the translation of this policy would result in even less federal financial support for tribal entities. They took heart in the pledge that the "administration intends to restore tribal governments to their rightful place among the governments of this nation." Government-to-government consultation is a key to tribal sovereignty, and while many presidents have paid lip service to this concept, few have given it teeth. With hopes trumping experience, tribal leaders took the president at his word and sought to engage his agency managers and members of Congress.

The Grand Rondes waded into this muddled political land-scape. Elizabeth Furse prepared an outline of proposed testi-mony that would satisfy the Department of the Interior's criteria for restoration. After the expected preliminaries, she stressed that this was a "justice issue" to remedy the travesty of termina-tion.[13] Furse thought the Grand Rondes' "star witness" should be someone who could speak compellingly about the dispersion of tribal peoples and the poverty that ensued. Again, she relied on Kathryn to make a powerful presentation to the legislators and asked her to end on a note of hope about what restoration would mean for the tribes.

In a matter of months, Kathryn made three trips to Washing-ton, D.C. She and Furse still tease each other about the rigors of those tight-budget travels: taking the "red-eye" for cheap fares; arriving sleepless on the very morning they had to make a pre-sentation on Capitol Hill; staggering to meeting rooms, trailing their suitcases behind them; finding "economy-class" lodging at "no-tell motels"; and walking miles because the price of a taxi seemed out of reach.

Kathryn was present when the Grand Ronde Restora-tion Bill was introduced on September 14, 1983. Congressman AuCoin had told her: "You watch. When I put that bill in the hopper, it will take on a life of its own." *Hopper?* Kathryn had wondered. From her work in the cannery in Alaska, she visual-ized the stained and reeking hopper where they put the salmon, and she could not transfer that image to the floor of the U.S. House of Representatives.

AuCoin's impression of Kathryn on that day remains vivid. He recalls her as "a woman who spoke to me through her silence and through her gaze . . . with incredible internal energy, moral energy . . . a silence that was louder than words. It was just a fleeting impression, but it was one that was accurate."[14]

Once the bill was formally introduced, Kathryn and AuCoin issued a joint press release on the stationery of the Confederated Tribes of the Grand Ronde. Simultaneously, on the West Coast, Kathryn's son Frankie held a press conference for the Oregon media. A month later, both Kathryn and Frankie testified in the Longworth Building Congressional Committee Hearing Room

OHS Neg. OrHi 101587

KATHRYN, KAREN, FRANK, AND ELIZABETH FURSE TESTIFYING IN SUPPORT OF
GRAND RONDE RETORATION, 1983

before the House Interior and Insular Affairs Committee. Witnesses in support included Kathryn's teenage daughter Karen (representing tribal youth); Ken Smith, a Warm Springs Indian from Oregon and assistant secretary of Interior for Indian affairs; Silas Whitman, executive director of the National Congress of American Indians; and Cynthia Darcy, staff member of the American Friends Service Committee on National Legislation.

Kathryn led off, speaking in Chinuk-Wawa, the language of her father and Molalla Kate:

> *Kah-ta miga? Niga locket sewash Tillicum pe niga klooshe tum tum pus nanitch mesika. Nesika chagwa seah illahu pus nensika mitlite resika wa wa mesika.* [How are you? My four tribal people and I are happy to be here. We have come a long way from our homes to talk to you.] . . .

As Vice-Chair of the Grand Ronde Tribal Council, I bring you greetings from my People: descendants of a People who began our passage through Oregon's unwritten history 127 years ago. How fortunate we are that they persisted so we, who came after them, could be here. . . . Chosen by our tribal council to come here, we will be weaving a picture for you of our land, our People, our culture and our Spirit, the basics of an Indian nation.

Kathryn knew she had only a short moment to convince her audience of the critical need for the restoration bill, but she could not refrain from speaking pointedly about the travails of her tribe. Again her father was her muse, as she thought about his daring in addressing the graduation attendees at Chemawa over seventy years earlier. She didn't mince words:

> We are speaking up today for our "right to exist." In the eyes of the government, we, as a terminated tribe, have been "statistically dead" for twenty-nine years. It has taken nine of those years—nine long struggling years—to reorganize, elect a new tribal council, and do research to work toward our goal. . . . We were recognized once; we need to be recognized again. As a comparatively small tribe, each member is vital to us, so each time one is lost, we can't help but feel that they might still be with us if they had continued health services. Many of our members are unemployed now, but we wonder perhaps if they'd had access to continued educational assistance, if they would be in skilled labor jobs now. Most important is our iden-tity—both individual and tribal. . . . Our children, especially, need this identity. So we need to return to our rightful place within the family of Indian Nations. Lastly, the land. All the valuable timber land that was lost, with proper management, could be supporting us today. . . . All these services are due for our People; we've already paid dearly for all of them.
>
> Once we were happy and free in our own lands; we were seldom hungry, for there was plenty for everyone. Land was always regarded as a living entity and sacred to my People, but it became important, too, to the white invaders.

Les AuCoin was getting nervous, because he had repeat-edly stressed that this restoration bill was not about return of the Grand Ronde land base. But Kathryn could not ignore what land meant to the tribes. She felt as though she were speaking on behalf of all Native people. She had the floor, and she needed to lay the groundwork for what was to come.

Propelled by the occasion to "speak truth to power," she recited the terrible litany of injustices:

> Our lands, means of existence, even part of our dignity, were taken long ago, encouraged by missionaries, army officers and government agents intent on ridding this country of our Indian existence. But the Grand Rondes were strong and continued to live through the years of the allotments and land cessions, weaving their beautiful baskets as they conversed in the Chinook Jargon, gathering their traditional foods and living in the new homelands they had now come to know and love so well. They knew they had seven treaties and that no other people had such a unique relationship with its government. . . . The People were all living together now, and like their ancestors, the strands of their heritage were held tightly in their hands. But soon another change would be forced upon them.
>
> In 1954, our second "Trail of Tears" began; this time they called it "termination" . . . legislation that forced us to surrender our identity as a federally recognized tribe, all our remaining lands and all social services. Families began to leave Grand Ronde or, worse, were separated. . . . Termination was a disaster.

Kathryn almost forgot that she was in an august congressional space, and her heart took over again:

> You can look at me and see that I'm an Indian—if you could look clear into my soul, you'd see that I'm an Indian. Yet, like my people, in the eyes of the government, I am not. My parents and grandparents were Indians; my parents attended and met at Chemawa School during the times when it wasn't considered "in" to be Indian. Yet I learned to be proud of my heritage through their lives and their teachings. I remember the conversations and laughter, using the Chinook Jargon . . . the traditional foods and the sweathouses. Although I lost [my parents] at age ten, my Indianness remained as strong as ever.

As a member of a recognized tribe ... I was able to attend
Chemawa, too, yet my children do not have that choice today.
There is a brand new health clinic there, but my people cannot
use it. The "Indian preference" jobs are not for us, either.

Like history repeating itself, our people have endured
much, but they have endured. We're here today having walked
through twenty-nine years of termination. But like our ancestors, we have continued to hold tightly to those strands of our
heritage, forever mindful of the coming generations.

*Oor klooshe icta klooshe resika wawa yuqua. Sahalie tyee nanitch
saharlie mesika.* [This has been good talk here in this place. May
our Father above watch over you.][15]

Elizabeth Furse had prepared Kathryn for the snail's pace of
congressional business. She warned that only a fraction of the
bills presented in Congress each session are passed. The Grand
Ronde advocates were relying heavily on a "guardian angel" on
the Senate side—Susan Long, legislative aide to Senator Hatfield, was a strong supporter and shepherded the bill once it
reached the Senate—but much work remained to be done in the
House.

Frankie followed Kathryn's testimony by describing the
specific effects of termination on the Grand Rondes. He cited
the 1982 report commissioned by the tribal government to document the conditions in which tribal members were living. He
summarized it as showing that "the Grand Ronde Indians are
lagging behind their white neighbors in health, employment,
and education." In fact, twenty-five percent of tribal members were suffering from "chronic health problems," and the
same number were "in need of medical attention" but could not
afford to secure it.

In a damning conclusion, Frankie detailed the results of Congress's assimilation policy:

The tragic irony ... is that not far from Grand Ronde is
the Indian Health Services facility at Chemawa Indian School.
This is a modern, efficient facility, but our People cannot make
use of its services because we are terminated. . . .

> In 1982 the average unemployment figure for all Oregonians was 11.3 percent. . . . For Grand Ronde Indians, unemployment stands at 37.6 percent.

Young tribal members, in particular, were suffering. Frankie spoke from experience as he continued:

> Our People are dropping out of school and are finding themselves unemployable. Only 52 percent of tribal members finish high school compared to the statewide rate of 75 percent. Termination cut off the opportunity for tribal members to compete for Indian scholarship funds [or] to enter Indian schools.[16]

The formal testimony of the Grand Rondes was set to finish with Karen, then sixteen, who was to read a short statement. Furse had selected her on the spur of the moment to speak for tribal youth living near the former reservation. Karen identified herself to the committee as a junior at Willamina High School who taught Indian Culture and Heritage to children at the Grand Ronde grade school through the Title IV program. She stressed how important it was that Indian children develop a sense of their Indianness:

> Becoming restored is something altogether new, but important to me. All my life, I have only known termination. People ask me what tribe I am, and when I tell them, they've never heard of it. That, in itself, would mean a lot to me: for people to know that I am part of the Molalla Tribe of the Grand Rondes, and how proud I am to be a member of my tribe. Younger children of the tribe feel the same as I do. . . . [IIR 3885] will make us as one again . . . a People, to be known again by our Government as Indians.[17]

Virtually every federal official who encountered Kathryn Harrison during the session was struck by her overwhelming spiritual authority. Putting it in Christian terms, Senator Hatfield said he felt the moral force of the "Holy Spirit speaking through her."[18] Describing a meeting in his office, Congressman AuCoin said: "I had this uncanny sense as Kathryn was talking—and I know that this sounds melodramatic—that Kathryn's words to me at that meeting were like echoes from her ancestors. I can't put it any other way. She had a moral force that you couldn't just ignore, even if you wanted to." Clearly, Kathryn was the leader of this delegation pressing for passage of the Grand Ronde Restoration Bill. She communicated a sense of rightness about the issue and stood witness for generations of crimes against her people. AuCoin reported that he had never "felt anything quite so mystical" as Kathryn's testimony that day. "Even though it was a small tribe," he said, "there were transcendent issues here. . . . She was the personification of all that spiritual force."[19] Elizabeth Furse's star witness had made her case.

When Kathryn and her cohorts returned home, she wrote a letter to her family describing the trip with Frankie and Karen. She couldn't resist a little boasting:

> We knocked 'em dead, I guess, as everyone came up to us afterwards saying how well it all went. They told us from the beginning that "no one attends hearings on Indian issues," but they came to ours. Even Channel 6 KOIN TV from Portland who filmed most of the first witnesses and myself. It was shown here that same evening. I was saying, "You can look at me and see I'm an Indian . . . yet in the eyes of the Government, I'm not." On the last day, I went to the swearing-in of the new President's Commission on Reservation Economies, and Frankie went with the rest of the attorneys to a meeting with the Liaison people from the Senate and the House as well as AuCoin's aide, to discuss the land issue. Then we all went on to Senator Hatfield's office . . . and now it has gone through the mark-up without any opposition. . . .
>
> So, with that, I'll close by saying, we're almost "Indians," thank God.
>
> With love and prayers, Mom

Kathryn and Elizabeth Furse returned to Washington, D.C., in November for the floor votes. During those critical sessions, Kathryn gripped the arms of her chair so hard that her hands were stiff. At last the bill passed. She and Elizabeth were exhausted. They simply walked across the street to the nearest café, where they sat and celebrated quietly. Back home in Grand Ronde, tribal members were driving around in throngs, shouting and honking their car horns to mark the momentous event. Thanks to Frankie, word had spread quickly through the small community.

The Grand Ronde Restoration Act passed the Senate without amendment by voice vote on November 11, 1983, and was cleared for White House approval. It was presented to President Reagan on November 14, and he signed it eight days later. On November 22, 1983, the act became Public Law 98-165. That very day, health-care benefits were extended to the nearly three thousand enrolled Grand Ronde members scattered throughout the western United States. Other benefits quickly followed.

The terse language of the law belies its deep significance for the Grand Rondes:

> Restoration of Federal recognition, rights and privileges
>
> (a) Federal recognition . . . Federal recognition is extended to the Confederated Tribes of the Grand Ronde Community of Oregon and the corporate charter of such tribe . . . ratified by the tribe on August 22, 1936, is reinstated. . . .
>
> (b) Restoration of rights and privileges . . . all rights and privileges of the tribe and the members of the tribe under any Federal treaty, Executive Order, agreement, or statute, or under any other Federal authority which may have been diminished or lost under [termination] are restored, and the provisions of [termination] shall be inapplicable to the tribe and to members of the tribe after November 22, 1983.
>
> . . .
>
> Notwithstanding any other provisions of law, the tribe and its members shall be eligible, on and after November 22, 1983, for all Federal services and benefits furnished to federally recognized Indian tribes without regard to the existence of a reservation for the tribe.[20]

Four months later, Kathryn celebrated her sixtieth birthday. She had just been named interim chair of the Tribal Council for the Confederated Tribes of the Grand Ronde Community of Oregon. She was so preoccupied with the duties of everyday tribal governance that she barely marked the passage into her seventh decade. Frankie took her out for a turkey dinner; then she returned to work.

The first year after restoration was a whirlwind. Tribal leaders and elders organized a formal restoration ceremony, where they honored all who had helped. They wrote and adopted a new constitution and presented it for approval by the Department of the Interior solicitors. It passed on November 10, 1984, with 145 votes for and 14 against. The few negative votes may have stemmed from lingering concern about hunting and fishing rights or from a mistrust of anything the federal government required.

The preamble set the tone for future tribal affairs:

> We . . . establish our tribal government in order to form a better tribal organization, secure the rights and powers inherent in our sovereign status and guaranteed to us by Federal Law, preserve our culture and tribal identity, promote the social and economic welfare of our people, protect and develop our common resources, maintain peace and order, and safeguard individual rights.[21]

The tribal leaders may have modeled their constitution on others, but the emphasis on sovereignty, culture, and tribal identity was all their own. And while the ink was barely dry on the congressional minutes, the Grand Rondes under Kathryn's leadership were already mounting a campaign for the return of their ancestral lands. Their unusually rapid success with the restoration legislation did not prepare them for the four long years it would take to regain a land base. But they came from a long line of patient and determined people.

11

Land!

The Creator made our bodies from the earth. . . . What shall I do? Shall I give the lands that are a part of my body and leave myself poor and destitute?—Owhi, Yakama treaty negotiator, Official Proceedings

In 1985, the Grand Rondes held their first annual powwow since restoration. Kathryn's family gathered. Patsy, Gene, and Jeannie came from Alaska; Raymond, Kathy, and Tommy came from Washington; and Roger came from New Mexico. Frankie and Karen were living in Grand Ronde and Diane and David in nearby Portland.

As interim chair of the tribe, Kathryn presided with pride. Roger, an aspiring artist, had entered a contest to design the tribal logo. The prize was fifty dollars, and competitors were identified by number rather than name. His was the winning design. A round seal in the shape of a rawhide Indian dreamcatcher, it depicts a forested Spirit Mountain with five feathers hanging from it to symbolize the five confederated tribes—Kalapuya, Chasta, Umpqua, Molalla, and Rogue River.[1]

The powwow drew a big turnout of tribal members, members of other tribes, and non-Indians. Organizers set up tables with crafts displays and conducted traditional dance competitions, awarding prizes to dancers who came from all over the Northwest. Les AuCoin delivered his official remarks, and the tribal members gave him a standing ovation. Hundreds shook

LOGO OF THE CONFEDERATED TRIBES OF
THE GRAND RONDE, DESIGNED BY ROGER
HARRISON, 1983

his hand as he left the podium and headed for the exit. Elders in full regalia cooked and served traditional foods, and a drumming group from Warm Springs performed. Kathryn was upset that she could not afford to pay the drummers, since the council had been able to budget only a hundred dollars to buy honoring gifts.

During this period, Kathryn was re-elected for her first official term on the Tribal Council. The new tribal constitution provided that nine members would be selected to serve until the first general election in September 1987. After that, terms would be staggered, with three members that year elected to one-year terms, three to two-year terms, and three to three-year terms.[2]

In the busy first few years of federal recognition, the tribal community needed to establish systems for access to federal pro-

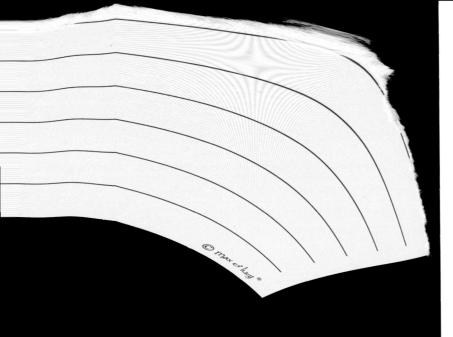

grams, to write proposals for grants for which the tribe was now eligible, to hire professional staff and consultants, and to develop ways of communicating with its far-flung members. Kathryn found the energy to begin another round of political maneuvering. She spent her time largely on the top two priorities set by the council: securing political support both internally and externally for a specific land base and restoring tribal members' hunting and fishing rights in the surrounding area. With these tangible steps, tribal leaders sought to make restoration "real" to their people and to provide incentives for the extended tribal family to return to Grand Ronde.

With scant support from other restored tribes, the Grand Rondes muscled their way onto the board of the Oregon State Commission on Indian Services, a legislatively created agency at the state capitol designed to improve intertribal access to state programs and facilitate government-to-government communication with state officials. The following year, Kathryn was appointed vice-chair of this important commission. In that capacity, she met regularly with tribal leaders, urban Indian representatives, and state legislators and executives, including newly elected Governor Neil Goldschmidt. The position required frequent trips to Salem and elsewhere around Oregon during the crucial period of stabilizing the Grand Ronde tribal infrastructure. Each new political contact enhanced the prospects of success for the Grand Rondes' long-term agenda.

In November 1985, the Grand Rondes published a reservation plan calling for a land base slightly exceeding seventeen thousand acres. This plan included timberland formerly held by the terminated tribes as well as their sacred site, Spirit Mountain. Predictably, it generated much public consternation. At public hearings, non-Indians voiced fears about their own access to hunting and fishing grounds, "tribal fences" around locally used recreation areas, and competition with private timber companies. The timber industry was showing signs of stress, and its corporate leaders did not welcome tribal logging.

One of the leading opponents was John Hampton, a timber baron with operations headquartered in nearby Willamina. Les AuCoin described him as giving "ballast to the more marginal

MAP OF THE TRASK MANAGEMENT UNIT

types who had these fevered hallucinations about bad things that were going to happen" if the Indians regained their land.[3] Both Senator Hatfield and Congressman AuCoin recall Hampton as the political heavyweight of the opposition group. Because of his personal wealth and his role as a major employer, he lent more credibility to the opposition group in the minds of the local, state, and federal elected officials.

Tribal council members had their hands full appearing at city and county hearings, sport fishermen's meetings, and hunt clubs and generally attempting to allay the fears of interest groups. Because of her experience and her track record, people turned to Kathryn to speak for the tribe. Working with Congressman AuCoin and Senator Hatfield, the tribal community crafted a strategy that would let them compromise while still achieving their objectives. In July 1987, two bills were introduced in Congress, one designating a 15,665-acre reservation and the other setting aside a much smaller tract of approximately 5,000 acres.

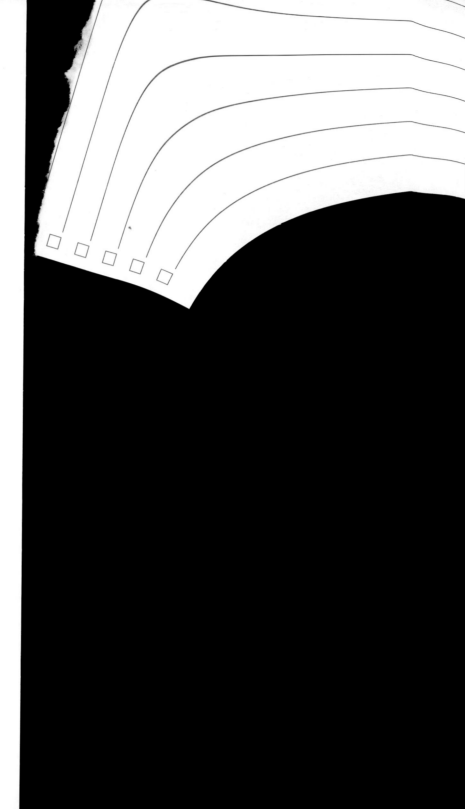

Ever the pragmatic politician, AuCoin noted wryly that th[ ]islative tactic "helped refine the issues before us." In Apri[ ]he testified in favor of creating a "mid-size" reservation [ ]the House Committee on Interior and Insular Affairs.

Since restoration, the Grand Rondes had been inv[ ]litigation over hunting and fishing rights initiated by loc[ ]groups. In January 1987, this issue was finally resolved by a jud__cially ratified consent decree. Pursuant to the decree, the tribal fisheries staff established licensing and regulation procedures for a large area known as the Trask Management Unit, stretching approximately forty-five miles from the city of McMinnville to the Pacific Ocean. Local hunters and fishers resented this "takeover," while the tribes saw it as regaining control of their ancestral lands and exercising stewardship over the resources.[4]

Kathryn participated in a marathon of daily meetings, working from dawn until well after dusk. Tribal officials had to reach out to members scattered throughout a six-county "service area" and make them aware of the programs now available to them. The limited tribal staff also had to attend to basic community needs, such as issuing tribal enrollment cards to all members eleven years and older so they could access health, education, and social services and be licensed to hunt, fish, and gather on local lands.

Kathryn always found time to continue her broader community service and to honor the memory of her parents. At the 1987 Career Fair at Oregon State University in Corvallis, her old neighborhood, Kathryn told the assembled students:

> The first ten years of my life were the most important. My parents stressed . . . growing mentally, physically, and spiritually. The teachings of my parents instilled pride. . . . We owe it to them, our ancestors, to set examples, so we can be looked back upon as we look to them. We need to leave a few footprints to guide those of tomorrow.[5]

In August 1987, Congressman AuCoin held a field hearing in the gymnasium of the Grand Ronde Elementary School to listen to local testimony about the proposed reservation. Over two

OHS Neg. OrHi 570

KATHRYN AND MARK MERCIER WITH LES AUCOIN
AT THE LAND RESTORATION BILL CEREMONY, 1988

hundred people appeared, and Kathryn led off testimony in support of the 15,665-acre reservation:

> In 1975 when our work began on our reservation effort, my people had a vision of a homeland and a chance to become self-sufficient. Many hours of hard work by a lot of people went into our fight to reverse the termination era that was forced upon us by the U.S. government in 1954. . . . Tonight I feel close to my ancestors, and I feel it is fitting that we are meeting here in view of Spirit Mountain like they must have done so many times, gathering together, long ago.[6]

AuCoin says he will never forget entering the gym that day, his mind filled with thoughts of the restoration celebration that had taken place at the same site three years earlier. He had braced himself for an onslaught of testimony in opposition to the bill, and his staff had set the stage by arranging the testimony into panels of conflicting camps—first tribal members, then representatives of the timber industry and other opponents. He had the tables moved side by side and then he engaged Kathryn and

John Hampton in conversation, issue by issue. In this way, they were able to break through a logjam over exportation of lumber versus sales to local mills. The tribe agreed to forego export opportunities, and the issue was laid to rest.

When local witnesses repeated scare stories about tribal plans to close access to the land, AuCoin would say: "Hold that thought. Now let me ask the Tribal Council: Are you really going to bar access for hunters and fishers to your lands?" Tribal leaders, well briefed on these issues, would make reasonable proposals, such as closing the land only for fire danger or other legitimate management concerns. Then AuCoin would get the opponents to concede that they had no problem with that approach.

The dialogue went on all night. As AuCoin remembers it:

> The gym was packed with people who were at sword points going in. But as the evening wore on, and the horror stories were alleged, and . . . we would go back and forth between the two panels, finding that really what we had here was an attitudinal problem, not a substantial problem between the two sides, the audience started trickling out. . . .
>
> The audience had come for a lynching, packed to the rafters, and by about halfway through, the conflict had so much air taken out of it that people didn't see any great theater here and went home. And more than that, the opposition panel was really left with no argument. There were Mark Mercier [Grand Ronde tribal chair] and Kathryn sitting at the table well prepared, brilliantly prepped. I was never more proud of them as a group of people who had struggled so much, as I was at that moment.[7]

To Kathryn's great disappointment, Congress adjourned in November 1987 without acting on the reservation bill. The Grand Rondes quietly celebrated the fourth anniversary of their restoration as a landless tribe by holding a potluck supper in a former "home for the aged," eating traditionally prepared venison stew and salmon. Fortunately for the tribe, Les AuCoin, along with Mark Hatfield, had substantial seniority in Congress

smoke signals

OCTOBER 1988

THE CONFEDERATED TRIBES OF THE   GRAND RONDE COMMUNITY OF OREGON

PRESIDENT REAGAN SIGNS RESERVATION BILL

President Reagan signed legislation creating a 9,811 acre reservation for the Confederated Tribes of Grand Ronde on September 9, 1988.

Reagan's signature on the reservation bill ends an almost five year effort by the Tribe to establish a landbase, and opens the way for the Tribe to build for its future.

The bill immediately puts the reservation lands, located in Yamhill County, into trust for the Tribe with the U.S. Department of Interior.

Income from the reservation, estimated to be 800,000 to one million dollars annually, will be used to supplement existing tribal education, housing, and health programs, and for economic development.

"This caps an extraordinary effort by the Grand Ronde Tribe to regain lost ground," Oregon Senator Hatfield said in a news release. "Tribal recognition is important to provide the right to be self-governing. The creation of a reservation is equally vital because it gives the tribe the opportunity to be self-sustaining", said Hatfield who sponsored the legislation in the Senate.

"This new reservation sets straight past injustices, gives tribal members the chance to improve the quality of their lives, and protects and promotes economic opportunities around the entire area. The community as a whole has done itself proud by working to put together this compromise," said Representative Les AuCoin who sponsored legislation in the U.S. House.

The Grand Ronde Indian Reservation, established on September 9, 1988, is 9,811 acres.

* The Act turns over to the Tribe all accrued timber receipts beginning on the date of enactment of the Act. Receipts from timber which has been removed from the reservation area do not apply.

fishing or trapping rights other than those already in effect under the Consent Decree entered into on January 12, 1987 between the State of Oregon and the Confederated Tribes of Grand Ronde.

SMOKE SIGNALS ANNOUNCES THE RESERVATION BILL IN OCTOBER 1988

by 1988. Both were determined to push the reservation legislation through. After a December luncheon with Kathryn, where she lobbied him fiercely, Oregon's Governor Goldschmidt supported them.

In March 1988, the AuCoin-Hatfield Compromise Bill was introduced, proposing a reservation of almost ten thousand acres. The bill repeated the Grand Rondes' agreement to restrict the export and purchase of timber for twenty years. It also required that thirty percent of timber revenue be reinvested to support tribal economic development ventures. The land designated was Yamhill County timber grant lands; but to maintain the local tax base, AuCoin had BLM lands exchanged for them. It was estimated that the tribe would receive approximately one million dollars in timber revenue, boosting them on their path to self-sufficiency.

The following month at a congressional hearing, Representative Ben Nighthorse Campbell—a Cheyenne tribal member from Colorado and acting House committee chair—acknowledged that "terrible mistakes" had been made during the termination era. Once again Kathryn was present, bearing witness to the "difficult . . . journey from termination back to our rightful place in the family of Indian nations."[8] The bill languished over Congress' summer recess, but Senator Hatfield was waiting to shepherd it through the Senate when the session resumed after Labor Day.

Kathryn passed an anxious summer. Art Bensell, the mentor who had encouraged her first steps in tribal governance at Siletz, died in May. The annual Grand Ronde powwow took place in August, and tribal members pressed her with questions. "How long before we will have a reservation? Will it ever come to be?" Finally, as promised, Hatfield whisked the bill through the Senate, and President Reagan signed it the week after Labor Day. The language was strong and clear:

> Subject to valid existing rights, including . . . all valid liens, rights of way . . . and easements existing on the date of enactment of this Act, all right, title and interest of the United States in and to the land described . . . is hereby held in trust for the use and benefit of the Confederated Tribes of the Grand Ronde Community of Oregon. Such land shall constitute the reservation.[9]

The Grand Rondes had regained their heritage, their ancestral land base.

The tribal newspaper, *Smoke Signals*, published Kathryn's reflections in its next issue:

> I thought about the treaties and the promises that were made . . . and it seemed like history was repeating itself. . . . We had to give a lot to get this land . . . but I went back and compared it to what our ancestors sacrificed, what they suffered. . . . Then, too, this land was taken away, and I always felt that it was our duty to regain [it]. . . . Once it's ours, I'd like to just go up and walk on it. And then to be buried on our land.

OHS Neg. OrHi 101612

TRIBAL LEADERS HONORING SENATOR MARK O. HATFIELD (CENTER) IN 1984:
FROM LEFT, WOODY PATAWA (UMATILLA), SUE SHAFFER (COW CREEK), DEE
PIGSLEY (SILETZ), ZANE JACKSON (WARM SPRINGS), KATHRYN HARRISON
(GRAND RONDE), AND VERNON KENNEDY (BURNS-PAIUTE)

My bones will mix with the bones of our ancestors. That's the
way it's supposed to be.[10]

Kathryn's fondest hope was for her grandchildren to take their
first steps on Grand Ronde land that went beyond the borders of
the cemetery where the tribe had begun its struggle for restoration.

Congressman AuCoin characterized the reservation bill
process as consolidating Kathryn's "personal growth, political sophistication, and personal confidence." He reports: "I just
don't know how it could have been done better. They wrote the
book . . . of how to calmly, ethically, follow the case for restoration and reservation—to reach out and show how others who
are not tribal members would be served by their support of the
tribe's agenda."[11]

Senator Hatfield agrees. He makes it a point to ask his
constituents, "Where do you think we got the land in the first
place?" Native people may have been the First Americans, but

the Euroamericans, Hatfield insists, were the Original Thieves. He recognizes the legitimacy of the claims Kathryn made to him long ago, and he gives her full credit for convincing his colleagues that the new legislation was simply a matter of setting things right.[12]

After the euphoria of the reservation's renewal subsided, the everyday business of governance again dominated Kathryn's life. The tribe's first priority was to establish an American Indian residential treatment center for young substance abusers. The Grand Rondes leased the former Turnaround Center in Keizer to house approximately forty youths from Oregon, Washington, and Idaho. Named Nanitch Sahallie—which in Chinuk-Wawa means "Look to the sky!" or "Seek up high!"—it opened in April 1989. Kathryn viewed this service to young addicts and alcoholics as the fruition of her life's work and paid close attention to its staffing and programming. If something like it had been available to her own children decades before, Frank's curse might not have echoed in succeeding generations.

The reservation legislation required the Grand Rondes to commit one third of the total revenue earned from their land to economic development over the next twenty years. The Tribal Council devoted much of its time to adopting an appropriate economic development strategy. They secured an Administration for Native Americans grant to do the planning. After a contract for NAPOLS legal assistance was approved, the drafting process began, leading to scores of ordinances. Kathryn sat on the NAPOLS statewide advisory board. Tribal council met every Wednesday evening, usually for three hours, and special subject committees met other evenings as well, keeping Kathryn's schedule full to bursting.

Now that the tribe had recovered a land base, Kathryn proposed that the council set up several dedicated endowment funds to better meet tribal community needs in perpetuity. Pat Mercier, the tribal accountant at that time, credits Kathryn with valiant work to preserve the tribe's infrastructure.[13] Four endowment funds were established: for education, health, housing, and elders' retirement. Tribal members applied for stipends through the relevant departments, whose recommendations were reviewed by Tribal Council. The Grand Rondes have embraced the goal of sufficiently endowing the accounts so the principal will never have to be invaded.

Kathryn was no longer governing part-time. Council business became her career. She made frequent trips to Washington, D.C., offering congressional testimony for appropriations and lobbying on substantive Indian policy issues that affected the Grand Rondes. She spent a good deal of time in Salem, too, occupied with state legislative matters. She also continued to serve on the state Commission on Indian Services. Her new career did not coincide with new wealth. Tribal council members were paid only when they attended official meetings and then at the minimum wage of five dollars per hour. Kathryn's two oldest sons, Frankie and Tommy, often supplemented Kathryn's monthly stipend with a hundred dollars from their logging incomes.

Kathryn again ran for office in September 1989. That month's issue of *Smoke Signals* dubbed her "one of the most respected Native American women in the entire nation." She won handily. By this time — one year after regaining reservation land — the tribe was earning approximately $1.2 million annually in timber revenue. Kathryn was photographed at the summer powwow in her buckskins and dance shawl with an eagle feather in her hair, standing taller than ever.

Slowly the Grand Rondes began plowing some of their profits into new ground. Their first acquisition was five and a half acres along Highway 18 (the main thoroughfare to the Oregon Coast) to house the growing Natural Resources Department. This property later became the site of the Grand Rondes' Spirit Mountain Casino. As timber prices fell, the tribe looked elsewhere for economic development opportunities.

In 1990, Kathryn revisited her birthplace in Corvallis, where Oregon State University had asked her to speak to its political science students about the workings of tribal government. By now, she was recognized across the state as an expert in the administration of Native American programs. When Patsy and Gene visited from Alaska that summer, they were so impressed by progress at Grand Ronde that they began to consider moving

back to Oregon. Finally, there was the prospect of some employment and stability for them.

The Tribal Council was pursuing the immediate priorities
of education, health, jobs, housing, and community support
for elders (transportation, nutrition, gatherings, and a panoply
of social services). Kathryn also concentrated on the long-term
need for cultural resource protection. With the passage of the
federal Native American Graves Protection and Repatriation
Act (NAGPRA) in 1990, she became concerned with the logistics
of repatriation. Museums were taking the position that items
had to be returned to individual tribes, not to confederated tribal
governments, and confusion and delay were the order of the day.
In early spring of that year, Kathryn went to Washington, D.C.,
to meet with the curator of the Museum of Natural History and
the chair of the Department of Physical Anthropology about
repatriation issues.[14]

Kathryn was also meeting with the Siletz Sacred Lands Committee about a Kalapuyan burial near Sweet Home. She hoped
to bring the ancestral remains and accompanying artifacts home
to their proper resting place. The British Museum in London
held the artifacts that a Reverend Summers had collected from
the newly removed Grand Rondes in the 1860s, which merited
another repatriation request. The tools, ceremonial items, sacred
sites, and remains of her ancestors have always called to Kathryn for protection, and she tried to meet regularly with archaeol-
ogists at Oregon State University and the University of Oregon
to keep up with their latest research interests and to enlist their
support in documenting the provenance of Grand Ronde artifacts.

That April, near the end of his term of office, Governor Neil
Goldschmidt signed a proclamation purporting to recognize the
unique government-to-government relationship between the
state of Oregon and the nine federally recognized tribal governments within its borders. The document proclaimed that the state
and the tribes "have historical relationships and unique rights
shaped by federal and state constitutions, statutes and treaties
with the United States government and executive orders of the

Courtesy of Kathryn Harrison

KATHRYN HARRISON IN REGALIA, AGE SIXTY-FIVE

President" and that Oregon "accepts the fundamental principle and integrity of the government-to-government relationship."[15] It was a positive step, and the tribes were able to use the proclamation to remind state officials of their duties.

Kathryn doubted that the governor or his staff truly appreciated what it would mean to consult with tribal leaders and their professional staff on an equal basis. State officials paid lip service to the concept, trotted the tribal leaders into the governor's office for photo ops, and promptly ushered them out. Dee Pigsley, the Siletz tribal chair, remembers, "We weren't even on his screen."[16] Tribal leaders elsewhere in the country fared no better and sometimes far worse. In the East, they were often ignored altogether; in the Midwest and in Oregon's neighboring states, Washington and California, they sometimes met with outright hostility. In June 1990, the two gubernatorial candidates, Secretary of State Barbara Roberts and Attorney General Dave Frohnmayer, seemed to take tribal government officials more seriously. After Roberts became Oregon governor, she signed the first gaming compact with the Grand Rondes.

As the tribes learned that they had political muscle, Kathryn renewed her activism. She was involved in planning a major conference sponsored by the Oregon Council for the Humanities, which she hoped would raise the profile of tribal people around the state. In October 1990, over four hundred attendees gathered in the Oregon Convention Center in Portland. Tribal experts from each of Oregon's nine federally recognized tribes spoke about their history and cultural traditions, and scholars from several Oregon universities filled in the account of Oregon's Native people. Kathryn shared the stage with such national Indian figures as Pulitzer Prize–winning poet and novelist N. Scott Momaday and future Assistant Secretary of Interior Ada Deer.[17]

By 1991, the Grand Rondes were holding their own in the national arena. When Kathryn attended national conferences and announced she was from Grand Ronde, she was no longer greeted by blank stares. That year, the projected revenues of the Grand Rondes were over $8 million. Their governing mechanisms were in place and functioning well. They were fiscally responsible, and their leaders had earned national recognition. Unlike midwestern states such as Wisconsin and Michigan, they had a supportive congressional delegation. Finally, they felt they belonged to the family of Indian nations, and they were on the verge of soaring.

Then their sense of security began to collapse. The George H. Bush administration began to dismantle affirmative action policies in education and federal grants. Budget cuts loomed in three different cabinet departments: Health and Human Services, Housing and Urban Development, and Interior, which was crucial to the tribes. As fish runs dwindled, tribal fishers sometimes faced armed non-Indians on riverbanks in nearby Washington state. The logging industry was crumbling. A conservative U.S. Supreme Court began to erode tribal court jurisdiction and, thereby, tribal sovereignty. Even Kathryn, the unreformed cheerleader, found it hard to keep up her spirits.

Then, in September 1991, as federal institutions and local economic forces seemed to line up against tribal interests, fate dealt Kathryn a crushing personal blow.

12

Mourning

Woman's hair cut short. Washes hair with piece of deerskin (doesn't touch with hands), doesn't paint or comb. Uses scratching stick for one year. — Molalla Kate describing mourning customs, 1934

Shortly after Labor Day weekend in 1991, Kathryn's oldest son, Frankie, age forty-three, slipped and fell to his death in a hiking accident near Cape Foulweather on the Oregon Coast. An obituary appeared in the September issue of *Smoke Signals:*

> Frank H. Harrison. [B]orn in Pendleton, Or. on January 15, 1948 to Frank and Kathryn (Jones) Harrison. He had resided in Molalla, Or. for 4 years and is a member of the Confederated Tribes of Grand Ronde, the Molalla Band and Rocky Boy Chippewa. Mr. Harrison testified in Washington, D.C. for restoration of tribal status, then was Chairman of the Restoration Ceremonies. He had served on many tribal committees, including the tribal council for four years. Mr. Harrison worked as a chaser for Grim Brothers Logging in Estacada.
>
> He graduated from Southwestern Community College and served in the U.S. Army in Germany during the Vietnam conflict. Frank was an avid hiker and mountain climber, having scaled Mt. Shasta, Mt. Rainier, Three-Fingered Jack and Mt. Hood twice. He also enjoyed hunting and fishing.

Courtesy of Kathryn Harrison

FRANKIE BY AN OLD-GROWTH TREE

He is survived by his parents Frank Harrison of Condon, Or. and Kathryn Harrison of Grand Ronde; brothers Thomas of WA, Raymond . . . of Portland, Roger of Salem and David Harrison of Portland; sisters Patsy (Gene) Pullin of Alaska, Jeanette Harrison of Brownsville, Kathryn (Jim) Coley of Hillsboro, Diane Harrison of Alaska and Karen Harrison of New Mexico. Funeral services were held on Thursday, September 12, 1991 at the Church of the Nazarene in Grand Ronde. Interment followed at the Grand Ronde Tribal Cemetery.

Searching for comfort, Kathryn relived her last moments with Frankie. He had visited the family Labor Day weekend, leaving on Monday afternoon to go fishing and take photographs at the beach. Kathryn's last words to him were, "Don't come back until you've got enough for all of us."

When he didn't come home by Thursday night, Kathryn was worried, but she reminded herself that he was an adult. She waited until Friday to notify anyone that he was missing. People around the reservation kept reporting they had seen him in the woods on Spirit Mountain or in his pickup on a back road. Kathryn now believes these "sightings" were manifestations of the Native belief that the recently dead return to their favorite places for a last visit.

When Kathryn called Tommy to tell him Frankie was missing, Tommy hurried from Washington to help organize the search. He called his father, and Frank drove in from Condon, where he had remarried and was back at work sporadically in the logging industry. On Sunday afternoon, the Coast Guard spotted Frankie's body in a crevice at the base of a cliff below Otter Crest Outlook. They notified Tommy, who called the house and spoke to Jeannie, asking her to break the news to Kathryn.

The Coast Guard first told the family it would be too difficult to retrieve Frank's body from the site. Tommy insisted, pledging to his mother, "I won't let them leave my brother down there." Kathryn's gut wrenched at the thought. To separate human bones from their homeland was against every tenet of tribal spirituality, and she could not let her son return to the earth in that remote place.

They recovered Frankie's broken body on Monday afternoon. After eight days of exposure to the weather and the salt air, the body was in such bad shape that Tommy would not let his mother see it. The casket would remain closed. Kathryn insisted that Frankie be wrapped in a Pendleton Chief Joseph's blanket the Siletz people had given her as a token of appreciation for serving on their council. Frankie had gone to school in Siletz, and the tribe had a place in his heart. Three of his pallbearers were from Siletz. Tommy later commented that "Frankie would have been proud, because so many pretty girls came to mourn him."

After the funeral, the family gathered at Kathryn's trailer on Ash Avenue. Frank and his wife sat in the front yard; Kathryn did not invite them to come inside. Flowers began to arrive from other tribal governments and from Frankie's co-workers at the logging company in Estacada. Elizabeth Furse, Kathryn's companion on many a red-eye flight during Grand Ronde restoration efforts, came to be with her.

KATHRYN AND HER FAMILY (WITHOUT FRANKIE AND DAVID) AT A POWWOW IN
AUGUST 1991, TWO WEEKS BEFORE FRANKIE DIED

Instinctively, Kathryn went into her small bathroom, took
her scissors from the shelf, and cut off her braid. "Woman's hair
cut short," her Aunt Kate had taught. Thus Kathryn signified
that part of her was gone. "I cut my mourning hair forever,"
Kathryn says. She has never again let her hair grow long.

Senator Mark Hatfield sent a note of condolence from Washington, D.C., where Congress was in session. He regretted not
being able to attend the funeral but sent his wish that "the support of your friends and loved ones can in some way help to ease
your grief."

At her home, Kathryn keeps a cedar chest that Frankie built
in high school. She carried it from Pendleton to Alaska, back
to Siletz, down to Coos Bay, and finally home to Grand Ronde.
The chest is filled with photographs Frankie took of his travels,
now joined with condolence letters.

One fall day ten years after Frankie's death, I asked Kathryn
if she would take me to Frankie's grave and let me photograph

her there. We went together to the cemetery, where Kathryn described the scene after her son was laid in the ground. Frank Sr. wanted to have his photograph taken by the grave site with Kathryn and his remaining children. "I did a bad thing," Kathryn confessed. Even then, when the pain of Frankie's death might have transcended all acrimony between the former spouses, "I couldn't bring myself to stand there with him. He wasn't part of our family. He wasn't a real father to those children." So Kathryn stood aside as they took the photo.

Not long after Frankie's burial, his brothers and sisters went to the site of his accident and placed a wooden cross at the spot where Frankie slipped and fell to his death. Kathryn went with them, but the path was steep and slick, so she did not climb to the top. Waiting alone at the bottom of the trail, she felt she could never be whole again.

Kathryn wrote a short tribute to her son in the Grand Rondes' 1991 *Annual Report,* summarizing his contributions to the tribe. With typical understatement, she commemorated Frank's service on the Tribal Council and his testimony at the restoration hearings. "[He was] always thoughtful and considerate," she added. "Frank was a very good son to me."

After Frankie's death, Karen, who had been in college in Albuquerque, came home to live with her mother. She worked at the tribal offices as a receptionist and helped Kathryn through the long, lonely months of acutely missing Frankie. Kathryn describes this time as "a test of faith," when her spiritual roots in both Christian and Native traditions sustained her. She and Karen took trips to Estacada and Molalla to see where Frankie had lived and worked. "We wanted almost to reassure ourselves that he had been with us so recently," Kathryn said. The holiday season was bleak for all the Harrisons, who let it pass without celebration. Karen stayed with her mother a year before she returned to school in Albuquerque.

Kathryn made copies of her favorite photograph of Frankie by an old-growth tree and gave one to each of her children. When Tommy opened his boxed photograph, he sobbed uncontrollably. Kathryn had tried to get Frankie to carry the flag at the Grand Entry for the Grand Rondes' annual powwow, but he always demurred, saying that Tommy should have the honor since he had gone to Vietnam. In the summer of 1993, Tommy carried the flag in memory of his brother.

The family began to realize how much they had counted on Frankie, whose presence had been a binding force. He had been patient and considerate, and Kathryn is convinced that he saw himself as the family's surrogate father. He assumed the role of caretaker for his mother and his siblings, never taking the time to have a serious girlfriend. He had been the planner, the one who got them all together for events.

Slowly, Kathryn re-engaged with her tribal family. A new community center was to be dedicated in 1992, a first tangible sign of the tribe's new economic footing. Its grand opening was marked with a "box social" fundraiser. The Grand Rondes remained true to their customs, continuing to supplement their income with funds raised through community potlucks and bake sales. While the tribe as a whole was recovering its sense of well-being, individual tribal members still contended with inadequate health care, unemployment, and substandard housing.

Next a dental clinic was installed in the new community space. The tribal dentist and her hygienist invited tribal members as young as two years old to the clinic for a gentle introduction to dental care. Kathryn was proud and grateful that the next generation would be spared the ordeal of being toothless and unemployable by the time they were forty.

At the same time, Kathryn was faced with the issue of whether to run again for Tribal Council. She was approaching seventy and could have retired, but she saw no point in sitting home alone. She was beginning to feel restless, and she thought that shying away from public service was not the way to honor Frankie's memory. "I figured as long as I could keep going, I would," she explains. In July 1992, she declared her candidacy with a short statement to her constituents:

> It has been an honor and a privilege being elected to serve
> on the council. Those who know me know of the many hours
> spent this year in representing our tribe. There were many ups

and downs along with the hard work . . . but I attended every
meeting and activity with pride and dignity.

We have accomplished so much, so fast, but we still have a
long road to travel. I know I can help in carrying out the visions
of our people. . . . My thanks to everyone for your trust and
faith in re-electing me so we may continue our work together.[1]

The Harrisons congregated for the August 1992 summer
powwow, where they would hold Frankie's memorial giveaway. An age-old Indian tradition, the giveaway usually occurs
one year after a death. Kathryn knew the event would be well
attended, so she had gathered things for it throughout the year.
She bought beaded patches from Alaska, earrings from the
Southwest. Everywhere she went, she picked up something for
the memorial.

She had been in mourning for a year and was worried about
holding the memorial in conjunction with the powwow. In planning it, she sought the spiritual advice of an elder at Warm Springs.
Kathryn had been asked to take part in the dedication ceremony
for the powwow grounds, and the elder told her she could participate if the giveaway took place before the dedication.

Frankie's memorial was faithful to Native tradition, and people came from all over to join in the service. Some of Frankie's
possessions were given to close friends, while others got something new to remember him by. Kathryn made sure that Elizabeth Furse received a pair of beaded earrings.

Kathryn was elected to another three-year term on Tribal Council. In September 1992, she helped launch the Head Start Program in the Community Center. Its culturally appropriate cur-
riculum was designed to promote a "positive self-image relative
to the culture and heritage of the Confederated Tribes of Grand
Ronde."[2] Kathryn was also elected tribal vice chair and presided
over hiring an in-house tribal attorney and shepherding the
exponential growth of the tribe's Spirit Mountain Development
Corporation.

Kathryn's year of mourning had reinforced her dedication to
protecting her people's cultural resources so those who were gone

OHS Neg. OrHi 101571

KATHRYN WITH ELIZABETH FURSE AT THE GIVEAWAY FOR
FRANKIE, 1992

would not be forgotten. She quickly found a way to channel this
passion. In constructing a natural gas pipeline, the Northwest
Pipeline Corporation exposed Native American remains (most
likely Kalapuya) in a ditch near Brownsville, Oregon. Kathryn
voiced an immediate objection and told the project manager that
she would "support shutting down the project if it continued to
threaten burials." The company signed an agreement to prevent
future desecrations by keeping security and tribal monitors on
the site at company expense. They also paid the costs of re-interment.[3]

Through most of 1993, Kathryn took the lead on cultural
resource and gaming issues for the tribe. A coalition of Oregon tribes was sponsoring a bill in the Oregon legislature to
strengthen the cultural resource protection statutes. Senate Bill
61 was set for hearing in March, and Kathryn offered the main

testimony before the Senate Judiciary Committee. Just a week after her sixty-ninth birthday, she struggled with her emotions as she tried to convey to the assembled lawmakers the horrors of "grave-robbing" to Native people:

> It's hard for me to express our feelings to you about burial disturbances, so-called "digs.". . . I can't tell you the feelings that my people had [about a site in Canby, Oregon, near Molalla] when some of the earth had been removed from a sacred burial place and taken over to a horse arena. Once the earth was spread, to have seen the remains. Whether it be a thigh or a foot bone . . . they were the remains of my ancestors. There are no words to describe the hurt. It pierced my heart.[4]

At this point in her testimony, a senator from Klamath Falls, an admitted "recreational" pothunter, noticed that Kathryn's voice was cracking. Rising from the hearing table, he took her a glass of water. Coming into the session, the tribal coalition had feared this lawmaker would oppose the bill. After his sympathetic gesture to Kathryn, the tribal attorney leaned toward her and said, "Now we've got him!"

Louie Pitt Jr., director of intergovernmental affairs for the Confederated Tribes of Warm Springs, credits Kathryn Harrison as the backbone of the intertribal effort to afford more protection to Native American remains, sites, and artifacts. "We'd be buffeted in the legislative fray and, on the verge of compromising, I'd feel this skinny little elbow in my back, and there would be Kathryn, urging us to hold fast."[5] In July, Senate Bill 61 passed overwhelmingly in both houses. Governor Barbara Roberts signed it then presented the signing pen to Kathryn.

Meanwhile, in 1993, staff of the Spirit Mountain Development Corporation were devoting most of their time to the gaming facility project. Kathryn was on the negotiating team, working to achieve a gambling compact with the state pursuant to the terms of the new federal Indian Gaming Regulatory Act. The Grand Rondes were well aware that if they moved quickly, they could corner the market for tourism from the nearby Portland metropolitan area. The Cow Creeks had already developed a casino along Interstate 5, but it was three hours' distance from Portland. The Siletz, too, were seeking to establish a gaming facility, but they were bogged down in litigation over siting a casino near Salem.

It was also the year that Kathryn's son Roger graduated from the Art Institute in Santa Fe, New Mexico. The graduation ceremony took place at a crucial time in compact negotiations with the governor, and Kathryn decided not to attend. At the ceremony, the students sat at their desks on stage, surrounded by their families. Roger sat alone. Kathryn has tried to apologize to Roger, but he has never really forgiven her. It was an uncharacteristic decision for her, putting the Tribe over family. As she ruefully says, "Political leaders are easier to replace then mothers."

In addition to negotiating with the state, Kathryn had to persuade her fellow tribal members that it was in their best interest to proceed with plans for the casino. At Grand Ronde, in addition to the elected Tribal Council, a General Council held regular meetings. These were similar to New England town meetings, where all those present could speak their minds. Constitutionally, the General Council had power only over decisions to change the reservation boundaries or to amend the tribal constitution. Politically, it always made sense to run important decisions by the General Council, because it was the constituency that elected Tribal Council members.

In an effort to persuade the General Council to support the gaming plans, Kathryn asked Sue Shaffer, long-term chair of the Umpqua Band of Cow Creek Indians, to attend a meeting and relate how the Cow Creeks began their gambling operations. Tribal members had many questions about where the gaming revenues would go and who would handle the money, and the elders were uneasy about relying on gaming profits. Shaffer effectively calmed their fears. In the end, the General Council approved the proposal. With the last hurdle cleared, the negotiators reached agreement.

Governor Roberts made a trip to Grand Ronde to sign the gaming compact. The tribe was off and running.

November 1993 was the tenth anniversary of restoration, and the Grand Rondes celebrated in style. Les AuCoin was now working as a lobbyist for the tribe, trying to secure approval of the gaming compact from the Department of the Interior. At the celebration, he was moved to see Kathryn in the role of the tribe's grand matron. "I actually got gooseflesh again about this spiritual leader," he said. "I know I must sound as though I go into séances or something, . . . but she really has words that seem to come from generations past."[6]

Kathryn's palpable emotion in the presence of Native relics and her ability to convey profoundly personal feelings to a roomful of observers are recurring themes in her life story. At the repatriation ceremony at the capitol in Salem in January 1995, for example, when she was presented with a thousand fragments of disturbed artifacts, the Salem *Statesman Journal* reported that while "to most people, they look like flat, oval stones," Kathryn's voice "choked with emotion as she held one in her hand."[7]

The following month, Kathryn was elected to the board of directors of the Native American Rights Fund, a national nonprofit group of lawyers with expertise in federal Indian law. The group was established in 1972 to litigate precedent-setting issues on behalf of Native people. Through its work it helped guarantee adherence to the federal trust responsibility and developed exciting new areas in Indian law. The Grand Ronde tribal newspaper editorialized in February 1994: "A national appointment such as this not only reflects well on the Grand Ronde Tribe, but is a proud commentary on Kathryn's contribution . . . and dedication to the advancement of tribal people." Kathryn worked across America to enhance tribal sovereignty, protect natural and cultural resources, and promote human rights.

At the end of March 1994, Kathryn turned seventy. I was the newly appointed United States Attorney for Oregon, literally two weeks into the appointment, when the Grand Ronde Tribal Council invited me to meet with them on her birthday. I drove to the tribal office complex, a constellation of modular one-story buildings within sight of Spirit Mountain, the low, forested mound a few miles north of Grand Ronde where Kath-ryn's ancestors had harvested roots and berries, hunted deer and elk, and sought spiritual guidance. Tribal Chair Mark Mercier presided, but he deferred to the tribal attorney to outline the structure of the tribal system. The council presented me with a notebook filled with hundreds of ordinances, along with a desk ornament containing a commemorative coin marking the tenth anniversary of Grand Ronde restoration.

I was accustomed to dealing with large, reservation-based tribes such as the Navajo, Yakama, or Warm Springs. This small, more assimilated group could have seemed less sophisticated, less culturally intense, but I had listened to Kathryn at the recent repatriation ceremony and knew otherwise. Kathryn listened attentively to my responses to council members and was surely sizing me up. I was in for a grilling: How did I interpret the trust responsibility? Was I prepared to interact in a proper govern-ment-to-government relationship? Would I allow full faith and credit to tribal court orders? What would my office do to protect Native cultural resources?

When lunchtime was announced, I was relieved to get off the hot seat. After business matters concluded, the Tribal Council meeting room was instantly transformed into a community gath-ering place. Kathryn was roasted at a potluck featuring 1950s food, Jell-O and casseroles, and quiet humor. I had forgotten she had cut her hair short, and the gift I had brought for her was a beaded barrette. She gamely attached it to her gray curls.

I decided on the spot to ask her to say the invocation at my swearing-in ceremony, which was to occur three weeks later. She honored me by appearing for the occasion in full regalia, wear-ing a fringed buckskin dress and moccasins and carrying an eagle feather fan. My mother—who we would soon learn was terminally ill with liver cancer—sat by Kathryn in the front row of folding chairs assembled at Lewis & Clark College's Northwestern School of Law, smiling broadly and holding a bouquet of stargazer lilies. Chatting, she and Kathryn discovered that they shared the same birthday and formed an instant bond. My mother gave Kathryn the lilies as she left, and Kathryn compassionately took me under her wing when my mother died six weeks later.

13

Women Elders as the People's Heartbeat

A Nation is not defeated until the hearts of its women are on the ground. — Traditional Cheyenne saying

The Grand Rondes accord a place of honor to their women elders, the Aunties. In this they follow Native tradition. Of the Cherokee, for instance, it is said:

> In the times before the Cherokee learned the ways of others, they paid extraordinary respect to women.
>
> So when a man married, he took up residence with the clan of his wife. The women of each of the seven clans elected their own leaders. These leaders convened as the Women's Council, and sometimes raised their voices in judgment to override the authority of the chiefs when the women believed the welfare of the tribe demanded such an action. It was common custom among the ancient Cherokees that any important questions relating to war and peace were left to a vote of the women. . . .
>
> The Cherokees also had a custom of assigning to a certain woman the task of declaring whether pardon or punishment should be inflicted on great offenders. This woman . . . was sometimes known as Most Honored Woman or Beloved Woman.

> It was the belief of the Cherokees that the Great Spirit
> sent messages through their Beloved Woman. So great was her
> power that she could commute the sentence of a person con-
> demned to death by the council.[1]

Ila Dowd was the Grand Rondes' language-keeper and the
elder who recited the Lord's Prayer in Chinuk-Wawa to open
special events. Eula Petit mentored several young tribal activ-
ists, including Kathryn's son Frankie. Sam Henny is universally
respected for reviving the tribe's artistic basket-making tradition, urging her students in workshops to incorporate spiritual
motifs in their baskets. These and other women elders always
have front-row-center seats at powwows and cultural gatherings, a custom of respect observed at intertribal events throughout the Northwest. Tribal youths come early to set up folding
lawn chairs for the Aunties.

Always, Kathryn pays homage to the grandmothers.
Grandmothers often preside at family gatherings and sit in the
chair of honor, and they have the privilege of speaking first and
last. Even Meriwether Lewis and William Clark—who tended
to subscribe to the conventional white wisdom that Indian
"squaws" were no better than beasts of burden—noticed that
when they stayed with the Wanapams at the confluence of
the Snake and Columbia Rivers, a "centenarian . . . sat at the
best place in the house, and when She spoke great attention
was paid to what she said."[2] Today, grandmothers are also the
surrogates at parent-teacher conferences their children have
abdicated. In her seventies, while serving as tribal chair, Kathryn found herself packing school lunches for grandchildren in
the mornings and getting calls at the office when one of them
became ill during the day.

The grandmother is the ultimate authority figure for her children's children, stepping in when parents cannot or will not. She
is the one who takes the time to do the storytelling and pass on
the traditions. Kathryn's great-great-Aunt Kate played this role
in her life. Through her years of service as tribal chair, Kathryn
kept a photograph of Molalla Kate in her office as reminder and
an inspiration.

As Pat Durkin observes in *Heart of the Circle*, a collection of Edward Curtis's photographs of Native American women, "Together the photographs show a truth about tribal life that modern Native women recognize: native women are at the heart of their communities. . . . In agricultural tribes, they usually had the crucial responsibility of choosing the seeds to be saved for the next year's crops."[3]

Indian women are the designated culture-bearers for their people. In recognition of this role, Nisqually leader Billy Frank Jr. pays tribute to tribal women as "our evolvers," the ones who propel their people through the generations. Their contributions are symbolized in a Nisqually totem pole that replaces the traditional animal figures with the faces of women whose arms reach out to the children below.[4]

In large measure, Vine Deloria Sr. attributed the survival of Native American culture to its women. In a project studying five generations of Indian women, Deloria highlighted seven characteristics central to female Indian identity.

~Skill in creating a community of women to share both responsibility and pleasure in the daily tasks of life.

~Humor to temper the burden of responsibility these women bear individually and collectively.

~Willingness to defer, but not forego; the ability to sacrifice immediate goals for the well-being of family members.

~Modesty in demeanor and attitude; self-respectful comportment that brings honor to the individual and her family.

~Spirituality to nurture the welfare of the people.

~Tribal ideals and values, strengthened and conveyed to others through storytelling and history-keeping.

~Ability to serve as the community's conscience, curbing men's exercise of their power.[5]

This complex portrait holds true for most Indian women who rise to positions of leadership, either because they exhibit the expected behaviors as they strive to assume the mantle of power or because they are the women who best internalized their grandmothers' teachings and naturally ascend to power.

Time after time, in commenting on Kathryn's way of being in the world, observers single out the same traits: spirituality, modesty, respect for tribal values, willingness to defer immediate goals for long-term benefits, gentle humor, and courage to speak up when the situation calls for it. As in the story of the Beloved Woman, both Kathryn and her Chemawa friend Cecilia Bearchum delight in piercing the "hot air balloons" of some of their male peers. They try to do it with good humor, so that their targets respond with laughter. Many is the time Kathryn has reminded her male colleagues that "Ginger Rogers did everything Fred Astaire did, but she did it backwards in high heels."

In Native culture, dwelling on one's own misfortunes is seen as a mark of self-centeredness, and it is considered gauche for women to call attention to themselves. Kathryn models this behavior. In her witnessing and storytelling, Kathryn quickly moves from the individual to the collective, noting that her personal journey is parallel to the tribe's. Rather than reciting a litany of personal woes, she will say: "People always focus on the Indian Wars era, but the policies and events of the twentieth century took a toll that has been every bit as tough to endure and survive."

Listeners are sometimes taken aback by her blunt tone as she relates even the most chilling events. The crueler the circumstance, it seems, the flatter her delivery. Kathryn is convinced that the simplest description serves the purpose of truth-telling, and she takes care to avoid verbal adornment. In her straightforward style, she brings to mind the ancient Icelandic sagas that recount horrific events sparsely.

Scholars of tribal storytelling explain that reluctance to engage in emotional display has deep roots in cultural tradition. In *American Indian Women: Telling Their Lives*, Gretchen Bataille and Kathleen Sands point out that, as a group, Indian women tend to reveal themselves quietly and slowly, telling even highly dramatic stories in terms of everyday adjustments to life's curves.

> Like all women in all times, Indian women have been forced to be flexible, resourceful and tenacious. . . . They have spoken the anxieties of their people, and through their narratives have offered models of individual strength and action. . . . The nar-

rators have seen themselves as rather ordinary, presenting records of gradual attainment of personal satisfaction rather than
recounting of personal triumphs. They have seen themselves,
not as women on the margins of two cultures, but as women
who take pride in their ability to draw effectively on traditional
resources as they assert themselves in the plural society of contemporary North America.

In the same study, they conclude:

> American Indian women's [stories] tend to be retrospective
> rather than introspective, and thus may seem understated to
> those unaccustomed to the emotional reserve of Indian people.
> There is little self-indulgence on the part of Indian women nar-
> rators; events occur and are articulated in words conservative
> in emotional connotation. Even moments of crisis are likely to
> be described without much intensity of language, or emotional
> pitch may be implied or stated metaphorically rather than di-
> rectly. Such understatement is not an indication of repression
> or absence of emotional states but often evidence that the nar-
> rator simply takes that state for granted.[6]

Kathryn draws the curtain on certain scenes in her personal
life, even with her close friends. I have come to understand this
as an aspect of her Indianness.

Across time and cultures, age coupled with economic well-being
has unbridled tongues. Kathryn is grateful that she has reached
a ripe old age, where she can tell the unvarnished truth as she
sees it. For Kathryn, other gifts of maturation are a confident
spirituality and the certainty that she speaks from experience
common to other women and other Native people. Today, Kathryn dedicates herself to mentoring younger women.

In the last decade of the twentieth century, when so many
tribal women ascended to elected and traditional leadership
roles within their communities, a wonderfully supportive group
formed. On her own initiative, Dr. Bette Haskins, a sixty-year-
old Cherokee woman, contacted women tribal leaders from

around the country to ask if they would be interested in gathering informally to compare experiences. Bette, almost ten years younger than Kathryn, had a doctorate in education administration from the University of North Dakota. She and Kathryn had come to know each other when Bette was director of American Indian Studies at Harvard before she went on to work with the BIA in Washington, D.C., in 1993.

About a dozen women responded to Bette's invitation, and a date was set for a meeting in the nation's capital. Kathryn was still in mourning for Frankie and did not attend the first year. Her friend Sue Shaffer, chair of the Umpqua Band of Cow Creek Indians, went to the inaugural meeting and experienced a spiritual strengthening and a sense of collective problem-sharing that "lightened each individual's burdens."[7] This came at a time when many of the women leaders were resisting pressure for high per capita distributions of revenue from gaming operations. They reinforced one another's resolve to invest instead in the tribal infrastructure, for the long-term benefit of the tribe.

For the first five years, Bette Haskins's determination, along with seed money from Nabisco's corporate women's fund, kept the group going. Later they secured grants, hired staff, and adopted a logo and a name—Heart of the American Indian Women's Network (HAIWN). In keeping with her own tradition, Kathryn brought Bette a gift of beaded earrings when she first attended a meeting in 1992. The meeting was hosted by the Powhatans, the tribe that met the Pilgrims' ships when they landed in Massachusetts. All in all, Bette coordinated six conferences for the women leaders.

Kathryn came to look forward to each year's convocation. Frequently, the women of HAIWN gasped or winced at the expression of a truth they had considered a product of their own misperception or paranoia. Kathryn carried away from these sessions the growing realization that "women do all the work, and men take all the credit." She is convinced that over the years this phenomenon shadowed much of her work in Indian Country, both at Siletz and Grand Ronde.

Sue Shaffer says that all the women leaders have become more outspoken over the years, and she delights in watching

OHS Neg., OrHi 101613

MILDRED CLEGHORN, ADA DEERE, AND KATHRYN HARRISON AT THE
NATIVE AMERICAN RIGHTS FUND MEETING

the older women embolden the younger ones. The elders (Sue and Kathryn among them) make a conscious effort to convey the message "You can't be a shrinking violet and make things happen."

Not all the conversation at HAIWN meetings was political. Women compared notes about raising grandchildren on their own or lamented the ravages of alcoholism. Sometimes they scheduled meetings in conjunction with the National Congress of American Indians, but they remained an independent, pay-your-own-way group.

In their discussions, HAIWN members nominated elders to the Grandmothers' Hall of Fame. Kathryn always began with their founder, Dr. Bette Haskins. Closely following would be many of her regional contemporaries: Cecilia Bearchum (her Chemawa classmate and founder of the Umatilla language program); Bernice Mitchell (founder of the tribal Head Start Program at Warm Springs); Sue Shaffer; Pauline Ricks (fellow Tribal Council member when Kathryn was at Siletz); and Fern Alexander (eloquent spokesperson for the urban Indian population on the Oregon Commission on Indian Services).

Moving outside Oregon, Kathryn would nominate Marge Anderson (former chair of the Mille Lacs Band of Ojibwe, ousted because of her steadfast stand against per capita distribution of gaming proceeds); Mildred Cleghorn (recently deceased fellow Native American Rights Fund board member and chair of the Fort Sill Chiricahua, Warm Springs Apaches, who described herself as still a "prisoner of war"); Annie Descheny (Navajo elder and first female Tribal Council member); and Wilma Mankiller (former principal chief of the Cherokee Nation). Kathryn especially admired Mildred Cleghorn's Apache matrilocal tradition, in which the elder woman was the core of her extended family and her indomitable spirit made her a contemporary "warrior woman."

As a group, Kathryn would include the Yankton Sioux's Braveheart Society in this Indian Women's Hall of Fame. In Sioux lore, Braveheart women went out on the battlefield, brought home the wounded, and helped them recover. In the early 1990s, a central group of about seventy members revived the Braveheart Society. Each year since, they have taken two or three dozen young Sioux women out into the hills, where they celebrate coming-of-age rituals.

The Braveheart Society has focused its healing tradition on the women who joined, standing up for the emotionally and physically injured. In addition, the Society has taken on projects consonant with its mission of rescue. Its most publicized recent action was to demand the re-interment of deceased ancestors who were unearthed by fluctuations in water levels caused by a hydro-project on the Yankton Reservation. According to BIA staff on the reservation, Braveheart Society members are a force to be reckoned with. In Kathryn's mind, every woman tribal leader is a Braveheart, metaphorically picking up the wounded and bringing them home.

14

Gambling Winnings and Life's Losses

Klohowyam nesika tillisum!
Mith let lee lee cupa ook ilahe
> *Welcome our friends!*
> *Live long on this land.*

> —Chinuk-Wawa greeting at the main
> entrance to Spirit Mountain Casino

Visitors to the Grand Ronde casino are met at the door with two cultural reminders. The first is a traditional greeting: "Welcome our friends! Live long on this land." The second is a twice-life-size bronze sculpture by Oregon artist Rip Caswell, based on a drawing of a grandmother teaching basket making to her grand-daughter.[1] For the public, Kathryn describes it this way: "With a powerful sense of personal triumph and dignity over tragedy, this art embodies our tribe's respect and recognition for our culture, and for those who kept it alive from generation to generation." The sculpture is a commanding presence in the lobby of the casino, which opened its doors in 1995.

That fall, Kathryn was again up for re-election to Tribal Council, and by this time she was easily its most visible member. Much to her credit, the Grand Rondes began 1995 with projected revenues of $14.5 million and high hopes for a plethora of new jobs associated with the casino's arrival on the local scene.

The tribe was committed to sponsoring job training for the distinct skills needed to staff the casino.

In the early winter of 1995, *Smoke Signals* published the following list of prospective job openings:

Bingo: callers, admission, floor and sales clerks, cashiers

Slots: money changers, slot attendants and technicians, admin.

Pull tabs: roamers, booth attendant money counter, redemption

Keno: cashier, runners

Poker: dealers

Blackjack: dealers, administrative assistant

Casino Finance: cage cashier, retail cashier, admin. asst.

Corporate Finance: budget administrator, purchasing admin., payroll distribution, admin. asst., account specialist, accountants

Human Resources: receptionist, human resources asst., training administrator, training assistants

Management Information: records retention

Marketing: advertising promotions, sales reps, public affairs

Security: security officers, investigators

Food and Beverage: hosts, cashier, waiting staff, bussers, runner, cook, chef, servers, beverage servers, deli-cook, espresso attendants, café coordinator, catering staff

Casino Services: wardrobe, phone operators, mail room courier, receiving clerk, public transportation services

Surveillance: technician monitors

Facility Services: housekeeping, grounds crew

Guest Services: valet, valet attendant, coat checker

The tribe hoped to entice young people back home, and even Kathryn was impressed with the array of job skills the new enterprise would offer the Grand Rondes and others in the surrounding community. The tribal newspaper began publishing twice monthly in order to keep community members posted on fast-breaking events.

Kathryn's salary was still $25,000 a year. Tommy (now Kathryn's oldest son) continued to chip in when he could, sending Kathryn a check once a month with a note, "Just a son, trying to help out." Tommy had worked as a logger in Bellingham, Washington, for the past thirteen years. He seemed settled there, where he was an active participant in the Veterans of Foreign Wars and enjoyed the camaraderie of fellow Vietnam vets. Kathryn was tickled that his nickname among his friends was "Indian Tom," because it showed he was proud of his Indian identity. Since his "twin" Frankie died, he had become less outgoing and gregarious, and Kathryn worried as his guitar playing became more subdued.

As the casino neared opening, the tribal newspaper published a centerfold article entitled "Tribal Gaming: Myths and Facts." It was an attempt to help tribal members deal with the numerous questions that would soon come from their neighbors and others around the state. It identified nine of the most common misconceptions Indians and non-Indians alike hold about gambling and casino management. Kathryn tires of these often repeated discussions with critics of gaming. (See Appendix 2 for a discussion of the nine myths.)

To help counter the proliferation of such myths, one of the first employees Spirit Mountain Development Corporation hired was a marketing director. Soon afterward, they recruited a person of unimpeachable integrity to chair their Gaming Commission — Kathryn's younger brother, Bob Watson.

Bob Watson had served as director of the Department of Corrections for Oregon and Delaware and was highly regarded by law enforcement professionals in both regions. The Grand Rondes could not have engaged a better watchdog to allay fears about their gaming operation's conformance with the highest standards. Because of the high-caliber personnel that tribal leaders were able to attract, they secured an $18.9 million loan for the casino through the John Hancock Insurance Company. This was the first loan paid directly to a tribal government to manage its own casino.

The financing attorney who helped establish Spirit Mountain Gaming, Inc., affirmed that John Hancock's representatives

Courtesy of *Smoke Signals*, Toby McClary, photographer

SPIRIT MOUNTAIN

"were impressed with the Tribe and Spirit Mountain's planning and quality of staff." He noted that in his experience, "lenders are usually very cautious when dealing with Indian tribes, but Grand Ronde was treated the same way a large corporation or unit of government would be treated."[2] As it turned out, Hancock's investment was a wise one.

Because of their different surnames, few people were aware that Kathryn and Bob were sister and brother. In addition, Bob's rearing in a non-Indian home from the age of five led him to identify more with the dominant Anglo-Saxon culture than with his Native traditions. When Kathryn first re-established contact with Bob after she left Frank, she wrote him a letter asking whether he considered her "too Indian." Upon reflection, he said later, it hurt him that his sister might believe he had so little concern for their Native culture, and Kathryn's letter motivated him to contribute to tribal development.

Truth be told, Bob was proud of the woman his older sister had become. He subscribed to the tribal newspaper in 1995 and was pleased to see Kathryn featured in its May issue in a "spotlight" profile. Headlined "Vice-Chair Has Earned Respect in Indian Country," the article succinctly portrayed the person tribal members turned to for leadership:

> Almost anytime something is going on in Grand Ronde, Kathryn Harrison is there. And she's been there since the very beginning.
>
> She talks about the early '80's with a fondness — a fondness that comes with a memory of the way things used to be.
>
> Kathryn says, "Sometimes I'll ask someone about restoration. I'll say 'Remember when . . .' and then it will dawn on me that there aren't many people left who were around during that time."
>
> There's a certain amount of satisfaction and pride that comes with that sort of achievement. And where the Grand Ronde Tribe is concerned, restoration was the most important achievement ever.
>
> Kathryn has served on Tribal Council since 1980. . . . "I'd like to see more culture developed in the Tribe," she said. "Our culture isn't lost, but we can regain some with our youth."
>
> Kathryn also likes the idea of more programs for elders. Maybe a care center and places to live. "We promised the members that housing would be a priority for us. I want us to hold on to that promise."
>
> She enjoys reading nonfiction books about other tribes and recent trends in Indian Country. . . . Kathryn is known as a tribal leader and is very well respected by many people and organizations in Oregon. She has received many awards for her contributions to her people and the state.

Kathryn was re-elected that September to another three-year term on Tribal Council. This time her campaign statement included a specific platform for revenue disbursement: (1) health benefits for every tribal member, (2) a retirement plan, (3) job training, (4) housing assistance for elders, (5) child care for students and workers, and (6) eventually, per capita distributions coupled with investment counseling.

Kathryn was deeply concerned about pressure from her constituents to simply divide up the gambling proceeds. She did not want to see her community fritter away its newfound and possibly fleeting wealth. In her view, per capita distributions, though appropriate in returning wealth to the tribal community, could be excessive and subject to abuse, undermining investment in the tribe's future. "It makes my heart ache to see the short-sightedness of some of my fellow tribal people when they come into sudden money," Kathryn confides. "They run out and buy used cars and TVs. What have they got to show for it five years later?"

This well-articulated platform distinguished Kathryn from other candidates. She was a leader with a specific vision, an advocate of long-term investment. Moreover, she had the ability to implement that platform and the wisdom to assemble a team of reliable professionals, including the tribal attorneys, public affairs representatives, and her own brother, returning to chair the Gaming Commission.

Bob Watson readily admits that he was predisposed to oppose gambling because of his background in corrections. "I can't conceive of why it would be a good thing for the tribe," he first said.[3] But Bruce Thomas, then CEO of Spirit Mountain Development Corporation, was enthusiastic about involving Bob. He gave Bob the name of the manager at the Mystic Lake Casino near the Mall of America in Minnesota, and Bob visited the casino on his way west from Delaware. Mystic Lake, one of the most successful casinos in the United States, is owned by the Shakopee Mdewakanton Sioux (Dakotah) Nation, which achieved federal recognition in 1969. Within thirty years, they were able to donate over $25 million in gaming proceeds to community applicants through their charitable arm.

The Shakopees were pleased to show Bob the results of their venture into gambling. The gist of their presentation was simple: "Look at all the terrific things we're doing with this money." They proudly displayed "before and after" pictures of their living conditions. Bob was particularly impressed by evidence of newfound self-respect and increased safety in the community, due to their state-of-the-art fire protection system and other public improvements. He realized that "people were looking forward to the future, which they didn't do before gaming." After speaking with the architects of the casino at Mystic Lake, he was persuaded that this would be a good direction for the Grand Rondes to take. Kathryn considered Bob's return to lead the Gaming Commission one of the tribe's significant gambling winnings.

Attracted by the Grand Rondes' growing promise of prosperity, over two thousand visitors attended the annual August powwow in 1995. Spirit Mountain Gaming, Inc., had a job booth there. The $18 million annual payroll for the casino was expected to have a major impact on the economies of neighboring towns, particularly Willamina and Sheridan. More distant Salem and McMinnville anticipated collateral benefits.

When the casino opened in October as the largest gaming center in Oregon, over four thousand guests appeared the first day. Kathryn's children gathered—only Tommy and Raymond missed the gala—and Roger, Karen, and Patsy talked about returning to Oregon to work there.[4]

Already the magnet was taking hold. Kathryn's Chemawa classmate Cecilia Bearchum traveled from Pendleton to be with her, and the two of them stayed up all night laughing, reminiscing, and comparing notes.

The high excitement of the time was extinguished by a family tragedy that left Kathryn reeling. Five days after the casino opened, Tommy was riding as a passenger in his own pickup in Bellingham. The driver left the road and hit a tree, and Tommy was catapulted from the truck. He was taken to the hospital for observation and soon released to go home. Two days later, his landlady found him in the shower, dead at the age of forty-six from internal hemorrhaging.

Due to the circumstances of Tommy's death, an autopsy was required. Kathryn abhorred this procedure, which violated her traditional beliefs, but she too wanted to know the cause of Tommy's death. It was officially determined to be a lacerated liver. "Why did they send him home?" Kathryn wailed. "Couldn't they detect that?" At her children's insistence, she hired an attorney to represent the family during the process, which delayed the return of Tommy's body to the ground.

Tommy's burial service was later than any of the family would have wished. Many of his friends and co-workers came from

KATHRYN HARRISON AT HER SONS' GRAVES,
MAY 2000

Washington to relate their reminiscences of "Indian Tom." His mountain-climbing buddies and logging partners spoke of his skill and professionalism, recalling how safe they felt when they were with him. They told tales of the Deming Logging Show, where Tommy competed each year to raise funds for families who had lost loggers on the job.

Patsy wrote an obituary for Tommy that appeared in the November 15, 1995, *Smoke Signals*:

Tom E. Harrison, age 46, died October 22, 1995 in Bellingham, Washington.

He grew up on the West Coast and moved to Ketchikan, Alaska in the late 1960's. He graduated from Kayhi High School in Ketchikan in 1968. He was a state champion wrestler and later was a Golden Gloves boxer.

He enlisted in the United States Army and served in the Vietnam War from 1969–1972. He was awarded bronze and silver stars.

In 1982, he moved to Bellingham, Washington. He was a logger and a member of the Veterans of Foreign Wars.

He dearly loved his parents, sisters and brothers, nieces and nephews, and cousins.

He is survived by his mom, Kathryn Harrison of Grand Ronde; dad, Frank Harrison of Warrenton, Oregon; sisters Patsy Pullin of Ketchikan, Alaska; Jeanette McGarry of Brownsville, Oregon; Kathy Coley of Salem, Oregon; Diane Harrison of Portland, Oregon and Karen Askins of Lincoln City, Oregon. Survived also by his brothers, Ray Harrison of Salem, Oregon; Roger Harrison of Santa Fe, New Mexico; and David Harrison of Portland, Oregon.

He was preceded in death by his older brother, Frank Harrison.

Tom was fun to be around, as well as charming, witty and private. He loved to write and sing songs, play his guitars and harmonica. We will miss him.

The family would like to thank all of those who attended the funeral. We appreciate all the prayers, flowers, support, and kind words spoken.

Tommy was buried in his military uniform next to his brother Frankie in the Grand Ronde Tribal Cemetery.[5] Kathryn placed her ceremonial eagle feather fan in the casket. Her two eldest sons, born exactly a year apart, died almost exactly four years apart. Thanksgiving and Christmas 1995 were shrouded in Kathryn's memory, and the boys' joint birthday on January 15 was unbearable. Kathryn confesses that this time in her life was the closest she ever came to giving up.

15

Chairwoman

The respected member of many Indian communities is the one who shares and gives all of his / her wealth to others. As resources are available, the virtue is to share them and use the Grace of giving is a virtue to be admired. —Smoke Signals, April 18, 2000

Once again, Kathryn began a new year wondering if she had the energy to continue in tribal governance. She sometimes felt she was merely going through the motions. But in the next five years she would put her stamp on tribal administration, strongly inculcating the value of giving back. As she put it time and again, "The true value of the Grand Rondes' success is that we chose to build bridges to the culture that tried to obliterate us. The tradition of sharing will see us through." She reminded herself that the best way to honor Tommy's pride in his heritage was to work to improve conditions for the tribe.

Kathryn was in constant demand—as an official greeter for the many business and international delegations that wanted to see the "newly discovered" tribe, as oral historian at orientations for new Grand Ronde employees, as a speaker for various community organizations interested in learning about Indian culture. She delivered dozens of invocations, and she could have spent eight hours every day making the rounds of cultural gatherings. The March 1, 1996, *Smoke Signals* listed fifty-two such events.

The Grand Rondes began a policy of allocating their casino revenue to adjacent land purchases. First they bought the twelve acres next to the casino, the site of a local produce stand. Since the casino opened, land values had skyrocketed, but Tribal Council nevertheless set a high priority on preserving the quality of development in the surrounding area. They wanted to ensure that no pawn shops or adult video stores could be located nearby. The council also passed ordinances dealing with the regulation of liquor consumption in new tribal territory and establishing a housing authority.

Kathryn was particularly gratified by a 1996 town-hall meeting in the neighboring town of Willamina. Oregon Governor John Kitzhaber attended, along with Tribal Council members. John Hampton—the former chief executive officer of Willamina Lumber who had so vigorously opposed the Grand Ronde restoration and reservation bills for fear they would erode the economic health of the community—was there and commended the tribe on its management of reservation timber.

During this time, the tribe actively pursued the acquisition of an additional 7,500 acres of original reservation land currently in the portfolio of the Bureau of Land Management. Tribal attorneys negotiated effectively with Department of the Interior solicitors to regain the property and add it to the Grand Ronde land base. Casino officials also moved rapidly on a 36,500-square-foot expansion to the facility, adding jobs for another 150 people.

Tribal council members were acutely aware that future prosperity was not assured, since there were no guarantees of continuing gaming revenue. In Oregon and nationally, controversy still swirled around tribal gaming operations. The media and various governors' offices sounded alarms about individuals' and states' growing dependency on gambling. Oregon's gambling oversight task force was chaired by State Attorney General Ted Kulongoski, who had publicly expressed his concern about the proliferation of gaming.

In an April 1996 meeting, Kulongoski commented: "Five years from now, this will be totally out of control, and the public will take a very harsh approach to gaming." Five years have passed. Not only did this dire prediction prove unfounded, but five years later Ted Kulongoski was running for governor and courting the tribes assiduously. He was a guest of honor at Kathryn's 2001 retirement celebration in the casino, and he happily accepted tribal gaming proceeds as donations to his campaign.

Kathryn believed that the best way to oppose uninformed hysteria about casino operations was to patiently pursue tribal goals and let the public discover for itself what gaming was all about. (For a discussion of misconceptions about casinos, see Appendix 2.) This they did, as they flocked to Spirit Mountain casino.

Throughout the political turmoil, Kathryn maintained her focus on cultural resources. She volunteered to be the Tribal Council liaison to the Kwelth Tahlkie Culture and Heritage Society (loosely translated as Pride of Yesterday Culture and Heritage Society). Her sister Marie also served on the Society's board. The Society was established to (1) preserve the heritage and culture of the Grand Rondes, (2) provide facilities for the safekeeping and exhibit of articles and artifacts, (3) provide educational opportunities for students and scholars, and (4) "ensure that historical contributions by tribal members receive proper recognition."[1] In ensuing years, the fourth purpose became dominant.

Seeking to increase their participation in cultural events close to the hearts of the surrounding community and once again displaying their savvy public relations skills, the Grand Rondes decided to sponsor a float in the June 1996 Portland Rose Festival's Grand Floral Parade. The tribe's huge float, transported on a flatbed trailer, was titled "Nature's Spirit." It featured a coyote mother and her pup, created with fur made of native grasses. Tribal members in traditional garb rode the float along the four-mile parade route, while commentators read from previously distributed scripts describing the symbolism. The June 17 *Smoke Signals* explained that the float "celebrates the fun-loving spirit of Coyote and also represents the high value the Grand Ronde Tribe traditionally places on nature and the cycle of life with the mother and her pup." "Nature's Spirit" won the top prize, and Kathryn accepted the Sweepstakes Award on behalf of the tribe. Speaking of sustainability, she often said, "If we respect the cycle of life, the earth will return it to us sevenfold."

The casino's upscale restaurant, Legends, opened on Independence Day 1996. On its walls are photographs of Molalla Kate and of Kathryn as a child in the blue wool coat her mother made for her. Tribal members and their families were invited to Legends for a free lunch the weekend before it opened to the public. Legends is now advertised in all tourism brochures for the Oregon Coast as a gourmet dining venue.

Tribal council passed a supplemental budget for the casino in its first year of operation, a further indication of its success. With Kathryn's guidance in setting long-range objectives, the council established three landmark programs: (1) "health security," first for tribal elders, then for other members; (2) "elders' pension," so that every tribal person over fifty-five years of age would receive $100 per month; and (3) an "investment benefit" program to train tribal members in responsible fund management and to generate income for later years. The program allotted investment funds of $1,000 to every qualified member. Working with an investment counselor, each member chose from a menu of safe investment options. These three programs avoid the danger of a per capita distribution of gaming revenue, where the money has the potential to run through the fingers of individuals with short-term goals.

In July 1996, Kathryn prepared for Tommy's memorial giveaway. The family planned to hold the service shortly before the annual August powwow, as they had with Frankie's. Not quite a year had passed since Tommy's death, and Kathryn's aching sense of loss had not subsided. About the same time, a group of Oregon women lawyers invited Kathryn to speak at their Portland meeting. Asked how she had found the strength to recover from deep despair, she said, "I walked by those tombstones [of her ancestors and her children in the tribal cemetery] and remembered—that memory made me step a little higher."[2]

Over the course of the year, Kathryn was plagued by viruses that turned into bronchitis or pneumonia. Her family and friends worried about her. That autumn she moved to a two-bedroom rented house in Sheridan, close to tribal headquarters. Kathryn sees the irony in living in a town named after Gen. Philip Sheridan, source of the infamous 1869 quote, "The only good Indians I ever saw were dead."[3] The community honors his memory with an annual Sheridan Days festival. One year, the town asked the Grand Rondes to fund the event, along with a library named after the general. The tribe responded that if the citizens of Sheridan would come to terms with their history and change the community's name for the better, the Grand Rondes would gladly provide funding.

It was hard for Kathryn to leave her trailer on Ash Avenue in Grand Ronde, the home her children had helped her acquire, but she was becoming uncomfortable with the isolated tribal neighborhood's rumor mill, where "everyone watches my family's comings and goings." Kathryn believes devoutly in community, but she is quick to puncture romanticized notions of everything she holds dear, including sisterhood. "Sisters are wonderful when they work out," she says. "But there are also wicked stepsisters."

In September 1996, Kathryn was elected chair of the Grand Ronde Tribal Council. Her eight fellow council members elected her by a vote of four to four, with Kathryn breaking the tie. In time, Kathryn's predominantly male colleagues accorded her grudging respect for her way of conducting council meetings and representing the tribe to outsiders. Ed Pearsall, who joined the council in 1994, says about Kathryn: "[She is] one tough lady. When she has to, she can come at you with all guns." Today, he is frank in recognizing Kathryn's value to the tribe. "The woman is unbelievable in her stamina. [As] the outside face to the community, she can bring the public to tears."[4]

One of Kathryn's first official actions as chair of the tribe was to sign a construction contract for the new health and wellness clinic. By this time, Grand Ronde enrollment totaled 3,415 members, 1,377 of them under twenty-one years of age. Because of termination, most tribal members did not live on or near the reservation but were scattered around the state and the nation. The difficulty came in trying to communicate with each of them and respond to their concerns. Before the casino put the Grand Rondes on the economic map, no one had cared much about tribal membership. Now many distant constituents were clamoring for benefits and lower enrollment standards, so that children or grandchildren who were as little as one thirty-second Grand Ronde could get their share.

The Grand Ronde tribe marked thirteen years of restoration with a dinner and a mini-powwow in November 1996. Kathryn spoke briefly about the importance of recognizing the tribe's struggles and remembering those who had sacrificed. The council decided to invite no official guests to speak, opting instead to give tribal members the opportunity to talk about what restoration had meant to them. "You all are the *real* special guests," Kathryn announced. She reiterated the theme in her holiday letter to tribal members:

> One only needs to see a little cemetery office where we started, then look around at the many departments . . . each with its expert staff, to realize the progress made in serving our people. [W]hoever thought we would have our Spirit Mountain Casino . . . as a way of not only helping ourselves, but the whole community as well?
>
> Having had the drastic experience of being a terminated tribe for twenty-nine years, we know the value of . . . returning to our rightful place in the family of Indian Nations.
>
> Yes, the tribe has seen many changes since our beloved ancestors were forced to walk their "Trail of Tears" to this new homeland. As their descendants, we can reach back to their resilience, endurance, and spirituality as we face the new challenges.[5]

For the new year, Kathryn posed for a striking ad that appeared in newspapers around the state. A simple black-and-white photograph showed her in a traditional basket hat touting the tribe's tradition of "giving back." As part of their gaming compact negotiations with the state, the tribe proposed and then agreed to set up a charitable fund that would distribute six percent of net profits from the casino to an eleven-county "service area." The Spirit Mountain Community Fund (SMCF) was formally established in 1997, which rapidly created a public image of the Grand Rondes as an extraordinarily generous tribe.

OHS Neg., OrHi 101616

KATHRYN WITH ELIZABETH COLE BUTLER AT THE DEDICATION OF THE GRAND
RONDE GALLERY AT THE PORTLAND ART MUSEUM

The fund's creation created a furor in Indian Country. Other tribes accused the Grand Rondes of allowing themselves to be blackmailed in compact negotiations with the governor and creating an unacceptable precedent for tribes still in the negotiating process. Critics saw the fund as an infringement on tribal sovereignty and a "virtual tax."

Nevertheless, the tribe became a major player in the charitable community in Oregon. People got over whatever compunction they felt about using "gambling money" and made grant applications in droves. Over the years, SMCF has proved to be a marketing coup, and the Grand Rondes are known statewide as "the little tribe with the big heart."

Since its inception, the fund has disbursed over $30 million. Through judicious grant approvals, the Grand Rondes became partners in such diverse ventures as Life Flight, the Portland Art Museum, the Oregon Museum of Science and Industry, the Portland Classical Chinese Garden, the Willamina Fire District,

the Portland Baroque Orchestra, and many community librar-
ies, hospices, Head Start programs, domestic violence shelters,
and food banks. Trustees consist of three Tribal Council members, one gubernatorial appointee, one management official of
the Spirit Mountain Development Corporation (SMDC—the
tribe's economic development arm, which operates the casino),
and three non-tribal members selected by the Tribal Council in
consultation with the governor's office. Kathryn was one of the
Tribal Council appointees until her retirement.

In the foundation's first three years, the tribe deliberately
looked for naming opportunities in its grant-making process. In
the Portland area, virtually every major tourist attraction and
community cultural anchor now includes the Grand Ronde
name or Spirit Mountain logo. Under Kathryn's leadership, the
tribe also used grant occasions to educate the general public
about tribal history and culture, directing staff to help applicants
incorporate information about the tribe in written materials and
exhibits. The SMDC trustee on the board of the Spirit Mountain
Community Fund (SMCF) for the first eight years was the casino
marketing director, so the marketing theme is consistent.

Throughout 1997, Kathryn's days—and often her nights and
weekends—were filled with official presentations, meetings, and
trips to the sites of grateful beneficiaries of SMCF largesse. She
dedicated facilities, launched vehicles, hefted shovels at ground-
breakings, and doled out oversized "photo op" checks. At home
in Grand Ronde, Kathryn presided over the openings of the
tribal health and wellness clinic and the Grand Meadows Housing Development. Construction also began on the tribe's new
100-room hotel adjacent to the casino. Kathryn considered it her
great good fortune to sit on Tribal Council as the tribe reaped
the benefits of so many years of "seeding" efforts. She sometimes
pinches herself in wonder at the fast-pitched accomplishments of
the last two decades. As tribal members' quality of life tangibly
improved from month to month, practically everyone became a
believer.

Enrollment pressures have kept pace with increasing benefits, with multitudes of people claiming Grand Ronde affiliation.

Kathryn and the Tribal Council had to stem a potentially para-sitic tide. In the past, proof of family affiliation or an affidavit from an elder was enough to establish tribal membership. With BIA support, however, other tribes were adopting more stringent blood-quantum requirements, and the Grand Rondes needed to do the same. Families were faced with the dilemma of historic intermarriages, both among the different Indian tribes and out-side them. Finally, in March 1997, the council promulgated a new enrollment ordinance carefully crafted "to ensure the integ-rity and accuracy of the [Grand Ronde] roll."[6]

The enrollment ordinance—a complex, three-page docu-ment—outlines several avenues for tribal membership, all recog-nized as legitimate by the elders. First was the roll that Congress adopted at the time of restoration, establishing blood ties to a direct lineal descendant; otherwise, tribal members needed to have one-sixteenth blood quantum. The ordinance went on to provide for children born out of wedlock, children adopted by tribal members, and others who had close social and economic ties to the tribe, as evidenced by the acceptance of their votes in tribal elections. Provision was made for people to be adopted as honorary members of the tribe, as long as they did not share in tribal assets or participate in tribal governance. Application forms and appeal processes were specified. The February 15, 1997, *Smoke Signals* published a summary of the proposed ordi-nance, which most tribal members considered fair. The measure was endorsed at a General Council meeting; the members who supported its passage were re-elected.

Kathryn's father, Harry Jones, was a full-blood Molalla, so she was considered a fifty percent Grand Ronde tribal member. Because of that, Kathryn's children were one-quarter Grand Ronde from their mother's side. Kathryn shared her colleagues' concern about the enrollment ordinance. Would her great-grandchildren qualify for tribal membership no matter how many Anglos had married into the family?

Kathryn gets a familiar glint in her eye when she speaks of "card-carrying Indians": "Who else in America has to show evidence of what's in their blood? Indians and people with dis-eases!"

Tribal council functioned extraordinarily well during this period, as council members worked closely with the tribe's legal staff. When Kathryn was called upon to give testimony or to make a press statement in the national arena, she collaborated with legal counsel in drafting it. She recognized her limitations and relied on solid professional advice. Challenges came from every direction.

Particularly troubling was the increasingly hostile climate in Congress. Washington Senator Slade Gorton, a perpetual nemesis of the Pacific Northwest tribes, was promoting his anti-Indian agenda—this time through his chairman's markup of a BIA funding bill.[7] As a condition of receiving funding, Gorton demanded that tribal governments waive sovereign immunity, thereby subjecting themselves to lawsuits (although no such demand was made of state governments). Kathryn, hearing echoes of termination, spoke out strongly against this measure designed to undermine tribal self-determination. "When we worked towards restoration, we thought that it would end termination pressures," she said. "But we continue to face threats such as this one each year. No one seemed to care about us during our twenty-nine years of termination, but now that we are trying to help ourselves, they want to penalize us."

Behind the scenes, Kathryn was working quietly and effectively with Oregon's congressional delegation, educating them about issues in Indian Country. Congresswoman Elizabeth Furse, former restoration worker for the tribe and Kathryn's colleague and friend, hosted a meeting in Washington, D.C., to allow tribal representatives from Grand Ronde and Warm Springs to make presentations on tribal management and economic development. These efforts were fruitful. Once again, as their counterparts in Washington and Oklahoma expressed legislative hostility toward Indians, Oregon representatives supported the state's Native people. With the exception of Representative Bob Smith (I), Oregon's delegation held firm against a bill proposing taxation of tribal trust lands, which would have undermined the very concept of tribal sovereignty. Senator Ron Wyden (D) took the lead in opposing his fellow senator's attack on tribal sovereignty. With eighteen co-signers, he sent a letter criticizing Slade Gorton's proposal to the Committee on Appropriations:

> [The sovereign immunity waiver] is completely at odds with both the broad history of federal Indian policy and recent legislation concerning Indian tribes. Congress has consistently enacted statutes that reflect the principal goals of federal Indian policy: promoting tribal economic development, tribal self-sufficiency, and strong tribal government. Eliminating this basic right of Indian tribes without any consideration of the resulting effect does not further these objectives and is flatly inconsistent with Congress' policy of protecting the right of tribes to enact their own laws and be governed by them.[8]

Ultimately the tribes prevailed, and Gorton backed off on the issue, but Kathryn was concerned that he would stir up other battles. Ever since his days as state attorney general in Washington, when he fought tribal fishing and hunting rights, he had built his political base on fanning anti-Indian sentiment.[9] His latest frontal attack on tribal sovereignty created the conditions for a well-financed, intertribally coordinated effort to oppose Gorton's bid for re-election to the Senate in the 2000 election. The campaign against him succeeded, demonstrating the tribes' growing political clout.[10]

Despite the national turmoil, the Grand Rondes prospered. Kathryn took great satisfaction in the traditional blessing of the new health center and in watching the first residents move into the new housing development at Grand Meadows, across from the old tribal cemetery. Financial managers projected $63 million dollars in revenue for the coming year, $36 million from gaming alone.

The business reputation of tribal managers increased along with the tribe's steadily rising revenue. In 1998, the Grand Rondes issued a second bond offering to finance construction of a new governance center to house tribal executive offices and the tribal court. The bonds were given a triple-A rating, the highest possible. By securing them through a municipal bond insurance policy rather than a letter of credit from a bank, the tribe was able to save several hundred thousand dollars in interest. This was another national first in a Native–non-Native partnership.

When Kathryn moved into her chair's office in the new administration building, she hung the artworks and awards she most valued on her walls. First to go up was a watercolor of two swimming salmon painted by her brother Bob. Next came a collage of photographs and newspaper articles that began with Governor Roberts signing the tribe's first gaming compact and ended with the front-page news of the casino's opening. Awards from several women's organizations went on the wall opposite her desk, along with photographs of grandchildren, great-grandchildren, and Molalla Kate. Kathryn loved her view from a window facing Spirit Mountain and a meadow where she often saw quail and grazing deer.

The Grand Rondes have shown sensitivity to nature in locating and constructing new facilities. The tribe protected native vegetation when they built their casino, and they incorporated peeled poles (used traditionally in plankhouses so the bark won't ignite) into their elders' housing. A national magazine of best practices in tribal design featured the tribe as a model. David Harjo, director of economic development for the Grand Rondes, made the tribe's "green design" policy explicit in a 2000 interview with the Oregon *Business Journal,* stressing that the tribe chose to invest in "environmentally friendly" real-estate projects.

In 1998, Kathryn addressed President Bill Clinton's Council on Sustainability, sounding the theme that undergirds the Grand Rondes' philosophy as they enlarge their footprints on the land: "If we walk in concert with the earth, she will nurture us." Yakama Nation leader Ted Strong was present when the video of the presentation was played for President Clinton and Vice President Gore. He recalls Al Gore asking: "How can I enlist her?" He knew that Kathryn could help spread his environmental message.

In September 1998, Kathryn, by then almost seventy-five years old, was re-elected to Tribal Council and re-elected as tribal chair. In her candidate statement, she enumerated the highlights of her last term, with creation of the Spirit Mountain Community Fund at the top of the list, and listed what she hoped

OHS Neg., OrHi 101591

KATHRYN WITH HER BROTHER BOB AND HER SISTERS
NORMA AND MARIE, AUGUST 1991

to accomplish for the tribe in the next three years. On the list
was the creation of a Veterans' Memorial, where she hoped to
see Frankie's and Tommy's names engraved together.[11]

Also on Kathryn's to-do list were a recreational area for tribal
youth, a daycare center for working parents, more housing for
the people coming home to Grand Ronde, and the production
of a video to honor Grand Ronde ancestors. She reminded the
council: "We still haven't reached our full potential, and I am
willing to work toward higher goals for us all."[12] At year's end,
the tribe anticipated almost $74 million in revenue in the com-
ing year, and two of Kathryn's long-range projects were on the
drawing board: an educational and recreational center for youth
and an additional housing complex.

Kathryn has been frustrated by the tribe's failure to implement the vision of her Culture and Heritage Committee. She scoffs at the "pathetic sweat lodge built with nails" on tribal grounds, and worries as the construction of a Grand Ronde Cultural Center keeps slipping down on the list of priorities.

Although she did her utmost to support cultural programs while she was on the council, she feels that she failed to foster a full-fledged, tangible monument to the ancestors. Architectural plans were developed and then scrapped; consultants were hired and then let go. "If the Warm Springs and the Umatillas can build a cultural center," she says, referring to the spectacular and much-visited museums east of the Cascades, "why can't the Grand Rondes, with their wealth and proximity to Portland?"

One cultural program that did come into being on her watch is the Chinook Language Program headed by Tony Johnson, a Chinook tribal member and one of the next generation of tribal leaders. A descendant of Chinook chiefs, he speaks the jargon of Kathryn's father and Molalla Kate.

Tony was born on Willapa Bay in Washington and educated at the University of Washington and Central Washington University, where he studied anthropology, silversmithing, and American Indian Studies. He is also trained in his people's traditional arts, and his passion is the perpetuation of local Native language and culture. He has trained many classes of elementary school children at Grand Ronde to speak Chinuk-Wawa, to sing traditional songs, and to copy traditional designs in their artwork.

The impact of the Chinook Language Program is felt at elders' gatherings, where native speakers give invocations in jargon, and at tribal celebrations, where Tony's young students perform. He has involved the elders in school classes, and every one of his alums can recite the Lord's Prayer in Chinuk-Wawa:

Nfsayka papa NiLayt kHapa saXfli,
Our father who lives above,
L ush kHapa nfsayka tfNtfN Nayka niN.
Your name is good in our hearts.
L ush Nayka tay/I kHapa kanawi tilixaN.

May you be the chief of all people.
L ush Nayka Nunk kHapa ili/I, kakWa kHapa saXali
May you do on earth as you do in heaven.
Palach nfsayka nfsayka NfkNfk kanawi san.
Give us our food every day.
Pus nfsayka nfsachi weyk Nayka hayash salfks kHapa nfsayka.
If we are bad, don't be angry with us.
Pus Laska Nfsachi kHapa nfsayka,
If others are bad to us,
Weyk nfsayka Nfsachi kHapa Laska.
Don't (allow) us to be bad to them.
Mash Nfsachi saya kHapa nfsayka.
Throw evil far away from us.
L ush kWanisfN kakWa.
Good if always (it) is like this.

> —The Lord's Prayer as spoken by Ila Dowd
> and translated by Tony Johnson

To which Kathryn always adds a fervent "Amen!"

16

Curses of Wealth and Blessings of a Meteorite

Never again will we seize your children, nor teach them to be ashamed of who they are. —Kevin Gover, Assistant Secretary for Indian Affairs, in official apology to Native Americans on behalf of the Clinton administration, September 8, 2000

Increasing wealth led to infighting among tribes and tribal members. As Grand Ronde chair, Kathryn became embroiled in personnel matters and for the first time found herself threatened with a lawsuit contesting council decisions. She learned that she had not developed the hard turtle shell she imagined. She lost sleep and prayed over the controversies, but she felt more beleaguered than ever. The internal jabs were the hardest to take. "Why do we eat our own?" she lamented.

Some insight about the destructive internal dynamic came from Don Wharton, the attorney from the Native American Rights Fund (NARF) whose help had been invaluable during the tribe's restoration process. The transition to success, he concluded, is very difficult for people who see themselves as victims. He offered the analogy of the abused spouse, to which Kathryn could readily relate. Because of the self-blaming that victims invariably experience, accompanied by guilt for what they "allowed" to happen, the victims may turn on each other when the situation turns around. This is classic victim behavior, repeated in many oppressed groups. British novelist and philosopher Iris Murdoch observed the same tendency among intellectual Jewish survivors of World War II who sought refuge at Oxford University and "fought as expatriates will."[1] Victims of war atrocities, too, sometimes echo their brutalizers in their behavior toward fellow sufferers.

As early as 1983, at the time of restoration, Wharton warned tribal member Jackie Colton (now Jackie Whisler) to "watch out" as tides began to turn in favor of the Grand Rondes. He feared that she would become disheartened with the internal acrimony that was sure to ensue. Colton phoned him in the late 1990s to recall his advice, laughing ruefully.[2]

By 1999, sporadic outbursts of bickering and recriminations among staff and elected tribal officials had surfaced. There were accusations of nepotism, self-dealing, back-stabbing, and petty thievery; and Kathryn became a lightning rod for every dispute. Try as she might to understand what was happening, she became dispirited and felt personally assaulted. She found some relief in the support of her long-time friend and fellow tribal chair Sue Shaffer of the Cow Creeks. When a tribal member seeking employment accused Kathryn of acting in an arbitrary and capricious manner, Sue came to Kathryn's defense. In an "open letter" to the Grand Rondes, Sue vouched for her character and her dedication to tribal welfare.

> I have worked with Kathryn Harrison for the past twenty years on various issues of tribal concern. Mostly, these issues were for the preservation and enhancement of tribal government rights. I know Kathryn as a tireless, dedicated leader, one who has been "in the trenches," not only to protect the Grand Ronde Tribe, but to promote it as well.
>
> Through the years I have recognized her continued commitment to the well-being of the elders and to the future of tribal youth, through education, training and building their self-esteem. Above all, I know Kathryn Harrison as an honest person whose word is as strong as her signature. While exhibiting strength and foresight, she also demonstrates compassion for those whose problems she is trying to resolve.[3]

Although she appreciated Shaffer's efforts on her behalf, Kathryn was hurt that someone outside the Grand Ronde community should have to vouch for her integrity.

Another hard lesson learned in 1999, which Kathryn calls the "winter of her despair," was that sovereignty often strips elected officials of their privacy and the ability to work things out in the comfort of their own offices. She understood the need to confirm her constituents' expectations that tribal officials would deal with people openly and fairly, and she tried to instill a sense of consistency and stability in government. She worried that if the annual elections, where one third of the council seats were contested, led to a dramatic turnover, then outside observers might perceive that the Grand Rondes were in turmoil. For a fledgling government, this was a real concern. Kathryn was a savvy enough politician to realize that the system breeds and needs refreshing. The leaders' measured responses to this natural tension, however, is what reassures those both inside and outside, and that is what matters in the long run. If the elections devolved into public charges and counter-charges, then governance would suffer.

It was one thing for Kathryn to understand these concepts and quite another for her to live through the challenges and attacks. She could not help feeling bruised and angry. Her colleagues in the Heart of the American Indian Women's Network gave support, but they met only once a year. The cardinal rule of "acting like a sovereign," a tribal leader's prime responsibility, is not to air dirty laundry outside Indian Country, where people with other agendas might misperceive or even take delight in news of internal troubles. Kathryn found herself turning more and more to her professional staff (especially the tribal attorneys and intergovernmental affairs specialists), her brother Bob (still head of the Gaming Commission), and old friends like Sue Shaffer. She took heart in the small boosts to her morale that came with community honors and recognition.

In the bleak spring of 1999, when Kathryn most needed an emotional lift, it appeared from two different directions. In June, Governor John Kitzhaber appointed her to the Oregon Council for the Humanities in recognition of her work as a Native cul-

188 LEADER AS ELDER

ture-keeper. Then, in July, Kathryn and I began our oral taping sessions, which continued every other Monday over the next
two years.

When I first proposed to write a biography instead of an as-
told-to memoir for Kathryn's family and tribe, her response was
facetious: "Why me? I thought you were my friend!" When we
decided to donate any proceeds from the unwritten biography
to the as-yet-unbuilt tribal cultural center, Kathryn felt more at
ease with the project.

To set the tone for the interviews, I gave her a paragraph
from a John Steinbeck biography:

> Life is plotless, a random onslaught of facts and events that
> often lack discernible pattern or arc of development. Against
> this confusing reality, or perhaps because of it, we tend to de-
> velop a personal mythos: a story about ourselves and the way
> our lives have been lived. Virginia Woolf's narrator in *The Waves*
> says: "In order to make you understand, to give you my life, I
> must tell you a story." In Woolf's sense, we are all makers of
> fiction in the original meaning of that word. That is, we create
> the story of our lives, selecting certain details from others to
> find order, to discover an aesthetically satisfying form within
> the chaos of experience.[4]

This was our task—to tease the arc of Kathryn's lifeway from
the welter of particularities that made up her days and years.

Kathryn is a marvelous subject. Within the bounds of family
and tribal privacy, she is committed to truth-telling; she bears
witness to the ways her life has been blemished as well as the
ways it has been blessed. In keeping with ancient oral tradition,
she cares about recording events as precisely as she can. Her
memory is impeccable. Every detail Kathryn provided in the
course of our Monday tapings has been corroborated in subse-
quent interviews with others and in independent research.

Kathryn's early childhood recollections were etched by the
pain of suddenly losing both her parents. Ella's death, followed
quickly by Harry's, was "memory's first imprinting step, the
cornerstone of the temple we erect inside us in memory of the

dead."[5] Even as a child of ten, Kathryn consciously committed details to memory so they would not vanish from her life.

She is unflinching in her life's testimony:

> Everyone has some cross to bear. I'm always afraid to go out and tell people: "Seven of my ten children have been adversely affected by alcohol; my husband beat me. But if I can help one person by baring my soul, then I have to do it. You know, it's an everyday challenge, and someday people will recognize the truth of others' experience in their own ways. You need to muster the gumption to do it. I pray for strength every day. But sharing is the only way to make a whole.

When asked what she is most proud of, without hesitation Kathryn exclaims: "My kids!" She adds wryly, "I often said: 'Lord, don't let me be alone again.' So the Creator sent me *lots* of kids. I should have said: 'Lord, don't let me be mobbed!'" Between the ages of eighteen and eighty, she can remember only one brief period when she did not have at least one child or grandchild living with her.

At this stage of her life, Kathryn appears to be reconciled to the ongoing tug of war in her own psyche: the fear of abandonment versus the fear of being engulfed. Reflections in tribal terms were her people's fear of invasion in the nineteenth century and their fear of abandonment (termination and dispersal) in the twentieth.

In addition to our lively interviews, there were other respites from tribal bickering. Each summer, Kathryn's family gathered on the reservation. Together they revived habits of berry-picking and other harvesting, traveling to powwows and tending ancestors' graves. Summer 1999 saw the opening of a food bank at Grand Ronde (a laying away of provisions for the winter) and the signing of a co-management agreement with the U.S. Forest Service. A successor agreement was signed the following January with the Willamette National Forest, covering Kathryn's ancestral grounds. Kathryn told the *Oregonian*: "Hard work for a number of years came together today. . . . How nice to walk upon the land that our ancestors used, and maybe pick huckleberries

OHS Neg. OrHi 101626

KATHRYN (IN REGALIA, FRONT RIGHT) AND TRIBAL LEADERS AT THE WHITE
HOUSE WITH WITH HILARY CLINTON (CENTER IN BLANKET), 1999

in the same place they did, and walk the old Molalla trails, and tell our children and grandchildren how much it means to us."[6]

In August 1999, the tribe hosted its second annual Chinook Jargon Conference. In her keynote address to the audience, Kathryn vowed, "I will study it when I retire." Six years later, she has yet to find the time. Tony Johnson, still directing the Chinuk-Wawa program, helps her find phrases when she wants to begin a speech in her native tongue. It pleases her to think that her great-grandchildren may learn the language before she does.

Also in summer 1999, the Oregon Commission for Women honored Kathryn with its annual award. Hundreds attended the presentation banquet in October at Portland's Oregon Convention Center. In her acceptance speech, Kathryn spoke of her struggles as a daughter, mother, and wife. She thanked her fellow Tribal Council members, the Confederated Tribes of Warm Springs (who hosted a table at the event), her family, and three women elders who went to great effort to attend the event.

In December, Grand Ronde elders held a tribute dinner for Kathryn. They surprised her, leaving her speechless. More than eighty elders presented her with a bouquet of red roses and a beaded necklace. Kathryn managed one sentence of deeply felt thanks: "I have attended a lot of gatherings, but there is no greater honor than one given by your own people." Culturally speaking, Kathryn and the elders understood that only tribal tradition can confer status that is recognized by other native people. Sometimes blowhards, charlatans, and entertainers are rewarded by "outsiders" but scorned by tribal communities.

The Christmas week issue of *Willamette Week*, Portland's alternative newspaper, profiled the Grand Rondes in its cover story under the headline "Jackpot Nation." It began: "The tale of the Grand Ronde Indians' transformation from a disbanded tribe to the most lucrative gaming operation in Oregon is the stuff of legend. What's less well known is the story of their budding political power and how they're using it."[7]

Kathryn was apprehensive about the article as it was being written, fearing that it would fuel the pressures for per capita revenue distribution. On December 15, 1999, for the first time, dividend checks for $2,800 had been issued to each adult tribal member. *Willamette Week* prided itself on exposés, and Kathryn worried about publicizing a recent agreement with the Kalispel tribe in northeast Washington under which it would cede twenty percent of its profits for the next five years to the Grand Rondes in exchange for consulting services and a $5.8 million startup loan for its new casino.

Kathryn, Len Bergstein (the Grand Ronde tribe's public affairs consultant), and Justin Martin (the tribe's' governmental affairs specialist) spent many hours with journalist Patty Wentz filling in background on Indian Country issues. The time was well spent. Wentz began the article by describing a recent tribal budget meeting: "Five years ago, the Grand Ronde tribe was so broke that it didn't bother printing revenue columns on its annual financial statement. . . . Last year the Spirit Mountain Casino . . . made $50 million, not in revenues, but in profit." She proceeded to describe how the Grand Rondes had judiciously used the gaming windfall to "rebuild a culture." By donating six percent of the casino profits to the larger community through its charitable fund, she reported, the tribe "has turned the racial slur 'Indian giver' on its head."

Photographs showcased the tribe's new health center and administration buildings. Wentz speculated that the Grand Rondes' extraordinary success might be due to its proximity to Portland or to the "wisdom of tribal chairwoman Kathryn Harrison." The article quoted the governor's legal counsel praising the tribe's negotiating skills, and it characterized the tribe as "quiet and sophisticated" in the way it exercised its newfound influence in Oregon. As she entered the millennium year, Kathryn was pleased, proud, and relieved.

At the age of seventy-six, Kathryn was urged to take advantage of the savings and convenience of tribal housing, but she liked going home at the end of the day to what she called her "stub house" in Sheridan. Grandchildren sometimes came for sleepovers that lasted several days. Arriving at work between seven-thirty and eight in the morning, Kathryn would report on the lunch box she had filled, the school event she had attended, or the note she had sent to a grandchild's teacher. "You never stop being a parent," she explains.

Kathryn does not think of herself as old. "Old is when you can't see, hear, or walk around," she says. Keeping a schedule that would exhaust most baby boomers, she finds time to drop postcards to the elders when she is traveling, to send birthday cards and gifts to tribal staff and friends, and to comfort friends and family who are sick or bereaved. More than once I've heard someone say about Kathryn, "She walks circles around the rest of us."

February 2000 brought a crisis in Grand Ronde governance when four key Spirit Mountain Development Corporation figures resigned to open a private consulting business. Their departure from the SMDC followed a Tribal Council management retreat led by facilitators from Harvard's Kennedy School of Government, and rumors about possible ramifications flew around the community. At issue was the consulting contract with the Kalispels and overtures from other tribes in need of gaming startup assistance. Unless an experienced new SMDC management team was rapidly installed, public confidence in the tribe could erode, which would have a disastrous effect on casino operations.

The tribe's primary press contact and troubleshooter was Len Bergstein, president of Northwest Strategies and a member of the SMDC board. Len was a political power in Portland who seemed to have access to everyone. Justin Martin worked to reassure political officials in the state capitol. Between them, they persuaded the governor's office to issue a statement expressing confidence in the Grand Ronde tribe and the future of its gaming operations. Soon afterward, a headline in the *Oregonian* announced that the departures were not expected to hurt the tribe's enterprises. The governor's legal counsel predicted that there would be no "fundamental change in Spirit Mountain [because] true leadership has always come from the Tribal Council at Grand Ronde."[8]

Thus began a bout of insomnia for Kathryn. Ultimately, the transition was smooth, thanks to Bob Watson's steady leadership. The SMDC board came to Kathryn to say it had unanimously chosen her brother to lead the corporation. Always wary of the suspicion of nepotism, Kathryn would have been reluctant to suggest his appointment. Bob agreed to take the job for six months.

Len Bergstein watched the relationship between SMDC and Tribal Council unfold. Both the SMDC board and the council showered Bob with praise after he presented his first "state of the union" report, and Kathryn beamed. Evaluating their progress six months later, Len commented: "[Kathryn's] affection for Bob is obvious in private settings, but the real contribution of their relationship came after the [departure of the former managers], when the qualities of Kathryn and Bob's personal restoration spilled over into a healing environment for the casino." By putting its faith in tested and trusted hands, the tribe once again landed on its feet.

Tribal leaders' adroitness in addressing the crisis earned them kudos both within and without the community. The faculty of Harvard University's Kennedy School were impressed enough with the Grand Rondes' handling of the situation that they invited the tribe's intergovernmental affairs program to apply for a national award. They also welcomed Justin Martin as a master's candidate at the graduate school in the 2003–2004 academic year. As "interim steward," Bob Watson carefully presided over a new division of responsibility between the gaming and non-gaming components of SMDC, largely commercial real-estate ventures.

Meanwhile, the Grand Rondes were contesting the possession of a meteorite by the American Museum of Natural History in New York City. At sixteen tons, it was the sixth largest meteorite ever found in the United States, and tribal members considered it sacred. It had been found in the Willamette Valley on the Molallas' ancestral grounds, sold by a private landowner, and transported to New York City in 1906 despite the objections of tribal medicine men, who believed that rainwater collected in the meteorite's reservoirs had healing properties.

The Grand Rondes laid claim to the sacred "object of cultural patrimony" under NAGPRA. They short-circuited litigation by negotiating directly with museum officials, who were stunned that an "unknown" tribe in Oregon could stall the museum's plans for exhibiting the meteorite. Kathryn—in the company of tribal attorneys, two other Tribal Council members, and Justin Martin— made two trips to New York to confront an array of Wall Street lawyers.

The negotiations were surprisingly short and productive. What emerged was a classic Grand Ronde settlement:

> ~ The sixteen-ton rock the tribe knew as "Tomanowos" could remain in New York.
>
> ~ The Grand Rondes would have exclusive annual access to it for ceremonial purposes.
>
> ~ The museum would sponsor an internship program for Native American youth.
>
> ~ The museum's display would recognize the significance of the meteorite to the tribe.

~ If the museum should ever fail to display it, Tomanowos would be returned to the Grand Rondes.

Thus, tribal members were assured of access to Tomanowos for religious, historical, and cultural purposes, while the meteorite remained on display in New York City for millions of visitors to see. Museum President Ellen Futter said she felt honored to be a co-signer of such an "enlightened and progressive approach to . . . opportunities that lie within our traditions." The resolution reflected "mutual respect and understanding" and signaled "new possibilities for an ongoing and fruitful relationship." She ended by saying that it had been a "privilege and pleasure to work with our friends" at Grand Ronde. One has only to look at the quagmire of the decade-long litigation surrounding the human remains of Kennewick Man (called "the Ancient One" by the tribes) to realize what a coup this was for the Grand Rondes. [9]

Facing a phalanx of New York and national media after the completed negotiation, Kathryn used the occasion to recite the history of her people. Trying to convey what the moment meant, she said: "Look at the power this rock still has—it brought us all together here." Len Bergstein thought to himself, *She's done it again. This little old woman from this little old tribe has commanded everyone's attention.*

Bergstein earns his living training people to make public presentations, but he knows you cannot teach someone Kathryn Harrison's "uncanny knack of always saying the right thing to the right audience. She draws the relevance out, communicating across cultural barriers." Once again, the Grand Rondes' trademark pragmatism had set the tone. In a June 23, 2000, editorial, the *Oregonian* commended the settlement: "Settling disputes over artifacts that were taken from Native Americans was the reason for the 1990 Native American Graves Protection and Repatriation Act. But as the Grand Ronde have shown, that needn't always make someone the loser. When all can benefit, everybody wins."

In the museum exhibit, a description of the importance of Tomanowos to the Grand Ronde tribes appears alongside a description of its scientific history:

Museum of Natural History

Meteorite—Possibly, core of a planet colliding with another planet. Our Sun formed 4.5 billion years ago giving rise to comets, asteroids, and planets and all life on earth.

Only 600 of the 2,500 meteorites found on earth are made of iron. Over many centuries rainwater interacting with iron sulfide deposits produced sulfuric acid resulting in the large cavities that held rainwater.

Grand Ronde Community

Tomanowos—Representation of Sky People. Upon its descent, union occurred between sky, earth, and water. Traditions and the spiritual link with Tomanowos continue today.

Resting on the ground, Tomanowos collected rainwater in the basins. This rainwater served as a powerful purifying, cleansing, and healing source.[10]

To the dismay of the Grand Rondes, a peace-seeking tribe, the year 2000 embroiled them in one dispute after another. For nearly five years, the tribes had been engaged in discussions with the board of directors at Chemawa Indian School about acquiring a parcel of land Chemawa owned at the Keizer interchange on Interstate 5 near Salem. The Grand Rondes were interested in what they saw as another "win-win" possibility: they would work with Chemawa to develop a counseling program for students with special needs, and in exchange they would purchase the land at fair-market value and use it for economic development, offering job-training programs for Chemawa students in connection with any commercial development.

The proposal was no secret, but some other tribes felt they had been denied information about the negotiations. Dee Pigsley, chair of the Confederated Tribes of Siletz, publicly voiced the Siletz' anger in the spring of 2000. Because Chemawa was in the Siletz BIA "service area," the Siletz resented the Grand Rondes trying to intrude on their territory. Pigsley wrote a pointed letter, requesting that it be read into the record at the May meeting of the Affiliated Tribes of Northwest Indians (ATNI). The letter alleged:

The way the board, the school and the Education Department have gone about this is disgusting. Keeping information from tribes and operating in secrecy is not good. Bad-mouthing other tribes that ask questions is even worse. This is not the way to do business in Indian Country—when federal agencies treat us in this fashion, we protest loud.

No one should support this project without seeing the entire plan. If land is to be developed to benefit the students, all tribes should have the opportunity to participate. Chemawa is a school for all Indian people—all tribes with participating students should be included in the discussion and approval / disapproval process.[11]

The Siletz complaint sparked latent intertribal jealousies. Some Warm Springs residents, smarting over Governor Kitzhaber's refusal to approve an off-reservation casino the tribe had proposed, suspected the Grand Rondes of a scheme to grab trust land near the state capital. The ATNI meeting erupted into a barrage of charges and counter-charges, with the Coquilles, Coos, and Snoquomish supporting the Grand Rondes and the Siletz and Warm Springs opposing. The opponents aired their grievances publicly in a front-page article in the Sunday *Oregonian* on June 4, 2000. ATNI put options concerning Chemawa's future land development on its fall meeting agenda.

There was a legitimate concern that the Grand Rondes were throwing their weight around. In addition to the Siletz fear that the tribe was "horning in" on a thriving I-5 interchange near Keizer, Grand Rondes were also buying prime land in Portland. Other tribes were feeling bulldozed by the *nouveau riche* kids on the block, especially as their poorer neighbors were just beginning to build some economic power. The Grand Rondes' actions were perceived as having little to do with traditional claims or aboriginal rights.

Kathryn was deeply hurt by some of the statements made by people she had considered old friends and allies. She did not understand their mistrust, and she lost sleep trying to decide how to mend the breach. Notwithstanding the uproar about Chemawa belonging to "all tribes," Kathryn was the only tribal leader to attend the school's graduation ceremony that year. Sherman Alexie, the prize-winning Native American novelist from eastern Washington, gave the commencement address. Kathryn used the occasion to persuade Alexie to appear at the tribe's restoration ceremony in November, one of many instances when she capitalized on a contact and used it to her advantage.

The Chemawa dispute was still brewing when Kathryn attended the NCAI meeting in Alaska at the end of June 2000. It seemed to her that mistrust contaminated the atmosphere. Upon her return, she learned that the National Indian Gaming Commission had fined the Siletz for violations in their casino operation (five years later, Siletz was still contesting the NIGC findings), whereas the Grand Rondes had received a clear audit. The Confederated Tribes of Warm Springs were suffering the strains of a five-year battle to secure a more profitable site for their casino, closer to Portland, while by virtue of their reservation's location, the Grand Rondes' casino was ideally situated between the city and the coast. Kathryn attributed the resentment directed at the Grand Rondes over the Chemawa controversy to the pressures Siletz and Warm Springs leaders felt about gaming activities, which helped her interpret their actions more charitably.[12]

Kathryn was cheered by an emotional event at the Cow Creeks' casino. Tribal Chair Sue Shaffer hosted a dinner to launch the World War II Memorial project, complete with USO entertainment and a video presentation honoring veterans by national news anchor Tom Brokaw. Kathryn was asked to give the invocation. Elizabeth Furse delivered the keynote address, in which she paid tribute to tribal veterans throughout history. She paid homage to the Native American soldiers who had fought patriotically in America's defense, despite their historical treatment by the U.S. government. She finished her honor roll by naming Tribal Chairs Sue Shaffer and Kathryn Harrison "warriors" who were every bit as worthy as other historic battle leaders. Kathryn was surprised and teary at such praise. She bore many scars from political fights, but she had never thought of herself as a war hero.

Many of Kathryn's efforts came to fruition in the summer of 2000. The Elders Housing Project had its grand opening in August. A community-based cultural area was designated for tribal use. The Native American Gallery at the Portland Art Museum (to which Spirit Mountain Community Fund had donated $1 million) opened on powwow weekend. The standout event of the year came on September 8, 2000, at a ceremony in Washington, D.C., marking the 175th anniversary of the Bureau of Indian Affairs, Assistant Secretary of Interior Kevin Gover officially apologized for the "legacy of racism and inhumanity that included massacres, forced relocations of tribes and attempts to wipe out Native American languages and cultures." In a speech greeted by cheers and a standing ovation from over three hundred tribal leaders, Gover cited "poverty, ignorance, and disease" as the product of the BIA's work:

> This agency participated in the ethnic cleansing that befell the Western tribes. It must be acknowledged that the deliberate spread of disease, the decimation of the mighty bison herds, the use of the poison alcohol to destroy the mind and body, and cowardly killing of women and children made for tragedy on a scale so ghastly that it cannot be dismissed as merely the inevitable consequence of the clash of competing ways of life.

Kathryn had never dared hope that the federal government would issue such an apology. It was belated, and it might have come from higher up, but Kathryn lauds Gover's healing promise that "never again will we seize your children, nor teach them to be ashamed of who they are." She would love to be able to hold succeeding administrations to that pledge.

At the National Congress of American Indians meeting in November, the Grand Rondes were nominated for Harvard's Honoring Nations citation for excellence in intergovernmental relations. A particularly poignant moment at the NCAI plenary session was the appearance of Lynn Cutler, President Clinton's White House liaison to Indian Country. The outcome of the George W. Bush–Al Gore race was unknown at the time, but Cutler expressed her hopes that her administration's policy of honoring their trust responsibility to Native Americans would continue. As it happened, one of the first things the victorious Bush administration did was eliminate her position.

Kathryn returned home in time for the Grand Rondes' seventeenth annual Restoration Day celebration. The mood was buoyant. The tribe had just officially enrolled its 5,064th member. and it was clear that Senator Slade Gorton had been defeated in his bid for re-election. The tribe had financed television, radio, and newspaper advertisements highlighting Gorton's assaults on Indian rights and the environment, and the defeat of this powerful incumbent was viewed nationwide as an indication of increasing Native American political power.[13]

The first week in January 2001, Kathryn participated in the orientation for new members of Oregon's legislature. She began by recounting tribal history. She emphasized two points: (1) the need to codify the executive order mandating state agencies to honor the government-to-government relationship in their daily dealings with tribal professional staff, and (2) the need for state officials to meet with tribal leaders more often than once a year.

The following week, Kathryn flew to Hawaii for a retreat called by Senator Daniel Inouye (longtime Democratic chair of the Senate Select Committee on Indian Affairs) to consider how to address issues in Indian Country with the Bush administration. She was most concerned about what was going to happen to Lynn Cutler's tribal liaison position in the White House and wanted to press for the continuation of the Office of Tribal Justice within the U.S. Department of Justice. At that time, Bush's nominee for attorney general, John Ashcroft, was facing a tough confirmation battle in the Senate, and tribal leaders thought they might have the leverage to exact at least one important promise from him.

Forty-five tribes were represented at the summit in Hawaii, along with John Echo-Hawk from NARF and federal Indian legal expert Charles Wilkinson. Senator Inouye advised tribal leaders to be vigilant about the forthcoming changes in the Bush administration, warning that "a lot could be done differently, but subtly and incrementally."

At the meeting, tribal leaders decided that Ernie Stensigar, chair of the Coeur d'Alenes, chair of Affiliated Tribes of Northwest Indians, and vice president of the National Congress of American Indians, would be their point of contact for the Bush administration. They agreed that this arrangement would not obviate the need for frequent and substantive meetings between the president and tribal chairs, but they did not want to be relegated to photo ops in the Rose Garden. They would insist on being treated as heads of foreign governments.

The January 31 edition of the national Native peoples' newspaper, *Indian Country*, contained an "Open Letter" to President Bush by columnist Suzan Shown Harjo. Noting the absence of a Native member in the Bush–Cheney Transition Team, she urged the president:

> Do not let the federal agencies set up any task forces or study groups or reorganizations to figure out what is wrong in Native America and what should be done to fix it. All the needed information about the poor condition and status of Native Americans is well documented and undisputed, and knowledgeable Indians can easily provide any details that might not be readily available. . . .
>
> Direct the federal agencies to give the White House a list of lands they hold whose ownership is contested by Native Peoples, and to justify their continued federal jurisdiction over them. Also ask the affected tribal governments for their views and give them a fair hearing.
>
> Then, start returning some of the lands, beginning with those that are tribal churches and those that hold potential for bettering tribal economies.
>
> That, sir, would be a really big thing.[14]

Kathryn agreed, but she did not expect much to come of it. Many in Indian Country were surprised when the Bush administration entered into serious negotiations with the Klamaths in southern Oregon over the return of 700,000 acres of their original reservation from lands currently administered by the U.S. Forest Service. Kathryn commented: "It's like Nixon going to China and issuing the self-determination Executive Order."

Early in 2001, Kathryn informed the elders that she had decided not to run again for Tribal Council. When they protested, she reminded them that she was not indispensable, that the tribe's survival had always been a collective effort.

Well aware that "success breeds enemies," Kathryn worried that she might have outstayed her welcome in Grand Ronde circles. Some of the newly elected tribal leadership saw her as too accommodating to state officials and advocated attempting to assert control over the independent gaming commission and the independent charitable fund. They wanted to distribute tribal profits to tribal members as quickly as possible, and they wanted to terminate contracts with outsiders and fill the vacated positions with members of the tribe.

As others jockeyed for a seat on Tribal Council, rumors abounded concerning Kathryn's plans. In truth, she was vacillating. She wanted to make way for the next generation of leaders, but she felt that she still had plenty of energy and ideas and knew it would be difficult to sit on the sidelines.

Lobbyists approached her from all sides. Her children believed her exhausting schedule was what kept her young, and they urged her to run again. Bob Watson worried for the welfare of the tribe, saying: "[I am] frankly scared about what will happen at Grand Ronde when Kathryn steps down, because she carries a certain credibility with her." He saw in his older sister "something that holds people to a higher level of behavior than they might otherwise exhibit."[15]

Bob's worry was justified. It took four years to restore balance to tribal council after Kathryn resigned. Len Bergstein is convinced that history will measure the Grand Rondes by how sensitively they handle their neighbors' envy, how well they stave off corruption, and how astutely they diversify their economy. Heading the ideal tribal government, he envisions a triumvirate that would capitalize on different leaders' strengths and put their talents to the "best and highest use" for the tribe. Len would have nominated Bob Watson as CEO, with a vision to drive future planning. He would have asked Kathryn to remain as traditional culture-keeper and to "keep talking values" to those both inside and outside the tribe. To run the tribe's day-to-day operations, he would have hired a proven manager, preferably one of the mid-career tribal members who left Grand Ronde for college and then came home.[16] Unfortunately, none of Len's "Dream Team" materialized, although Kathryn keeps talking values, officially or unofficially, as the occasion warrants.

Kathryn stuck with her decision not to run again, mostly because she was weary of fighting the same battles again and again. Privately, she allowed that she would miss the income, now that council members were compensated at a "living wage" ($60,000 at the time of her retirement). She told her children they could no longer count on her financial support. Characteristically philosophical about this change in her circumstances, she remarked: "I never had anything to begin with, so why worry about it now?"

As the new year began, the Institute for Tribal Governance at Portland State University nominated Kathryn for the DC Advocacy Institute's "Leadership for a Changing World" Award. One of the letters submitted, from her restoration colleague Elizabeth Furse, picked up on Kathryn's theme of survival in modern times in spite of success:

> Kathryn Harrison was a leader when her tribe had nothing, as today she is the leader of a tribe that is the envy of many. . . . Kathryn is that rare leader—a person who remembers how it felt to be poor and disenfranchised, yet is able to deal with the challenges of success. . . . When Indian people think of their great [20th-century] leaders, Kathryn Harrison will be among that list.[17]

The year 2001 was Kathryn's final year of office. The National Indian Gaming Commission awarded the tribe a certificate of self-regulation, allowing the Grand Ronde gaming commission to oversee its own operations. Kathryn responded: "We have worked with dedication and diligence to operate our casino in a manner that is effective, fair and honest. This decision recognizes that effort."[18] The Grand Rondes were one of only two tribal governments in the nation to be granted self-regulation. On a personal level, Kathryn saw the award as gratifying affirmation of her managerial skills as well as her brother's.

In the first year after Kathryn stepped down from Tribal Council, the Grand Rondes recognized the need for her continued voice and carved out a new role for her as the "face of the tribe." She soon began to wonder if her message to the public truly reflected the views of tribal leaders. Bob Watson left his position at Spirit Mountain Development Corporation, and council members moved to consolidate their authority over all arms of tribal operations. Len Bergstein was told that his public affairs expertise was no longer needed, so he moved over to work with the Confederated Tribes of Warm Springs in their bid to site a casino near Portland. More and more, Grand Ronde political debate centered on increasing per capita distribution. Among the last elements of Kathryn's legacy was the tribal education complex, which was proceeding ahead of schedule.

One of Kathryn's last official acts before retirement was to lead a Grand Ronde delegation to New York City for the first annual ceremony reuniting tribal members with Tomanowos, their heavenly visitor. Staff of the American Museum of Natural History welcomed the group in the evening and had all the museum's alarms and security systems turned off. Tribal veterans had brought water from Oregon streams and rivers to fill the craters in the giant stone. Grand Ronde singers and drummers performed traditional music as the delegation celebrated the sacred moment.

Kathryn struggled to say a few words honoring the occasion. Looking at the meteorite, she pictured ancient warriors coming down the trail to dip their arrowheads into the holy water that gave them strength and courage. She could almost hear the meteorite asking, "What took you so long? I've been waiting to hear my people's language."

17

Looking Toward our Ancestors

Our leadership and direction emerge from the land up. . . . This relationship is continuously reaffirmed through our way of being in the world —"the good life." It is perhaps best remembered in phrases like "this is where my grandmother's and children's umbilical cords are buried."—Winona LaDuke, 1999

Kathryn plans ahead by honoring the wisdom of the past. The Chinuk-Wawa phrase "Kakwa Anqati; Kakwa Alta"—"If we want to always do well, we should always look toward our ancestors"—succinctly captures this ruling principle. The tribe's professional planners always begin by looking back, and Kathryn repeats this mantra of the elders to children in the hope that it will become embedded in contemporary tribal culture.

The summer before she retired, Kathryn expressed a yearning to return to the homeland of her great-great-Aunt Molalla Kate, near Molalla, Oregon. We planned a field trip as we completed our research for this book, arranging a meeting with Isabel Williams, director of the Molalla Area Historical Society, at the Dibble House, the Society's museum. The oldest house in Molalla, the Dibble House was completed in 1859, three years after Molalla Kate left on her Trail of Tears.

We were to meet on July 3, the day before Molalla's annual Buckaroo Days began with a Fourth of July rodeo. I picked

KATHRYN AND IVOR DAVIES AT DICKEY CREEK, AUGUST 2000

Kathryn up at her home in Sheridan. Driving through Woodburn reminded her of going to the Demolition Derby at the Woodburn raceway in the 1950s, when she and Frank were living in Silverton. It was a cheap form of recreation if you refrained from betting, and the derby was the only comic relief she remembers from those bleak, alcohol-hazed days.

A dozen members of the historical society were assembled at the Dibble House. Women were setting out food on a large table in the center of the old pioneer kitchen area, and a video camera was installed on a tripod. Kathryn was enthusiastically greeted by the descendants of the settlers who had welcomed Molalla Kate back from the Grand Ronde Reservation almost a century and a half earlier.

Ivor Davies was there. In 1913, at the age of six, he had attended the burial of "Indian Henry," Molalla Kate's step-brother.[1] Two fourth-generation women from the Dickey family came to meet Kathryn, eager to hear what she could remember about Molalla Kate. In their homes were baskets given to their ancestors by Kate's father's Northern Band of Molalla Indians, as well as metates (grinding stones) they had unearthed in their farm fields on Dickey Prairie. Champ Clark Vaughan, great-grandson of William Hatchette Vaughan ("Uncle Billy" to the respectful Molallas), brought along his self-published mono-graph, "Encounters with Molalla Indians — 1843–1906" about his great-grandfather's experiences with Kathryn's ancestors. Champ was restoring his family's pioneer homestead along the Molalla River and invited Kathryn to visit.

Kathryn was surprised to find such a large, formal gathering awaiting her. She quickly warmed to the occasion and offered tales of childhood experiences with her beloved Aunt Kate. A few residents told of finding artifacts scattered around the area and feeling "haunted," which prompted Kathryn to ask if they had ever sensed the presence of those who had gone before. Several people described supernatural moments and inexplicable sounds of human voices and activities around their prairie homes. They asked how they should respond. "Listen first," Kathryn advised, "and then ask, 'May I help you?' The spirits are restless and will make their needs known."

Kathryn's Molalla hosts asked if there was anything they could do for her. "Well," she said with a smile, "I'd like two Buckaroo tickets for tomorrow — in the covered section, please!" Two hours later we left, tickets in hand, apologizing for impos-ing on them on the eve of the holiday. "It's not every day we get to see a *real* Molalla Indian," they demurred.

The next day, Kathryn and her daughter Patsy drove to Molalla. They took their seats in the covered section at the Buckaroo, and the announcer formally introduced them to the crowd over the loudspeaker. Kathryn was in her element.

Ever since our visit, Kathryn and the descendants of Molal-la's earliest European emigrants have exchanged correspon-dence. Kathryn sent them a historic photograph of Molalla Kate, showing her flattened forehead. She also sent a copy of anthropologist Phillip Drucker's notes on the 1934 Smithsonian interviews with Molalla Kate. In turn, the Dickey family invited Kathryn to their prairie homes to see some of the Molalla tribal artifacts handed down through the generations, gifts from Chief Yel-kus's band. In August, the Molalla Area Historical Society arranged another field trip for us, this time to the site of the old

OHS Neg. OrHi 101620

KATHRYN AND HER SON ROGER WITH THE GRAND RONDE SPECIAL EDITION
PENDLETON BLANKET, 1999

Indian encampment on Dickey Creek, followed by a picnic in a
nearby park.

Not long after our excursion to Molalla, I received a worried
phone call from Kathryn. She had just finished briefing Tribal
Council on our meeting with the Molalla Area Historical Society
and was back in her office for a quick recess. "One of the newly
elected members wants to make a claim for their baskets! What
should I do? They want to bring the whole cultural resource
department and photograph and measure everything. Those
people were so wonderful to us. I don't want to offend them. I
don't want them to feel as though we were setting them up for a
repatriation!"

I tried to reassure her that because the items were gifts to
individuals from the original makers, the Grand Ronde tribal
government had no valid legal claim to them. Still, as Kathryn
well knew, council members may not have thought to consult
with tribal attorneys. If they rushed ahead and made a public
demand, she said, "we would all be embarrassed."

Following her instincts, Kathryn went back into the council
meeting and forcefully quashed the discussion, telling the person
who had come up with the proposal to "go concentrate on your

own tribe. You're not a Molalla!" Her colleagues know better than to cross Kathryn in such circumstances. They respect her moral leadership and know that protecting the tribe's cultural resources is close to her heart. Kathryn, still in command, was fulfilling her brother's prophecy about forcing people to rise to their higher selves.

For many people, Kathryn Harrison's life mirrors the lessons of many Pacific Northwest Indians whose lives have gone through dramatic change. She is conscious that she occupies this symbolic place, and she resists over-simplifying the parallels. Nonetheless, if the tale of her life can lead to a more empathetic and nuanced understanding of twentieth-century tribal affairs, she gladly tells it.

Kathryn stands as living testimony that just as children can withstand losing their parents in a dread epidemic, tribes can withstand being decimated by European diseases. As Kathryn overcame her suffering in an abusive foster home, tribes have overcome being herded onto reservations under the control of the United States War Department. As she made the best of an Indian boarding school's attempts to "assimilate" her, tribes have made the best of missionaries' and government officials' attempts to "civilize" them. Both Kathryn and the tribes have maintained their cultural identity by incorporating tribal rites into new ones.

Kathryn's saga of marriage to an alcoholic echoes tribal struggles against the predations of liquor and cigarette merchants who circled reservation boundaries. As surely as Frank failed to fulfill his responsibilities to his family, leaving Kathryn to deal with their ten children many times before she finally left him, the federal government abdicated its responsibility to the tribes during the termination era, leaving them to eke out a living in urban areas. Kathryn's years adrift, working as a migrant laborer, parallel the experience of tribes stripped of their land and uprooted, with government services suspended.

Kathryn found personal rehabilitation by returning to traditional cultural values. Likewise, tribal communities have found new life in rediscovering their old ways. Enlightened governmental policy such as the American Indian Religious Freedom Act has allowed tribal medicine leaders to once again practice in the open, bringing peace and trust in healing to afflicted elders. Both Kathryn and the tribes have negotiated successfully for their restoration. At eighty-one, Kathryn has not only survived but thrived, and the Grand Rondes' Phoenix-like comeback has become a contemporary legend.

18

Embracing Elderhood

*Ms. Harrison is a role model to countless others who look to her for
inspiration, counsel and leadership.* — Portland State University
President Daniel Bernstine, 2003

At its June 2003 commencement ceremonies, Portland State
University presented Kathryn Harrison with an honorary Doctor of Humane Letters. Elizabeth Furse, director of the university's Institute for Tribal Government, spoke of Kathryn's achievements:

> Kathryn is renowned as a community organizer, consensus
> builder, and peacemaker in a world where non-Indian and In-
> dian people frequently experience difficulties in understanding
> one another. . . . In her tireless dedication to her life's work, she
> continues to work on community solutions even though she has
> retired from elected office.[1]

Reporting on the event, the tribal newspaper identified Kathryn
first as "Tribal Elder," second as "former Tribal Chair," and third
as "Tribal Ambassador." The ranking reflects the traditions of
her people, and Kathryn shares these priorities.

Kathryn was thrilled to receive the degree, an honor she
never expected. She had assumed that the pinnacle of her educational achievement was her 1972 degree in nursing from Lane
Community College. Immediately she thought of her grandchil-

dren, who could now call her "Dr. Grandma." For Kathryn, the most memorable part of the graduation ceremony was hearing a voice in the audience call out "Jonesey!" and realizing that her Chemawa friend Cecilia Bearchum had driven four hours from the Umatilla Indian Reservation to be there.

By now, the tribe had retained Kathryn as a consultant to serve as its ambassador at community events. Working closely with Justin Martin, the tribe's intergovernmental affairs specialist, Kathryn arranged meetings with state and federal officials. She averaged five speaking engagements per month, helping to build political alliances and support for Grand Ronde development projects. She traveled tirelessly on the tribe's behalf. Initially, in 2002, her compensation for the year was $60,000. The next year her compensation was reduced to $25,000, and Tribal Council was split evenly about whether to renew Kathryn's contract on any terms. Cheryle Kennedy, who replaced Kathryn as tribal chair, broke the tie, voting to contract for another year of Kathryn's services. Later Kathryn learned indirectly that her contract was not in the tribal budget for 2004.[2] She was miffed and wounded, and her hurt was compounded as planning began for the twentieth anniversary of Grand Ronde restoration in November 2003. She was not asked to participate until the day before the celebration. Some of the original participants in restoration efforts boycotted the event, because they felt that the new planners gave the "founders" short shrift. It seemed to Kathryn that the internal harmony she had worked so hard to establish was slipping away. The tribe was losing respect for its history.

Kathryn's family had also entered a time of turmoil. In February 2003, Kathryn's oldest living son, fifty-two-year-old Raymond, was attacked as he was riding his bicycle home from work near Seattle. Severely beaten about the head, he was Lifeflighted to Harborview Hospital, where he underwent six hours of brain surgery. When Kathryn rushed to Seattle to sit by his bedside, doctors told her that Raymond might never be able to speak again. Memories of Tommy's release from the hospital only to die a day later flashed through her mind. But Raymond

DEAN MARVIN KAISER AND KATHRYN WHEN SHE RECEIVED AN
HONORARY DEGREE FROM PORTLAND STATE UNIVERSITY

astounded everyone by sitting up, eating and talking two days
after his surgery. Later, as Kathryn's daughter Karen moved out,
Raymond moved in with Kathryn at home.

Contract or no, Kathryn kept up her schedule of work for
the tribe. On several occasions, if she had not made the effort
to attend an event, the absence of a tribal representative would
have been noticeable. One prominent occasion was Senator Hatfield's eightieth birthday celebration in October 2003. Another
was former President Clinton's visit to Portland the following
month.

Kathryn was particularly upset when she was excluded
from a luncheon honoring the Hatfield Fellow for 2002. Chosen
and supplied with a stipend by the SMCF, Hatfield Fellows are
assigned for one year to a member of Oregon's congressional delegation in Washington, D.C. In classic Grand Ronde "win-win"
fashion, Hatfield Fellows are there to learn the ropes of federal
governance while simultaneously teaching their congressional
colleagues about Indian values and tribal government priorities.

Fellows can come from any tribe in Oregon; failing qualified candidates, they can come from anywhere in the Northwest.

"The Hatfield Fellowship was *my* idea!" Kathryn fumed. "I won't be an afterthought, after all these years!" She felt she was being "trotted out" by the Tribal Council only when it was convenient for them. "I was worried about superficial photo ops in the Bush administration," she said. "It never occurred to me that I would be treated so shabbily by my own tribe."

Through all her travails, Kathryn maintained her dignity and her determination to preserve the public face of the Grand Rondes. In November 2002, a reporter for the *Oregonian* contacted her. There were rumors that "things were falling apart" at Grand Ronde, the reporter told her. Kathryn did her utmost (as it turned out, successfully) to deflect the reporter's interest in writing a story for the paper.

Kathryn was also working behind the scenes on the casino's behalf. She could pick up the phone and easily get through to government officials, and the tribe's intergovernmental affairs staff took advantage of that access. In January 2003, she and Justin Martin met with Mark Hatfield to discuss off-reservation gaming pressures—specifically, the Warm Springs' continuing efforts to build a casino in the Columbia River Gorge. Senator Hatfield said his number one question always was, "Will it hurt any of Kathryn's programs?" Kathryn told him it would have an impact on the Spirit Mountain Community Fund's charitable giving. Hatfield immediately decided: "Then I'm against it!"

At public meetings, people often questioned Kathryn about their inability to "get through" to the new Grand Ronde council members. She would do her best to cover for the tribe. The Native American business analyst for Nike, for example, complained that no one returned his phone calls. Kathryn invited him to the casino, gave him a tour, and took him to lunch. Then she put him in touch with the proper tribal staff to coordinate employment opportunities for tribal members.

Oregon tribal leaders also questioned Kathryn about their deteriorating relations with the Grand Rondes, approaching her at regional meetings to complain about the tribe's high-handedness and one-dimensional perspective in dealing with them.

Kathryn does her best to avoid these conversations, following her own advice to "hold your head high and walk on by." A Siletz Tribal Council member commented on her careful demeanor at the September 2003 meeting of the Affiliated Tribes of Northwest Indians, noting that she was being a "model elder" and trying mightily not to second-guess others. Kathryn sits in the back rows with old friends and jokes with good nature about the *faux pas* the younger people make. "They'll learn," she knows, and she hopes she will be around to speak from experience when someone finally asks.

In November 2002, I ran into Kathryn in the San Diego airport on her way back from the annual meeting of the National Congress of American Indians. She was exhausted, having been on the road for three weeks, attending meetings on behalf of the tribe. I asked her what she had been doing. "Leave me alone," she snapped with a grin. "I'm concentrating on trying to be an elder!"

Kathryn regularly attends an elders luncheon, provided by a federal food grant, via a tribal shuttle. There political activism is still very much alive, and the fellowship of elders has become Kathryn's network and her source of information. When one of the new Tribal Council members startled everyone by campaigning at a funeral, the elders rebuked him. The traditional General Council, which meets once a month on Sundays and is heavily attended by elders, has begun to act more assertively, questioning Tribal Council's actions when it seems appropriate. The elders are mentoring potential candidates for the council among Grand Ronde's Gen-Xers. Always, they tell the stories. Kathryn was thrilled in the 2004 tribal elections when a well-schooled slate of three "reformers" won their seats with the largest voter turnout ever at Grand Ronde. In September 2005, two more members of the "reform ticket" won seats, giving them a majority, and former SMCF Director Angela Blackwell was named vice chair. Grand Ronde may be emerging from its post-Kathryn slump.

In his most recent book, Sherman Alexie, Kathryn's favorite writer, tries to put the angst in Indian Country into perspective:

Colonized, genocided, exiled, Indians formed their identities by questioning the identities of other Indians. Self-hat-
ing, self-doubting, Indians turned their tribes into nationalistic
sects. But who could blame us our madness? . . . We are people
exiled by other exiles, by Puritans, Pilgrims, Protestants, and
all of those other crazy white people thrown out of a crazier
Europe. We who were once indigenous to this land must im-
migrate into its culture.[3]

Finally, four years after Kathryn retired her leadership position at Grand Ronde, the hole left by her departure—the "madness"—is closing. One could say she should have done better
succession planning. There was only so much she could do.

The women's Braveheart Society at the Yankton Sioux Reservation is addressing this splintering of Native peoples by turning again to their traditional role of healing wounded warriors.
Faith Spotted Eagle, one of Braveheart's founders, calls it "rage
work." In ceremonies that date from time immemorial, they
welcome those who are hurting back to their culture. They try
to rechannel the rage that tribal members so often turn against
each other. Spotted Eagle defuses the "internalized oppression"
by storytelling around a fire.

Don Wharton, the NARF attorney who represented the Grand
Rondes when they achieved restoration in 1983, reveres Kathryn
for her enduring stamina. "It's hard to change the story," he says.
"The transition to success is a very difficult one to make for people
whose image of themselves is as victims. Kathryn Harrison is one
of the few tribal leaders who has managed to make it real."[4]

Today, Kathryn complains about the "young elders" who
take Indian names that weren't conferred by the tribe and suddenly show up at Grand Ronde to claim tribal benefits. Worse
still are the many imposters who borrow from Indian tradition to
fraudulently present non-Indian arts and crafts as Indian-made
or to hawk meaningless New Age services such as sweat-lodge
purification ceremonies and guided "rites of passage" in the wil-
derness. "These people are phony Indians and self-appointed
shamans," Kathryn says. "A real shaman emerges through the

Courtesy of *Smoke Signals* and Legends Restaurant, Brent Merrill, photographer

KATHRYN DANCING AT POWWOW

traditional path and is recognized by the tribe. The fakes and wannabes cheapen and commercialize authentic native culture." Louie Pitt of the Warm Springs calls New Agers the "new colonialists" and "nice guy racists" who "take over our sacred sites, our religion, our cultural traditions," and make no bones about trying to enrich their lives "at our expense." He remembers a conversation with Kathryn when she commented, "Yeah, they do it with a smile, but it still feels the same to me."[5]

In the five years that this book was in development, Kathryn often encountered Nisqually tribal leader Billy Frank Jr. at national meetings. Billy himself had been the subject of a book by Charles Wilkinson published in 2000 under the title *Messages from Frank's Landing: A Story of Salmon, Treaties, and the Indian Way.* Billy joked with Kathryn, "Is your book done yet?"

"Almost," she replied. "I don't have many secrets left."

"But Kathryn," Billy would scold. "You're not supposed to tell them everything!"

Kathryn threw up her hands and said, "Now you tell me!"

APPENDIX ONE
Chronology

NOTE: *Events pertaining directly to Kathryn Harrison's personal history appear in capital letters.*

pre-1787 Decades of imported disease decimate Indian populations.

1787 Northwest Ordinance guarantees Indian "property, rights and liberty."

1803 Meriwether Lewis and William Clark travel through fifty Indian nations, saved repeatedly by Native women (the Nez Perce guide through the Bitterroots was named "Furnishes White Men with Brains").

1843 KATHRYN'S GREAT-GREAT-AUNT MOLALLA KATE IS BORN.

1844 First settlers arrive on Molalla Prairie.

1851 First unratified treaty is negotiated with the Molallas.

1855 Molalla treaty is signed.

1856 "Trail of Tears" takes place to the Grand Ronde Indian Reservation.

1860 MOLALLA KATE'S FAMILY MAKES THEIR REBELLIOUS RETURN TO THEIR TRADITIONAL HUNTING GROUNDS.

1866 Oregon legislature prohibits whites from marrying anyone "with one-half Indian blood."

1877 Nez Perces are driven out of their homeland and are captured by U.S. Army near Canada-U.S. border.

1878 Reverend Summers collects Grand Ronde artifacts as "last remnants" of the tribe.

1887 Congress passes the General Allotment Act, dividing and dispersing Indian lands.

1890 U.S. Army slaughters women and children at the Battle of Wounded Knee.

1892	KATHRYN'S FATHER, JOHN HERALD "HARRY" JONES, IS BORN AT GRAND RONDE.
1894	KATHRYN'S MOTHER, ELLA FLEMMING, IS BORN ON FLEMMING ISLAND IN ALASKA.
1900	U.S. land survey shows that Indians have lost 95 percent of their lands.
1901	U.S. Census reports that Siletz Indians on the reservation have been reduced from 2,500 to 483; nationwide, Native people have lost 90 percent of their population.
1902	ELLA IS SENT TO INDIAN BOARDING SCHOOL IN OREGON.
1903	*Lone Wolf v. Hitchcock* (Secretary of the Interior) allows Congress to abrogate treaties with Indian nations in the interest of acquiring lands deemed federally significant.
1904	Chief Joseph dies without being allowed to return to ancestral land.
1905	HARRY IS ORPHANED AND SENT TO INDIAN BOARDING SCHOOL IN OREGON.
1905–6	Lewis and Clark centennial is commemorated.
1908	*Winters v. U.S.* recognizes tribal water rights, but states disregard the ruling.
1910	HARRY GRADUATES FROM CHEMAWA INDIAN SCHOOL AS VALEDICTORIAN.
1911	ELLA RETURNS TO ALASKA TO HELP ON THE FAMILY'S FOX FARM.
1911–13	HARRY PURSUES HIGHER EDUCATION AT SALEM BUSINESS SCHOOL AND WASHINGTON STATE UNIVERSITY IN PULLMAN.
1915	BIA superintendent declares Harry incompetent to manage his own family land.
1916	HARRY AND ELLA MARRY ABOARD STEAMBOAT IN ALASKA.
1917	KATHRYN'S OLDER BROTHER HAROLD IS BORN AT GRAND RONDE.
1919	Congress voids the president's power to establish reservations and recognize tribes.
1920	KATHRYN'S OLDER SISTER DOROTHY IS BORN IN ALASKA.
1921	Commissioner of Indian Affairs orders the suppression of Indian dances, dress, and ceremonies across the United States.
1924	KATHRYN MAY JONES IS BORN IN CORVALLIS.

Indian Citizenship Act is passed by Congress, making Kathryn the first official American in the Jones family.

1925   KATHRYN IS BAPTIZED IN THE METHODIST CHURCH.

1926   KATHRYN'S MOTHER WORKS AS HOUSECLEANER AND SEAMSTRESS; KATHRYN'S FATHER IS A HOUSEPAINTER.

1927   KATHRYN'S SISTER MARIE IS BORN IN CORVALLIS.

Indian Oil Leasing Act authorizes Secretary of the Interior to enter into leases without tribes.

1928   Meriam Commission Report criticizes allotment and Indian education system and advocates improved health care and protecting tribal rights and traditions.

1929   KATHRYN BEGINS KINDERGARTEN; BROTHER BOB IS BORN IN CORVALLIS.

1930   BIA job program puts Indian men in off-reservation placements in order to "assimilate" them.

1931   FEDERAL BANK FORECLOSES ON MOLALLA KATE'S LAND AT SILETZ; KATE DEFIANTLY "SQUATS" THERE.

1932   KATHRYN STARS IN THIRD-GRADE PRODUCTION OF "GOLDILOCKS" IN CORVALLIS.

1933   SISTER NORMA IS BORN, AND FAMILY MOVES TO SILETZ (LOGSDEN).

KATHRYN'S FATHER IS EMPLOYED IN INDIAN EMERGENCY CONSERVATION WORK PROGRAM AS PAINTER AND CARPENTER.

FDR authorizes Indian Emergency Conservation Work Program (parallel to CCC).

1934   KATHRYN'S PARENTS DIE IN THE FLU EPIDEMIC.

Indian Reorganization Act replaces Allotment Act and encourages economic development.

1935   KATHRYN'S SIBLINGS ARE SEPARATED IN FOSTER CARE AND INDIAN BOARDING SCHOOL.

1936   KATHRYN ATTENDS SEVENTH GRADE AT SILETZ SCHOOL WITH SISTER MARIE.

1937   KATHRYN AND MARIE ARE TAKEN TO LIVE WITH THE WATSON FAMILY IN BUXTON, OREGON.

1938   MOLALLA KATE DIES; KATHRYN GRADUATES FROM EIGHTH GRADE IN BUXTON.

Congress allows Secretary of Interior to sign tribal mining leases without the tribes' approval.

1939	KATHRYN FLEES FOSTER HOME AND BEGINS TENTH GRADE AT CHEMAWA INDIAN SCHOOL.
1940	Congress passes the Nationality Act reconfirming Indian citizenship; several states refuse to allow Indians the right to vote.
1941	KATHRYN BEGINS DATING FRANK HARRISON AT CHEMAWA INDIAN SCHOOL.
	The U.S. enters World War II; male Indian students are subject to the draft.
1942	KATHRYN GRADUATES FROM CHEMAWA AND MOVES TO PORTLAND.
	More than 25,000 Native Americans are fighting in the war, and more than 40,000 work in wartime industries.
1943	KATHRYN'S DAUGHTER PATSY (CHILD #1) IS BORN IN PORTLAND; KATHRYN MOVES TO MONTANA TO LIVE WITH HER OLDER SISTER DOROTHY.
1944	DOROTHY DIES OF PNEUMONIA; KATHRYN MARRIES FRANK HARRISON BUT REMAINS IN MONTANA AS FRANK SERVES OVERSEAS.
	Fifty tribes send delegates to the first National Congress of American Indians.
1945	FRANK IS DISCHARGED FROM THE SERVICE; KATHRYN JOINS HIM IN PORTLAND.
1946	KATHRYN'S DAUGHTER JEANNIE (CHILD #2) IS BORN; KATHRYN WORKS IN TOLEDO, OREGON, LUMBER MILL.
	Congress establishes the Indian Claims Commission to decide Indian land issues.
1947	KATHRYN IS LIVING AT SILETZ, WHILE FRANK DRIVES LOGGING TRUCKS.
1948	KATHRYN'S SON FRANKIE (CHILD #3) IS BORN IN PENDLETON.
	Congress establishes the Higher Education Grant Program for Native college students.
1949	KATHRYN'S SON TOMMY (CHILD #4) IS BORN IN PORTLAND.
	Hoover Commission urges the U.S. government to transfer responsibility for Indian services to the states and to enforce a policy of assimilation.
1950	Congress adopts programs to attract industry to reservation land and to relocate Indian families to urban areas.

1951   KATHRYN'S SON RAYMOND (CHILD #5) IS BORN IN PENDLETON, OREGON.

1952   KATHRYN'S SON ROGER (CHILD #6) IS BORN IN SILVERTON, OREGON.

BIA spends $500,000 moving Indians to urban areas; the National Congress of American Indians blasts relocation as "cultural destruction."

1953   KATHRYN IS LIVING AT SILETZ, WHILE FRANK WORKS IN A LOGGING CAMP.

Maine becomes the last state to accept the 1924 Indian Citizenship Act.

1954   KATHRYN IS A MIGRANT FARM WORKER IN OREGON.

Congress passes the Western Oregon Tribes Termination Act.

1955   KATHRYN'S DAUGHTER KATHY (CHILD #7) IS BORN IN HILLSBORO, OREGON.

1956   Indian Vocational Training Act provides job programs for tribal members in cities.

1957   KATHRYN'S DAUGHTER DIANE (CHILD #8) IS BORN IN SILVERTON.

1958   KATHRYN'S FAMILY WORKS ODD JOBS, MOVING SOUTH THROUGH IDAHO TO ARIZONA.

Over tribal protest, BIA project encourages non-Indians to adopt Indian children.

1959   KATHRYN WORKS AS A FIELD HAND, LIVING IN A FARM SHED, HAULING HER OWN WATER, AND RAISING EIGHT CHILDREN IN ARIZONA.

1960   KATHRYN'S DAUGHTER PATSY, AGE SIXTEEN, LEAVES HOME TO GET MARRIED.

President John F. Kennedy abandons the termination policy.

1961   KATHRYN'S SON DAVID (CHILD #9) IS BORN IN OREGON CITY; FAMILY MEMBERS ARE STILL MIGRANT FARM WORKERS.

About 500 Indians from 70 tribes attend the American Indian Chicago Conference and draft the Declaration of Indian Purpose, calling for a reduction in BIA power and the protection of Indian water rights.

1962   THE HARRISON FAMILY LIVES IN LEBANON, OREGON; THE ELDEST SONS LETTER IN SPORTS.

The National Indian Youth Council formed, enrolling 5,000 members.

1963   President Kennedy is assassinated.

1964   KATHRYN TURNS FORTY; SHE HAS NINE CHILDREN
       AND AN ABUSIVE, ALCOHOLIC HUSBAND.

1965   The BIA spends $11.5 million relocating Indians to urban areas
       (approximately half returned to their reservations within a
       year).

1966   KATHRYN'S SON FRANKIE GRADUATES FROM
       HIGH SCHOOL; THE FAMILY MOVES BACK TO
       PENDLETON.

1967   KATHRYN'S DAUGHTER KAREN (CHILD #10)
       IS BORN; THE HARRISONS MOVE TO ALASKA;
       KATHRYN'S BROTHER HAROLD DIES IN
       PENDLETON.

       The American Indian Law Center is founded at the University
       of New Mexico (at the time there were only 25 Native
       American attorneys in the United States).

1968   TOMMY GRADUATES FROM HIGH SCHOOL IN
       ALASKA AND VOLUNTEERS TO SERVE IN VIETNAM.

       The American Indian Movement (AIM) is founded; Congress
       passes the Indian Civil Rights Act.

1969   KATHRYN WORKS IN A FISH CANNERY IN ALASKA.

       Vine Deloria Jr. publishes *Custer Died for Your Sins: An Indian
       Manifesto*; the Marine Corps declassifies information about the
       Navajo "Code Talkers" of World War II; AIM "invades and
       occupies" Alcatraz Island; Indian author N. Scott Momaday
       receives the Pulitzer Prize for *The Way to Rainy Mountain*, his
       novel about an Indian veteran.

1970   KATHRYN LEAVES HER HUSBAND AND RETURNS
       TO OREGON WITH HER FIVE YOUNGEST
       CHILDREN.

       President Richard M. Nixon declares self-determination policy
       for Indian tribes; BIA budget has $10 million for economic
       development on reservations; the American Indian Press
       Association and the National Indian Education Association are
       founded; the Native American Rights Fund (NARF) begins
       providing legal services to tribes.

1971   KATHRYN GOES ON WELFARE AND ATTENDS LANE
       COMMUNITY COLLEGE IN EUGENE.

       AIM stages a counter-celebration at Mt. Rushmore on July
       Fourth and paints Plymouth Rock red on Thanksgiving.

1972   KATHRYN RECEIVES A NURSING DEGREE FROM

LANE COMMUNITY COLLEGE; TOMMY RETURNS
FROM WAR IN VIETNAM.

More than 1,000 Indians from 100 reservations participate
in the Trail of Broken Treaties Caravan to Washington,
D.C.; presenting a Twenty Points petition, they demand
BIA demolition, direct access to the White House by tribal
governments, and restoration of treaty-making powers; for six
days they occupy BIA headquarters.

1973   KATHRYN WORKS AS A NURSE IN LINCOLN CITY.

AIM stages a siege at Wounded Knee at the Pine Ridge
Reservation in South Dakota; Congress passes CETA,
providing jobs for unemployed Native Americans both on and
off reservations.

1974   KATHRYN (AGE FIFTY) WORKS AT SILETZ TRIBAL
ALCOHOL PROGRAM AND DIVORCES FRANK.

U.S. v. Washington (the Boldt decision) affirms treaty rights in
Northwest fishing cases.

1975   KATHRYN IS ELECTED TO SILETZ TRIBAL
COUNCIL; THE SILETZ BEGIN RESTORATION
EFFORT.

The Indian Self-Determination and Education Assistance Act
allows tribes to provide members with programs and services;
no longer must they rely on the BIA.

1976   KATHRYN WORKS ON SILETZ RESTORATION WITH
CHARLES WILKINSON.

The Indian Health Care Improvement Act increases the
availability of health care.

1977   KATHRYN LEAVES SILETZ.

Congress passes the Siletz Restoration Act.

1978   KATHRYN SERVES "MEALS ON WHEELS" TO
ELDERS IN LANE COUNTY.

Congress passes the American Indian Religious Freedom Act
and the Indian Child Welfare Act.

1979   KATHRYN MOVES TO COOS BAY AND ATTENDS
THE MIDWEST INTERTRIBAL SPIRITUAL
GATHERING, GAINING HER TOTEM, THE TURTLE.

AIM is formally dissolved following the deaths of the AIM
chairman's family.

1980   KATHRYN LEADS THE ALCOHOL REHABILITATION
PROGRAM IN COOS BAY.

The U.S. Supreme Court awards the Sioux more than $100

million as compensation for the Black Hills, taken a century earlier in violation of the Fort Laramie Treaty.

1981   KATHRYN MOVES HOME TO GRAND RONDE AND WORKS AS TRIBAL ENROLLMENT CLERK.

A federal commission report exposes corruption in BIA management and auditing.

1982   KATHRYN AND HER SON FRANKIE ARE ELECTED TO THE GRAND RONDE TRIBAL COUNCIL.

The Cow Creek Band of Umpqua Indians receives federal recognition.

1983   KATHRYN, HER SON FRANKIE, AND HER DAUGHTER KAREN TESTIFY BEFORE CONGRESS FOR GRAND RONDE TRIBAL RECOGNITION.

The Grand Ronde Restoration Act passes and is signed by President Ronald Reagan.

1984   KATHRYN (AGE SIXTY) IS ELECTED INTERIM CHAIR OF GRAND RONDE TRIBAL COUNCIL.

Sue Shaffer is elected tribal chair of the Cow Creeks.

1985   KATHRYN IS RE-ELECTED TO TRIBAL COUNCIL; RESERVATION PLAN IS MADE PUBLIC.

Wilma Mankiller is selected as principal chief of the Cherokee Nation.

1986   KATHRYN NEGOTIATES WITH THE BUREAU OF LAND MANAGEMENT FOR RETURN OF INDIAN LAND.

Klamath Tribes are restored in southern Oregon.

1987   KATHRYN IS RE-ELECTED, SERVING AS TRIBAL COUNCIL SECRETARY.

U.S. Supreme Court allows casino-style gambling on Indian reservations.

1988   GRAND RONDE RESERVATION ACT PROVIDES LAND BASE OF ALMOST TEN THOUSAND ACRES.

Congress passes the Indian Gaming Regulatory Act.

1989   KATHRYN IS RE-ELECTED TO TRIBAL COUNCIL; NANITCH SAHALLIE OPENS FOR TRIBAL ALCOHOL PROGRAM.

Coquille Tribe of Southwestern Oregon is federally recognized.

1990   TRIBE PURCHASES GRAND RONDE CASINO SITE ON HIGHWAY 18, A ROUTE TO THE OREGON COAST.

Congress passes the Native American Graves Protection and Repatriation Act.

1991   KATHRYN'S SON FRANKIE IS KILLED IN A

CLIMBING ACCIDENT ON THE OREGON COAST.
Tribes from Alaska to Florida rebury Indian remains previously
housed in museums.

1992 GRAND RONDE COMMUNITY CENTER OPENS;
KATHRYN IS RE-ELECTED TO TRIBAL COUNCIL.
More than 100 Indian groups are still waiting for the BIA
federal recognition process.

1993 KATHRYN AND GOVERNOR BARBARA ROBERTS
SIGN GAMING COMPACT AND OREGON SENATE
BILL 61, PROTECTING CULTURAL RESOURCES.
Ada Deer is named assistant secretary for Indian Affairs in the
U.S. Department of the Interior.

1994 KATHRYN (AGE SEVENTY) PRESIDES AT THE
SALEM REPATRIATION CEREMONY.
Three cabinet officials hold "Listening Conference" early in the
Clinton administration, inviting Indian leaders from all over the
country for a two-day session.

1995 SPIRIT MOUNTAIN CASINO OPENS; KATHRYN'S
SON TOMMY DIES AFTER AUTOMOBILE ACCIDENT.
Minnesota bans the sale of Crazy Horse malt liquor.

1996 KATHRYN IS ELECTED CHAIR OF TRIBAL COUNCIL;
SHE MOVES TO SHERIDAN.
BLM cedes 7,600 acres of timberland to the Grand Rondes.

1997 SPIRIT MOUNTAIN COMMUNITY FUND IS
CREATED; GRAND RONDE HEALTH CENTER
OPENS.
Class action suit allowed against BIA for mismanagement of
Indian trust accounts.

1998 GRAND RONDE GOVERNANCE BUILDING OPENS;
KATHRYN IS RE-ELECTED TRIBAL CHAIR.
U.S. Forest Service signs agreement for co-management with
tribes of forest lands.

1999 KATHRYN RECEIVES OREGON COMMISSION ON
WOMEN ANNUAL AWARD.
Heart of the American Indian Women's Network meets at
Agua Caliente.

2000 KATHRYN'S BROTHER, BOB WATSON, IS
APPOINTED ACTING MANAGER OF SPIRIT
MOUNTAIN.
Grand Rondes' meteorite repatriation lawsuit is settled in
New York City; at 175th anniversary of the BIA, Kevin Gover
apologizes for official racism.

2001   KATHRYN RETIRES FROM TRIBAL GOVERNMENT;
        TRIBE HIRES HER AS PUBLIC SPOKESPERSON.

        George W. Bush becomes president; White House tribal liaison
        position is abolished; John Ashcroft is appointed Attorney
        General; Gale Norton appointed Secretary of Interior; NCAI
        invites Clinton tribal liaison to annual meeting in Minneapolis.

2002   KATHRYN SERVES AS "PUBLIC FACE" OF GRAND
        RONDES.

        President Bush denies recognition to Chinooks, who greeted
        Lewis and Clark at Pacific Ocean.

2003   KATHRYN IS AWARDED HONORARY DOCTORATE
        OF HUMANE LETTERS FROM PORTLAND STATE
        UNIVERSITY; TWENTIETH ANNIVERSARY OF
        GRAND RONDE RESTORATION IS CELEBRATED.

        Spirit Mountain Casino is named number one tourist attraction
        in Oregon; Spirit Mountain Community Fund has donated $20
        million to charity.

2004   KATHRYN TURNS EIGHTY AND RECEIVES
        HONORARY DEGREE FROM HER ALMA MATER,
        THE LANE COMMUNITY COLLEGE SCHOOL OF
        NURSING.

2005   KATHRYN'S "AMBASSADOR" CONTRACT WITH
        GRAND RONDE TRIBE IS RENEWED.

        ROY TRACK JR., THE SON OF KATHRYN'S SISTER
        DOROTHY, DIES IN ARIZONA.

        Portland Art Museum exhibits Summers Collection of tribal
        artifacts; Lewis and Clark bicentennial is commemorated;
        Spirit Mountain Community Fund passes the $30 million mark
        in donations to charity.

APPENDIX TWO
Nine Myths about Indian Gaming

Myth No. 1: The Indian Gaming Regulatory Act (IGRA) created Indian gaming.

In fact, the tribes have been gaming since time immemorial, both among themselves, as in the hops harvest stick games, and vis-à-vis the European explorers and settlers, as when they "redistributed some wealth" during the Lewis and Clark foray into Indian Country. Native peoples consider gaming an amusing diversion, not in the least immoral as Puritan society believed. They see luck at gambling as a sign of strong spirituality, and individuals are able to confirm their social status by redistributing the surpluses gaming practices generate.

Indian nations consider the right to gamble an aspect of sovereignty. All IGRA does is regulate casino operations, in keeping with congressional oversight under the Commerce Clause.

Myth No. 2: Indian gaming is commercial, for-profit gaming akin to Donald Trump's operations in Atlantic City.

This is the claim that has fueled the most controversy in tribal gaming operations. As conceived, tribal casinos were a way to fund government programs, as the Grand Rondes have done with their health clinic, education center, community center, elders' housing, and numerous other programs for the benefit of tribal members. The rub comes with per capita distribution, and the media are fixated on a few tribes' "instant millionaires." The fact is that most Native Americans still live below the poverty line, suffer from poor nutrition and related diseases, and have difficulty finding employment. Gaming proceeds go into the tribal general treasury, and tribal councils must decide how to allocate the revenue.

Myth No. 3: Tribal gaming is an unregulated magnet for organized crime.

In fact, Indian gaming is more heavily regulated than commercial casinos. In Oregon, the state police and the FBI keep close tabs on tribal operations, in addition to individual tribal gaming commissions. The gaming operations have been remarkably secure and free of graft. During my more-than-seven-year tenure as United States Attorney for the District of Oregon, the only case brought from Grand Ronde was referred by the tribe itself against a recently hired dealer from Las Vegas.

Effective tribal leaders recognize the vulnerability to corruption and organized crime that comes with the gaming territory and can do a great deal to mitigate the danger. With a strong, independent gaming commission, the Grand Rondes have been particularly vigilant in this regard. They take the lead in enforcing their own regulations because it is in their own interest to maintain a reputation for running a clean shop. An important safeguard of sovereignty is to demonstrate that they can enforce the law without outside supervision.

Myth No. 4: Indian people do not pay taxes.

Native Americans pay all taxes required by state and federal law. Although Congress has exempted them from some of the taxes non-Indians pay (including property taxes).[1] They have voluntarily made payments to state governments in lieu of taxes while negotiating gaming compacts. Spirit Mountain has significantly contributed to the tax base in Yamhill and Polk Counties. In recognition of the additional burden on public services that the casino may impose, the Spirit Mountain Community Fund has supplemented those contributions by funding law enforcement and medical and education services in the surrounding towns. By all measures, the casino has been an asset to the state's economic development.

Myth No. 5: IGRA has not worked.

In a February 2005 article for *The Christian Science Monitor,* Brad Knickerbocker wrote, "Since passage of the Indian Gaming Regulatory Act in 1988, the number of casinos has grown to more than 300 with a total annual business of nearly $13 billion." Indian gaming is proving a boon to states where IGRA has been faithfully implemented.[2]

Congressional oversight hearings have been replete with testimony about the benefits of Indian gaming. In fact, when negative publicity appeared in *Time* about mismanagement in other states, dozens of Oregon organizations wrote public letters to the newspapers praising their experience with Indian casinos in Oregon.

Myth No. 6: IGRA infringes on states' rights.

Many parts of IGRA were originally proposed by the states and have been held to be constitutional. IGRA merely requires state governors to negotiate with tribal governments, recognizing their sovereignty. The states have no powers over tribal governments except those expressly delegated by Congress.[3] Oregon's governors have had respectful and constructive relationships with Oregon's tribal leaders in hammering out the details of Oregon's gaming compacts.

Myth No. 7: Tribal gaming drains resources from surrounding communities.

The opposite is true, as evidenced by the turnaround in local support for neighboring casinos. The Umatillas released a report for their area showing that all economic indicators were up dramatically since the opening of their Wildhorse Casino in 1997. Tribal efforts to contribute to neighboring communities as well as to other Indian reservations reflect the traditional gifting of surplus that confirms the social status of the well-to-do.

Myth No. 8: Better economic development alternatives to gaming are available to tribes.

History has not shown this to be true. If better alternatives were available, tribes would pounce on them. Spirit Mountain

Development Corporation is constantly on the lookout for ways to diversify the tribe's economy.[4]

Myth No. 9: Tribal gaming has little public support among non-Indians.
Tourism figures put the lie to this allegation. Spirit Mountain Casino has consistently been one of the top tourism draws in Oregon. In a 2004 state report by the Tourism Bureau, the casino was the most visited site in Oregon, ahead of such natural wonders as Multnomah Falls or Crater Lake. Exit surveys show tremendous consumer satisfaction, and the parking lot is jammed at all days and all hours. Tribal buses run continuously between the major metropolitan areas and Grand Ronde, transporting recreational gamblers, corporate party groups, and people with tickets for shows by nationally known entertainers.

Notes

Chapter 1

1. An *Anchorage Times* article of 1983 described Flemming's pioneering days.

2. Claus M. Naske, William Hunt, and Lael Morgan, *Alaska* (New York: Harrison House, 1983), 127–28. Ethnohistorian Lael Morgan has written about the decimation of Alaskan Natives, particularly the Eyaks.

3. *Smoke Signals*, November 15, 2000. These objects and remains were later donated to the Smithsonian in Washington and only recently repatriated.

4. Velma Wallis, *Two Old Women: An Alaska Legend of Betrayal, Courage and Survival* (Fairbanks, Alaska: Epicenter Press, 1993), 45.

5. Kathryn once obtained a copy of this note from Bureau of Indian Affairs archives in Seattle. She has lost the piece of paper but remembers the simple text.

6. Hubert H. Bancroft, *History of the Northwest Coast* (San Francisco: A.L. Bancroft, 1884), 109.

7. Mourning Dove, *A Salishan Autobiography*, ed. Jay Miller, (Lincoln: University of Nebraska Press, 1990), 166.

8. Earl Shorris, "The Last Word: Can the World's Small Languages be Saved?" in *Harper's Magazine*, 301:1802 (August 2000), 38. See also Elizabeth Kolbert, "Last Words: a Language Dies," in *The New Yorker*, June 6, 2005, 46–59.

Chapter 2

1. See Alvin M. Josephy Jr., *The Indian Heritage of America* (New York: Alfred A. Knopf, 1968), 323–29; *A Walk Toward Oregon: A Memoir* (New York: Alfred A. Knopf, 2000); Lionel Youst, *She's Tricky Like Coyote: Annie Miner Peterson, an Oregon Coast Indian Woman* (Norman: University of Oklahoma Press, 1997), 33, 38; Carolyn M. Buan and Richard Lewis, eds., *The First Oregonians* (Portland: Oregon Council for the Humanities, 1991), 39–45.

2. Letter from the Commissioner of the Department of the Interior, Office of Indian Affairs, to Superintendent, Grand Ronde School and Agency, January 11, 1902.

3. Interview with Robert Kentta by Kristine Olson, November 5, 1999; interview with Delores "Dee" Pigsley by Kristine Olson, May 12, 2000 [hereafter Pigsley interview].

4. Documented in Harrison family papers, in Kathryn's possession.

5. Interview with June Olson, by Kristine Olson, August 27, 1999.

6. From the perspective of 1492, the percentage of Native land lost by the Indians is greater still.

7. See Josephy, *Indian Heritage*, 350–51; Charles F. Wilkinson, *Blood Struggle: The Rise of Modern Indian Nations* (New York: Norton, 2005), 43–51.

Chapter 3

1. Joseph Lane to Secretary of War, *Annual Report of the Commission of Indian Affairs* (Washington, D.C.: GPO, 1850), 129.

2. Patricia R. Baars, *Near Neighbors: Cross-Cultural Friendships in Dickey Prairie and South Molalla* (Oregon City: Clackamas County Education Service District, 1989).

3. Champ C. Vaughan, "Encounters with Molalla Indians — 1843-1906," self-published monograph, (2000), 3.

4. United States Congress, 1852: 44–1, 44–2.

5. Terence O'Donnell, *An Arrow in the Earth: General Joel Palmer and the Indians of Oregon* (Portland: Oregon Historical Society Press, 1991), 261–80.

6. Baars, *Near Neighbors*, 13.

7. See Robert Boyd, *The Coming of the Spirit of Pestilence: Introduced Infectious Diseases and Population Decline Among Northwest Coast Indians, 1774–1874* (Seattle: University of Washington Press, 1999).

8. Affidavit of Hoxie Simmons, age eighty-five, State of Oregon, County of Lincoln, September 18, 1957.

9. Baars, *Near Neighbors*, 11.

10. Ronald B. Lansing, *Juggernaut: The Whitman Massacre Trial, 1850* (San Francisco: Ninth Judicial Circuit Historical Society Press, 1993).

11. Philip M.S. Drucker, *Notes, 1934*, p. 30, 4516 (78), vol. 1, National Anthropological Archives, Washington, D.C.

12. John McLoughlin, chief factor of the Hudson's Bay Company Columbia Department, retired in 1846, moved to Oregon City with his family, and became a leading citizen of the Oregon Territory. See Dorothy Nafus Morrison, *Outpost: John McLoughlin and the Far West* (Portland: Oregon Historical Society Press, 1999).

13. Interview with Patricia Baars by Kristine Olson, September 16, 1999.

Chapter 4

1. Mr. Hobart and Miss Wilson grew fond of each other and later married. During World War II, Mr. and Mrs. Hobart bought Kathryn's extended family homestead from the Federal Land Bank for "one dollar consideration." Lincoln County land records, County Clerk's office, Newport, Oregon.

2. Janet Campbell Hale, *Bloodlines: Odyssey of a Native Daughter* (Tucson: University of Arizona Press, 1998), 50.

3. Stick games are gambling events and tournaments played with four bones—two with stripes and two without. Eleven sticks are used to keep score. It is a game of psychology, with each team chanting to distract the other side. The team captain chooses a person to hide the bones in his hands. The other team must pick which hand hides the striped bones. In the contests, teams often enlisted medicine men to use their powers on the team's behalf. There were individual bets as well as team bets. Stick games were called *lo-wick-sha*, which means *to gamble*. They are still played at powwows.

4. Robert Carlton Clark, Robert Horace Down, and George Verne Blue,

A History of Oregon (Evanston, Ill.: Row, Peterson and Company, 1926–1931), 17, 21, 35.

5. Ironically, Harry had spent the early fall months renovating two rooms in the clinic for the use of local Indian families who were unable to make it up to the BIA Hospital in Washington.

6. Interview with Maude Lane by Kristine Olson, January 21, 2000 [hereafter Lane interview].

Chapter 5

1. Lane interview. Albertina Kerr Youth and Family Center records show that Norma Jones, an Indian of "legitimate" birth was admitted on November 27, 1935.

2. Interview with Marie Jones Schmidt by Kristine Olson, February 22, 2000.

3. Indian Child Welfare Act of 1978, Public Law 95-608, 25 U.S.C., Section 1902.

4. Interview with Robert Watson by Kristine Olson, May 12, 2000 [hereafter Watson interview].

Chapter 6

1. Child Study Association of America, ed. *The Indian Girl: Her Social Heritage, Her Needs and Her Opportunities* (Washington, D.C.: GPO, 1935).

2. Brenda J. Child, *Boarding School Seasons: American Indian Families, 1900–1940* (Lincoln: University of Nebraska Press, 1998).

3. Wilma Mankiller and Michael Wallis, *Mankiller: A Chief and Her People* (New York: St. Martin's Press, 1993), 7.

4. Benis M. Frank, introduction to *Warriors: Navajo Code Talkers*, by Kenji Kawano (Flagstaff, Ariz.: Northland Publishing Company, 1990), 1–13.

5. In Kathryn's official file at the National Archives in Seattle.

Chapter 7

1. David McCullough, *Truman* (New York: Simon & Schuster, 1992), 860.

2. Helen Pearce, "Folk Sayings in a Pioneer Family of Western Oregon," in *California Folklore Quarterly*, 5 (1946), 236–7.

3. Sixty years later, in 2003, the National Congress of American Indians drew four thousand delegates.

4. See Josephy, *Indian Heritage*, 345–65; Vine Deloria Jr., *Behind the Trail of Broken Treaties: An Indian Declaration of Independence* (Austin: University of Texas Press, 1985), 29–32; Vine Deloria Jr. and Clifford Lytle, *American Indians, American Justice* (Austin: University of Texas Press, 1983), 147, 156.

5. House Concurrent Resolution 108 of 1953.

6. Jeff Zucker, Kay Hummel and Bob Høgfoss , eds., *Oregon Indians: Culture, History and Current Affairs* (Portland: Oregon Historical Society Press, 1983), 77.

7. Deloria and Lytle, *American Indians, American Justice*, 20.

8. Josephy Jr., *A Walk Toward Oregon*, 261–62.
9. Barbara Kingsolver, *The Poisonwood Bible* (New York: Harper Collins, 1999), 383.

Chapter 8
1. General Services Administration, National Archives and Records Office of the Federal Register, "Public Papers of the Presidents of the United States: Richard Nixon, 1970" (Washington, D.C.: GPO, 1971), 564–76.
2. In 2004, thirty-two years later, Kathryn returned to Lane Community College to be honored as one of their notable alumni.
3. Wilkinson, *Blood Struggle*, 45.

Chapter 9
1. Wilkinson, *Blood Struggle*, 271–303.
2. Memorandum from Don Wharton to Elizabeth Furse, May 5, 1982.
3. Testimony of Kathryn Harrison before the U.S. Senate Committee on Interior and Insular Affairs, March 30, 1976, 1–3, transcription in Harrison family papers in Kathryn's possession.
4. Winona LaDuke, *All Our Relations: Native Struggles for Land and Life* (Cambridge, Mass.: South End Press, 1999).
5. Interview with Mark Hatfield by Kristine Olson, June 8, 2000 [hereafter Hatfield interview.]
6. Mankiller and Wallis, *Mankiller*, 186.
7. See Peter Matthiessen, *Indian Country* (New York: Viking, 1984). He recounts the saga in chapter seven, pp. 201–20.

Chapter 10
1. Letter from Les AuCoin to Kathryn Harrison, January 19, 1982.
2. Hatfield interview.
3. Ibid.
4. LaDuke, *All Our Relations*, 82.
5. Wilkinson, *Blood Struggle*, 190–1.
6. Interview with Les AuCoin by Kristine Olson, June 16, 2000 [hereafter AuCoin interview].
7. Ibid.
8. In author's possession.
9. Lawrence M. Hampton, "The Indian Reorganization Act," in *The Aggressions of Civilization: Federal Indian Policy Since the 1880s*, ed. Sandra L. Cadwalader and Vine Deloria Jr. (Philadelphia: Temple University Press, 1984), 131–48.
10. Furse was later elected to Congress from Oregon and continued to champion Native issues there.
11. Interview with Kathryn "Kat" Brigham by Kristine Olson, February 10, 2000.
12. *Smoke Signals*, November 1, 2003, 4.
13. Interview with Elizabeth Furse by Kristine Olson, January 16, 2000.

14. AuCoin interview.

15. Testimony of Kathryn Harrison in support of HR 3885 before the House Interior and Insula Affairs Committee, October 18, 1983, 1-5, in Harrison family papers.

16. Testimony of Frank Harrison in support of HR 3885 before the House Interior and Insula Affairs Committee, October 18, 1983, 2-3, transcript in Harrison family papers in Kathryn's possession.

17. Testimony of Kathryn Harrison in support of HR 3885 before the House Interior and Insula Affairs Committee, October 18, 1983, 1, transcript in Harrison family papers in Kathryn's possession.

18. Hatfield interview.

19. AuCoin interview.

20. Public Law 98-165, enacted by the U.S. Congress, November 11, 1983.

21. Constitution of the Confederated Tribes of the Grand Ronde Community of Oregon, submitted for adoption to the qualified voters of the tribe, November 10, 1984. http://www.grandronde.org/Legal/Docs/index.html (accessed October 5, 2005).

Chapter 11

1. Early restoration committee letterhead included the Tillamook and the Chinook, but tribal council decided to name only the top five, based on current population figures. The latter two tribes have since sought restoration independently, only to be rebuffed by the George W. Bush administration.

2. This system is used to this day. Kathryn served five consecutive three-year terms.

3. AuCoin and Hatfield interviews.

4. The first issue of *Smoke Signals*, April 1987, makes it clear that two items dominated the tribal agenda that spring. Foremost was the effort to line up local support for the reservation bill. Second was securing health-care services, primarily blood-pressure monitoring for tribal members with diabetes and treatment for alcohol abuse.

5. *Smoke Signals*, May 1987.

6. Ibid., September 1987.

7. AuCoin interview

8. *Smoke Signals*, May 1988.

9. 25 United States Code Section 713(f), enacted September 9, 1988 as Public Law 100-425.

10. *Smoke Signals*, November 1988, 11.

11. AuCoin interview.

12. Hatfield interview.

13. Interview with Don Wharton by Kristine Olson, January 6, 2003.

14. Under the headline "Archaeological Committee: A Committee in Action!" the spring 1990 issue of *Smoke Signals* gave a detailed report.

15. Oregon State Archives, Governor Neil Goldschmidt, Proclamation, April 10, 1990.

16. Pigsley interview.

17. The following year the Oregon Council for the Humanities published the proceedings as *The First Oregonians*. The book proved so popular that the OCH plans to publish an updated second edition in 2005, to be funded in part by the Grand Ronde Tribes' Spirit Mountain Community Fund.

Chapter 12

1. *Smoke Signals*, July 1992.
2. Ibid., August 1992.
3. Ibid., December 1992.
4. Ibid., May 1993.
5. Interview with Louie Pitt Jr. by Kristine Olson, August 21, 1999.
6. AuCoin interview.
7. Gail Oberst, "Chinook Artifacts Returned to Indians," *Statesman Journal* (Salem), January 26, 1994.

Chapter 13

1. Mankiller and Wallis, *Mankiller*, 207.
2. James P. Ronda, *Lewis and Clark Among the Indians* (Lincoln: University of Nebraska Press, 1984), 166.
3. Pat Durkin, *Heart of the Circle: Photographs by Edward S. Curtis of Native American Women* (San Francisco: Pomegranate Artbooks, 1997), 12-14.
4. Billy Frank Jr. acceptance speech at Ecotrust Awards Dinner, Portland, Oregon, November 6, 2003.
5. See Gretchen M. Bataille and Kathleen Mullen Sands, *American Indian Women: Telling Their Lives* (Lincoln: University of Nebraska Press, 1984), 18–19.
6. Bataille and Sands, *American Indian Women*, 17.
7. Shaffer interview.

Chapter 14

1. The grandmother depicted is Martha Jane Sands, a tribal member from early reservation days; Lon Mercier, her great-great-grandson, made the drawing. Kathryn was a partial model for the piece, lending the details of her ear, hand, and foot.
2. *Smoke Signals*, March 17, 1995.
3. Watson interview.
4. In due time, Roger became a blackjack dealer at the casino to finance his artistic pursuits, Karen was hired as a secretary to SMDC, and Patsy (who returned to Oregon in 1996) was named director of Employment Services.
5. The Grand Ronde tribe customarily honors veterans with a Pendleton blanket. The all-wool blankets, available in many colors and designs, have been manufactured by Pendleton Woolen Mills in eastern Oregon for more than a century. In the 1990s, the company introduced a Grand Ronde logo blanket, based on a design Kathryn and other tribal members at the casino put together and then took to the elders for approval. Kathryn describes the

blanket this way: "The logo is in the center, and the motifs are hands for the elders; something to represent hills, valley, and forest; and coyotes because Coyote—the logo of the casino—is the changeable trickster, who can bring you good look or bad luck." Roger, as designer of the tribal insignia, received the first logo blanket made. The tribal office still sells the popular blanket.

Chapter 15

1. *Smoke Signals*, May 1, 1996.

2. Kathryn Harrison, acceptance speech for Woman of the Year award given to Oregon Women Lawyers in July 1996, reprinted in *Advance Sheet* (Fall 1996), 5.

3. Roy Morris Jr., *Sheridan: The Life and Wars of General Phil Sheridan* (1869; reprint, Crown Publishers, 1992), 97. See also Dee Brown, *Bury My Heart at Wounded Knee: An Indian History of the American West* (New York: Holt, Reinhart & Winston, 1970), 170.

4. Interview with Ed Pearsall by Kristine Olson, September 25, 2000.

5. *Smoke Signals*, December 16, 1996.

6. Enrollment Ordinance, Tribal Code, Sec. 4.10 (a) (2). http://www.grandronde.org/Legal/Docs/Enrollment3-2004_1.pdf (accessed October 5, 2005).

7. Charles Wilkinson confirms this view of Senator Gorton in his recently released *Blood Struggle: The Rise of Modern Indian Nations*, (New York: Norton, 2005), 203.

8. *Smoke Signals*, October 1, 1997. Oregon Attorney General Hardy Myers opposed the provisions, and the Clinton White House threatened a veto.

9. Fay G. Cohen, *Treaties on Trial: The Continuing Controversy over Northwest Indian Fishing Rights* (Seattle: University of Washington Press, 1986).

10. Eric Pianin, "Tribes Take Aim at Old Foe: Rights Issues Spur Campaign to Oust Senator Gorton," *Washington Post*, April 3, 2000.

11. The memorial was completed in 2003, after Kathryn's last term ended. Not only does it bear her sons' names, but a nearby bench where elders can sit is named in her parents' honor. Kathryn donated the bench because she wanted Ella's name to be remembered along with those of her sons. Her mother is the only woman thus commemorated.

12. *Smoke Signals*, June 15, 1998.

Chapter 16

1. Peter Conradi, *Iris: The Life of Iris Murdoch* (London: W.W. Norton, 2001), 371.

2. Wharton interview.

3. Sue M. Shaffer to Whom it May Concern, August 17, 1999, in author's possession.

4. Jan Parini, *John Steinbeck* (New York: Henry Holt, 1995), 2.

5. Sue Miller, *While I Was Gone* (New York: Random House, 1999), 109.

6. Courtenay Thompson, "Willamette Forest, Tribes Agree on Collaboration." *The Oregonian*, January 28, 2000.

7. *Willamette Week*, Portland, December 22, 1999, 1, 20–9.

8. *Oregonian*, February 10, 2000.

9. See Roger Downey, *Riddle of the Bones: Politics, Science, Race, and the Story of Kennewick Man* (New York: Copernicus, 2000).

10. "News and Notes," newsletter of the American Indian Ritual Object Repatriation Foundation, Fall/Winter 2000.

11. Delores Pigsley, "A Prepared Statement," May 5, 2000.

12. The Warm Springs plan to site a casino off-reservation in Cascade Locks in the Columbia River Gorge was approved by Oregon Governor Ted Kulongoski in May 2005, only to be rejected by Secretary of the Interior Gale Norton. The Department of Interior left the door open for the Warm Springs to re-apply once the land was purchased and taken into trust.

13. See Eric Pianin, "Tribes Take Aim at Old Foe: Rights Issues Spur Campaign to Oust Senator Gorton," Washington Post, 2000.

14. Suzan Shown Harjo, "Open Letter to President Bush," *Indian Country Today*, January 31, 2001.

15. Watson interview.

16. Interview with Len Bergstein by Kristine Olson, July 20, 2000.

17. Elizabeth Furse, letter of nomination to D.C. Advocacy Institute, January 20, 2001, in author's possession.

18. *McMinnville News Register*, February 20, 2001.

Chapter 17

1. Ivor Davies died in September 2005 at the age of 98.

Chapter 18

1. *Smoke Signals*, June 15, 2003.

2. In 2005, Kathryn's contract as tribal ambassador was renewed on a per diem basis.

3. Sherman Alexie, *Ten Little Indians* (New York: Grove Press, 2003), 40.

4. Wharton interview.

5. Pitt interview.

Appendix Two

1. For a discussion of congressional exemptions, see Deloria and Lytle, *American Indians*, 223–25, and Charles F. Wilkinson, *Indian Tribes as Sovereign Governments* (Oakland, Calif.: American Indian Lawyer Training Program, 1988), 43–45.

2. Ron Karten, "The Punch of Tribal Casinos," *Smoke Signals*, March 15, 2005, provides an overview of the major contributions tribal casinos are making to the country's economy, especially rural economies.

3. For a primer on state authority in Indian Country, see Wilkinson, *Indian Tribes*, 33–48.

4. For a balanced discussion of gambling and its alternatives in Indian Country, see Wilkinson, *Blood Struggle*, 329–56.

Bibliography

Books

Albom, Mitch. *Tuesdays with Morrie*. New York: Doubleday Press, 1997.

Alexie, Sherman. *Old Shirts and New Skins*. Los Angeles: American Indian Studies Center, UCLA, 1993.

Alexie, Sherman. *Ten Little Indians*. New York: Grove Press, 2003.

Allen, Paula Gunn. *The Sacred Hoop: Recovering the Feminine in American Indian Traditions*. Boston: Beacon Press, 1992.

Allen, Paula Gunn, ed. *Voice of the Turtle: American Indian Literature*. New York: Ballantine, 1994.

Axtell, Horace, and Margo Aragon. *A Little Bit of Wisdom: A Conversation with a Nez Perce Elder*. Lewiston: Confluence Press, 1997.

Baars, Patricia R. *Near Neighbors: Cross-Cultural Friendships in Dickey Prairie and South Molalla*. Oregon City: Clackamas County Education Service District, 1989.

Bataille, Gretchen M., and Kathleen Mullen Sands. *American Indian Women: Telling Their Lives*. Lincoln and London: University of Nebraska Press, 1984.

Bernstein, Alison R. *American Indians and World War II: Toward a New Era in Indian Affairs*. Norman: University of Oklahoma Press, 1991.

Boyd, Robert. *The Coming of the Spirit of Pestilence: Introduced Infectious Diseases and Population Decline Among Northwest Coast Indians, 1774--1874*. Seattle: University of Washington Press, 1999.

Brown, Dee. *Bury My Heart At Wounded Knee: An Indian History of the American West*. New York: Holt, Rinehart and Winston, 1970.

Buan, Carolyn M., and Richard Lewis. *The First Oregonians*. Portland: Oregon Council for the Humanities, 1991.

Cawley, Fr. Martinus. *Father Crockett of Grand Ronde*. Lafayette, Ore.: Trappist Abbey, 1985.

Child, Brenda J. *Boarding School Seasons: American Indian Families, 1900—1940*. Lincoln: University of Nebraska Press, 1998.

Child Study Association of America, ed. *The Indian Girl: Her* Social *Heritage, Her Needs and Her Opportunities*. Washington, D.C.: GPO, 1935.

Clark, Robert Carlton, Robert Horace Down, and George Verne Blue. *A History of Oregon*. Evanston: Row, Peterson and Company, 1926--1931.

Cohen, Felix. *Handbook of Federal Indian Law*. Washington, D.C.: GPO, 1942.

Conradi, Peter. *Iris: The Life of Iris Murdoch*. London: W.W. Norton and Company, 2001.

Davis, Mary B., ed. *Native America in the Twentieth Century, An Encyclopedia*. New York: Garland Publishing, 1994.

Deloria, Philip J. *Playing Indian*. New Haven: Yale University Press, 1998.

Deloria, Vine Jr. *Custer Died for Your Sins*. Norman: University of Oklahoma Press, 1988.

————. *God Is Red*. New York: Dell Publishing Company, 1973.

————. *Behind the Trail of Broken Treaties: An Indian Declaration of Independence*. Austin: University of Texas Press, 1985.

————. *Red Earth, White Lies*. New York: Scribner's, 1995.

————. *We Talk, You Listen: New Tribes, New Turf*. New York: Macmillan, 1970.

Deloria, Vine Jr., and Clifford Lytle. *American Indians, American Justice*. Austin: University of Texas Press, 1983.

Dippie, Brian W. *The Vanishing American: White Attitudes and U.S. Indian Policy*. Lawrence: University of Kansas Press, 1982.

Downey, Roger. *Riddle of the Bones: Politics, Science, Race, and the Story of Kennewick Man*. New York: Copernicus / Spring-Verlag, 2000.

Drucker, Philip M. S., *Notes, 1934*. Washington, D.C.: National Anthropological Archives.

Echo-Hawk, Walter, Elizabeth Sackler, and Jack Trope, eds. *Mending the Circle: A Native American Repatriation Guide*. New York: American Indian Ritual Object Repatriation Foundation, 1996.

Edwards, G. Thomas. *Sowing Good Seeds*. Portland: Oregon Historical Society Press, 1990.

Fadiman, Anne. *The Spirit Catches You and You Fall Down: A Hmong Child, Her American Doctors, and the Collision of Two Cultures*. New York: Farrar, Straus and Giroux, 1997.

Forbes, Jack D. *Columbus and Other Cannibals*. Brooklyn: Autonomedia, 1992.

Getches, David H., Charles Wilkinson, and Robert A. Williams Jr. *Cases and Materials on Federal Indian Law*. 3rd ed. St. Paul, Minn.: West Publishing Company, 1993.

Hale, Janet Campbell. *Bloodlines: Odyssey of a Native Daughter*. Tucson: University of Arizona Press, 1993.

Hauptman, Lawrence M. *The Aggressions of Civilizations: Federal Indian Policy Since the 1880's*. Philadelphia: Temple University Press, 1984.

Hauptman, Lawrence M., and James D. Wherry, eds. *The Pequots in Southern New England: The Fall and Rise of an American Indian Nation*. Norman: University of Oklahoma Press, 1990.

Hazen-Hammond, Susan. *Timelines of Native American History*. New York: The Berkeley Publishing Group, 1997.

Johnson, Nancy. *Redefining Success: Women's Unique Paths*. Portland: Sybil Publications, 1995.

Josephy, Alvin M. Jr. *The Indian Heritage of America*. New York: Knopf, 1968,

————. *A Walk Toward Oregon*. New York: Random House, 2000.

Kawano, Kenji. *Warriors: Navajo Code Talkers*. Flagstaff, Ariz.: Northland Publishing Company, 1990.

Kimball, Chris. *Navajo Code Talkers: A Brief History*. History and Museums Division, USMC, 1982.

Kingsolver, Barbara. *The Poisonwood Bible*. New York: Harper Collins, 1999.

Klein, D., and G. Ackerman. *Women and Power in Native North America*. Norman: University of Oklahoma, 1995.

Kroeber, Karl, ed. *American Indian Persistence and Resurgence*. Durham: Duke University Press, 1994.

Krupat, Arnold. *Native American Autobiography: An Anthology*. Madison: University of Wisconsin Press, 1994.

LaDuke, Winona. *All Our Relations: Native Struggles for Land and Life*. Cambridge, Mass.: South End Press, 1999.

Lansing, Ronald B. *Juggernaut: The Whitman Massacre Trial, 1850*. San Francisco: Ninth Judicial Circuit Historical Society Press, 1993.

Mankiller, Wilma, and Michael Wallis. *Mankiller: A Chief and Her People*. New York: St. Martin's Press, 1993.

Matthiessen, Peter. *Indian Country*. New York: The Viking Press, 1984.

McCullough, David. *Truman*. New York: Simon & Schuster, 1992.

Miller, Sue. *While I Was Gone*. New York: Random House, 1999.

Mudge, Zachariah Atwell. *Sketches of Mission Life Among the Indians of Oregon*. New York: Carlton and Porter, 1854.

Naske, Claus M., William Hunt and Lael Morgan. *Alaska*. New York: Harrison House, 1983.

Niethammer, Carolyn. *Daughters of the Earth*. New York: Macmillan Publishing Company, 1977.

Oberdorfer, Don. *Senator Mansfield: The Extraordinary Life of a Great American Statesman and Diplomat*. Washington, D.C.: Smithsonian Books, 2003.

O'Donnell, Terrence. *An Arrow in the Earth: General Joel Palmer and the Indians of Oregon*. Portland: Oregon Historical Society Press, 1991.

Parini, Jan. *John Steinbeck: A Biography*. New York: Henry Holt and Company, 1995.

Philp, Kenneth R. *Termination Revisited: American Indians on the Trail to Self-Determination, 1933—1953*. Lincoln: University of Nebraska Press, 1999.

Pierpoint, Claire Roth. *Passionate Minds: Women Rewriting the World*. New York: Alfred A. Knopf, 2000.

Polishuk, Sandy. *Sticking to the Union: An Oral History of the Life and Times of Julia Ruuttila*. New York: Palgrave Macmillan, 2003.

Quintasket, Christine. *Mourning Dove: A Salishan Autobiography*. Lincoln: University of Nebraska Press, 1990.

Ronda, James P. *Lewis and Clark Among the Indians*. Lincoln: University of Nebraska Press, 1984.

Ruby, Robert H., and John A. Brown. *Esther Ross: Stillaguamish Champion*. Norman: University of Oklahoma Press, 2001.

Sekaquaptewa, Helen. *Me and Mine*. Tucson: University of Arizona Press, 1969.

Silko, Leslie Maromon. *Almanac of the Dead*. New York: Simon and Schuster, 1991.

————. *Yellow Woman and a Beauty of the Spirit: Essays on Native American Life Today*. New York: Simon and Schuster, 1996.

Stockel, H. Henrietta. *Chiricahua Apache Women and Children: Safekeepers of the Heritage*. College Station: Texas A and M University Press, 2000.

Swann, Brian, and Arnold Krupat, eds. *I Tell You Now: Autobiographical Essays by Native Americans*. Lincoln: University of Nebraska Press, 1987.

Szasz, Margaret Connell. *Between Indian and White Worlds: The Cultural Broker*. Norman: University of Oklahoma Press, 1994.

Tapontsang, Adhe. *Ama Adhe: The Voice That Remembers — The Heroic Story of a Woman's Fight to Free Tibet*. Boston: Wisdom Publications, 1997.

Trudell, Richard, ed. *Indian Tribes as Sovereign Governments*. Oakland: American Indian Resources Institute Press, 1988.

Wallis, Velma. *Two Old Women: An Alaska Legend of Betrayal, Courage and Survival*. Fairbanks: Epicenter Press, 1993.

Weaver, Jace. *Other Words: American Indian Literature, Law and Culture*. Norman: University of Oklahoma Press, 2001.

Wilkinson, Charles F. *Indian Tribes as Sovereign Governments*. Oakland: American Indian Lawyer Training Program, 1988.

————. *Fire on the Plateau: Conflict and Endurance in the American Southwest*. Washington, D.C.: Island Press / Shearwater Books, 1999.

————. *Messages from Frank's Landing: A Story of Salmon, Treaties, and the Indian Way*. Seattle: University of Washington Press, 2000.

————. *Blood Struggle: The Rise of Modern Indian Nations*. New York: Norton, 2005.

Wong, Hertha Dawn. *Sending My Heart Back Across the Years: Tradition and Innovation in Native American Autobiography*. New York: Oxford University Press, 1992.

Youst, Lionel. *She's Tricky Like Coyote: Annie Miner Peterson, an Oregon Coast Indian Woman*. Norman: University of Oklahoma Press, 1997.

Youst, Lionel, and William R. Seaburg. *Coquelle Thompson: Athabaskan Witness*. Norman: University of Oklahoma Press, 2002.

Zucker, Hummel and Hogfoss, eds. *Oregon Indians: Culture, History and Current Affairs*. Portland: Oregon Historical Society Press, 1983.

Articles

Back, Brian. "Grande Ronde Tribe Sinking Dollars into Pearl District." *Business Journal*, June 2, 2000.

Bourland, Greg. "A Pox on Our House." *New York Times Magazine*, September 22, 2002.

The Chemawa American, February 28, 1905.

The Chief. Chemawa School Annual, 1942.

Fogarty, Mark. "Building More Than Houses." *American Indian Report*, Vol. xvi, No. 7, July 2000.

Heart of the American Indian Women's Network, Newsletter, Vol. 3, No. 1, January   2000.

Knickerbocker, Brad. "Gains on the Reservations." *The Christian Science Monitor*, February 15, 2005.

Kolbert, Elizabeth. "Last Words: A Language Dies," *The New Yorker*, June 6, 2005.

Miller, John J. "Honest Injun?" *National Review*, March 28, 2005.

Oberst, Gail. "Chinook Artifacts Returned to Indians." *Statesman Journal*, January 26,   1994.

Pearce, Helen. "Folk Sayings in a Pioneer Family of Western Oregon." *California Folklore Quarterly*, Vol. 5, 1946.

Pennelly, Amanda. "Tribes, Funding Board at Odds." *Portland Tribune*, April 6, 2004.

Pianin, Eric. "Tribes Take Aim at Old Foe: Rights Issues Spur Campaign to Oust Senator Gorton." *Washington Post*, April 3, 2000.

"Relics of Ancient Race." *Lincoln County Leader*, November 2, 1933.

Shorris, Earl. "The Last Word—Can the World's Small Languages be Saved?" *Harper's Magazine*, Vol. 301, No. 1802, August 2000.

Smoke Signals, Publication of the Grand Ronde Tribe, 1987--2005.

Thompson, Courtenay. "Tribes Claim Willamette Meteorite." *The Oregonian*, November 17, 1999.

_____. "Willamette Forest, Tribes Agree on Collaboration." *The Oregonian*, January 28, 2000.

_____. "Four Top Spirit Mountain Officials Exit Casino." *The Oregonian*, February 10, 2000.

_____. "Tribe Decides Meteorite's Site Right" and following editorial. *The Oregonian*, June 23, 2000.

_____. "Teaching Amid Turmoil at Chemawa." *The Oregonian*, June 4, 2000

Willamette Week, Vol. 25, Issue 7, November 22, 1999.

Interviews

AuCoin, Hon. Les. June 16, 2000, Portland, Oregon.

Baars, Patricia. September 16, 1999, Canby, Oregon.

Bearchum, Cecilia. February 13, 2000, Mission, Oregon.

Bergstein, Len. July 20, 2000, Portland, Oregon.

Brigham, Kathryn ("Kat"). February 10, 2000, Mission, Oregon.

Case, Lillian (Dada) Van Pelt Larvie. October 30, 1999, Mission, Oregon.

Deloria, Sam. November 20, 2003, Albuquerque, New Mexico.

Fitzgerald, John. April 27, 2000, Seattle, Washington.

Furse, Hon. Elizabeth. January 16, 2000, Tierra del Mar, Oregon.

Goodman, Edward Clay. April 27, 2004, Portland, Oregon.

Harrison-Samson, Diane. September 18, 2000, Portland, Oregon.

Harrison, Kathryn Jones. July 1999-June 2005 (weekly).

Hatch, David. February 20, 2004 and May 26, 2005, Portland, Oregon.

Hatfield, Hon. Mark. June 8, 2000, Portland, Oregon.

Johnson, Tony. November 15, 1999, Grand Ronde, Oregon.

Kentta, Robert. November 5, 1999, Siletz, Oregon.

Kentta, Verna Miller. December 6,1999, Siletz, Oregon.

Lane, Maude. January 31, 2000, Siletz, Oregon.

Molalla Historical Society members. July 3, 2001, Molalla, Oregon.

Olson, June. August 27, 1999, Grand Ronde, Oregon.

Pearsall, Ed. September 25, 2000, Grand Ronde, Oregon.

Pigsley, Delores ("Dee"). May 12, 2000, Keizer, Oregon.

Pitt, Louis Jr. August 21,1999, Mission Longhouse near Pendleton, Oregon; November 22, 1999, Warm Springs, Oregon; March 31, 2005, Tierra del Mar, Oregon.

Pullin, Patsy and Gene. July 31, 2000, Grand Ronde, Oregon.

Schmidt, Marie Jones. February 22, 2000, Milwaukie, Oregon.

Shaffer, Sue. July 7, 2000 and September 6, 2000, Roseburg, Oregon.

Simmons Austin, June. March 6, 2003, Gervais, Oregon.

Spotted Eagle, Faith. January 24, 2001, Seattle, Washington.

Vaughan, Champ Clark. July 3, 2001, Molalla, Oregon.

Van Pelt, Jeff. October 30,1999, Mission, Oregon.

Watson, Robert. May 12, 2000, Grand Ronde, Oregon.

Wharton, Don. January 6, 2003, Boulder, Colorado.

Index

About the Author

KRIS OLSON INTERVIEWING KATHRYN HARRISON

Jennifer Jasaitis, photographer

A graduate of Wellesley College and Yale Law School, Kris Olson served as law clerk to two federal judges, as an assistant U.S. Attorney for ten years prosecuting federal criminal cases, and as Professor and Associate Dean at Lewis and Clark's Northwestern School of Law for another ten years. She was United States Attorney for the District of Oregon from 1994 to 2001 (appointed by President Clinton) and Senior Counsel to Congressman Earl Blumenauer (D. Oregon) from 2001 to 2003. Kris was a member of Attorney General Janet Reno's Advisory Committee on Native American Issues, and she has served as a consultant to tribal governments concerning cultural resource protection and the development of tribal court systems.

Kris has published extensively in professional journals on cultural resource protection, criminal justice policy, sex discrimination, and federal Indian law. She and her husband, Les Swanson, divide their time between their homes in Portland, Oregon; in Tierra del Mar on the Oregon coast; and at Mt. Adams in Washington State.